THE MEDIEVAL CHURCH IN ENGLAND

by
DOROTHY M. MEADE

CHURCHMAN PUBLISHING: 1988

© Copyright Dorothy M. Meade 1988

The Medieval Church
In England
by
Dorothy M. Meade
was first published in 1988
by

CHURCHMAN PUBLISHING LIMITED
117 Broomfield Avenue
Worthing
West Sussex BN14 7SF

Publisher: E. Peter Smith
and Distributed to the book trade
by
BAILEY BOOK DISTRIBUTION LIMITED
Warner House
Wear Bay Road
Folkestone
Kent CT19 6PH

Churchman are represented in Australia, Canada,
New Zealand and the United States

ISBN 1 85093 074 0

All Rights Reserved

Printed in Great Britain by
Biddles Limited of Guildford

FOREWORD

I would like to thank the staffs of the Durham libraries – the Dean and Chapter Library, the University Library and the County Library (City Branch) – for their assistance.

Medieval sums of money can sound deceptive to the general reader – a penny is of little value now yet it was a day's pay for a ploughman (a well-paid worker) in the first half of the fourteenth century. Because of this I have transposed medieval pence and pounds into comparative present-day amounts. Edward III (1327–77) paid £5 for a vest, said to have belonged to St Peter, and William Woods[1] reckons this to be the equivalent of £1,000 in modern money. I have taken this as an approximate guide although it has its pitfalls, for inflation altered values then as now.

The former county names (i.e. those existing before the boundary changes of 1974) have been retained as they are still well-known and were in use during the centuries covered by the book.

Scriptural quotations are from *The New English Bible* of 1970. The spelling of quotations from contemporary documents has been modernised.

D.M.M.

---

[1] Woods, William. *England in the Age of Chaucer* (1976), 70.

CONTENTS

INTRODUCTION 1

CHAPTER ONE: THE PARISH CLERGY
1. Training 3
2. Minor orders 3
3. A celibate priesthood 5
4. Major orders 6
5. Benefit of clergy 7
6. The parish and its incumbent 8
7. The priest's spiritual work 10
8. Assistant parish clergy 11
9. Clerical dress 11
10. Forms of address of the lower clergy 12
11. Priests' houses 12
12. Income 14
    (a) The glebe 14
    (b) Tithes 14
    (c) Oblations 16

CHAPTER TWO: CHRISTIAN LIFE
1. Birth and baptism 18
    (a) Born into the Church 18
    (b) Original sin 18
    (c) Godparents 19
    (d) Naming 20
    (e) The ceremony outside the church 20
    (f) At the font 21
    (g) Confirmation and communion following baptism 22
    (h) Churching 22
2. Confirmation 23

3. Confession   24
   (a) Obligatory confession after 1215   24
   (b) An annual rite   25
   (c) The seal of confession   28
   (d) Absolution   28
   (e) Penance   29
4. Mass   31
5. Marriage   34
   (a) Bethrothal   34
   (b) Impediments to marriage   34
   (c) At the church door   35
   (d) Inside the church   36
   (e) The wedding-breakfast   37
   (f) The blessing of the marriage-chamber   38
   (g) Divorce   38
6. Parish officials, employees and performers   39
   (a) Churchwardens   39
       (i)   Upkeep of the parish church   39
       (ii) Churchwardens' and sidesmens' reports   40
       (iii) Peter's pence   41
   (b) The sexton   42
   (c) The nightwatchman   42
   (d) The ringers   42
   (e) Travelling workmen and artists   43
   (f) Miscellaneous occupations   44
   (g) Church plays   44
   (h) Organists and singers   46
   (i) The parish meeting   47
7. Superstitions   48
8. Saints and pilgrimages   51
   (a) Pilgrimage   51
   (b) The making of a saint   53
   (c) The cult of the Virgin Mary   54
   (d) The journey   56
   (e) At the shrine   57
   (f) Illness and causes of cures   58
9. Indulgences   59
   (a) Prospect of purgatory   59
   (b) The Roman jubilees   60
   (c) The Canterbury jubilees   61

	(d) A private indulgence	62
	(e) Pardoners	62
10.	Sanctuary	64
11.	Rites for the sick and the dead	68
	(a) Visitation of the sick	68
	(b) The rites for the dying	71
	(c) The funeral	72
	(d) Memorial observances	75
	(e) Chantries	77
	(i) The multiplication of masses	77
	(ii) Perpetual chantries	78
	(iii) Soul-masses and the Black Death	79
	(iv) Chantry colleges	80
	(v) Chantries in hospital chapels	80
	(vi) Religious gilds	81
	(vii) Numbers of intercessory institutions	82
12.	The Jews	82

CHAPTER THREE: THE CHURCH'S YEAR

1.	The development of the ecclesiastical calendar	94
2.	The celebration of holy days	96

CHAPTER FOUR: BISHOPS AND ARCHBISHOPS

1.	Dioceses, provinces and cathedrals	106
2.	Consecration, the insignia and enthronement	108
3.	Choosing a bishop	110
4.	The Archbishop of Canterbury's right to crown the sovereign	112
5.	The Archbishop of Canterbury's right to marry the sovereign	113
6.	The lords spiritual	113
7.	Diocesan duties	114
8.	The consistory court and its personnel	115
9.	The bishop's court	116
10.	Archdeacons and their chapters	116
11.	Suffragan bishops	118

CHAPTER FIVE: MEMBERS OF THE RELIGIOUS ORDERS

1. Monks, canons and nuns — 121
   - (a) The monasteries — 121
   - (b) The monks — 123
   - (c) Life in the medieval monastery — 124
   - (d) Obedientiaries — 126
   - (e) Abbots and priors (heads of houses) — 126
   - (f) Nunneries — 128
   - (g) Visitations — 132
   - (h) Social impact — 132
2. Friars — 135
   - (a) The first friars — 135
   - (b) The introduction of the Dominicans and Franciscans into England — 135
   - (c) Dominican and Franciscan nuns — 137
   - (d) Carmelite, Augustinian and Crutched friars — 138
   - (e) Confraternities — 138
   - (f) Opposition of parish priests and monasteries — 139
   - (g) Support of royalty — 139
   - (h) Friars during the Peasants' Revolt — 140
   - (i) Development of buildings — 140
   - (j) Criticism of the friars — 141
   - (k) The Observant friars — 142
   - (l) Number of friaries and their occupants — 143
3. Knights of the military orders — 143
   - (a) The Knights Hospitallers and the Knights Templar — 143
   - (b) The suppression of the Templars — 146
   - (c) The Hospitallers after 1312 — 148

CHAPTER SIX: THE PAPACY

1. Early development — 151
2. Government — 152
3. Property and income — 154
4. Papal provisions — 155
5. Sojourn in Avignon — 158
6. The Great Schism — 158
7. The last chance to reform — 159

CHAPTER SEVEN: ECCLESIASTICAL AUTHORITY AND NON-CONFORMITY

1. Heresy — 161
2. John Wyclif — 162
    (a) Oxford — 162
    (b) Lutterworth — 168
3. The Lollards — 174
    (a) The missionaries — 174
    (b) The language of the people — 177
    (c) Women Lollards — 181
    (d) Persecution — 182
    (e) Death by burning — 185
    (f) Richard Hunne — 189
    (g) The Lollards and the Reformation — 192

LIST OF ILLUSTRATIONS — 199

INDEX — 200

INTRODUCTION

The early Church formed by the followers of Jesus was a simple affair based on evangelistic journeys and house meetings. After Christianity became the state religion of the Roman empire in 392 it developed into a powerful institution. Through its acquisition of land and wealth its leaders were equivalent to secular rulers and so it wielded great influence in the decisions of men. It was the fount of Christian knowledge and asserted that its ministrations were the only means of salvation. By the Middle Ages kings and commoners alike accepted this and admitted its supremacy.

All were aware that the Church of which they were members possessed absolute authority, issued its own laws, punished the disobedient, claimed to have the entry into heaven and brooked no alternative opinions. For the most part they were content to have it so, but the inquiring human spirit could not be subjugated forever. During the medieval centuries the Church was forced to come to grips with those of its flock who reached an independent outlook and who raised critical reactions in people's minds.

The ecclesiastical organisation was based on a system of parishes and at the heart of each was the church. This was the most distinctive building in the parish, being noticeably different from the dwelling-houses near it – bigger, higher, more carefully constructed, probably of different material, usually set on an east-west alignment and surrounded by a spacious churchyard. It was the focus of community life, both religious and social, and the parishioners spent much time and effort on its maintenance and improvement. By a custom that developed into an established requirement they were financially responsible for the nave and its accretions, while the rector bore the cost of the chancel.

Everyone attended church – or was supposed to do so – on Sunday mornings in order to hear the priest say mass. There were also occasional visits to mark great personal events, baptism, marriage, funeral and, finally, burial in the consecrated churchyard.

Because of its size it was natural that the parishioners should use their part of the church for purposes other than religious. Fire-fighting equipment was kept there; if a market was held nearby, the church was the natural shelter in bad weather and the buying and selling continued under its roof; similarly, out-door social events took place there, if rained off; the feast following the annual parish meeting was usually held in the nave; the room over the porch might be hired by the local trade gilds, used for the signing and storing of legal documents or for the occupation of the sexton, night-watchman or chantry-priest; in emergencies, such as flooding, the tower could become a refuge, and some were surmounted by lanterns for the guidance of travellers. In these many ways the parish church was indispensable to village and town life.

The churches gave visible expression to the beliefs of the universal Church and they developed to accommodate new rites and practices. In some cases, because they were adequate for the needs of their small congregations, they remained little changed. Many were altered so that the original structure is almost hidden by the later additions of porches, aisles, transepts, chantry-chapels, the lengthening of the chancel or the raising of the nave roof. Some were totally rebuilt in one architectural style. All bear witness to the worship of the Church and the lives of the people. Whether they were struggling communities or munificent individuals, the parishioners cared for the religious building in their midst because it was an integral part of their lives and a symbol of their local heritage.

THE PARISH CLERGY

1. TRAINING

The Church was in theory a democratic institution in which the lowest member could and did rise to the highest place. (The only Englishman to become pope, Nicholas Breakspear [Hadrian IV], was the son of a humble townsman of St. Albans). It could offer employment to all ranges of ability and there were always plenty of candidates. The most ambitious and intelligent of these obtained influential posts in the king's court, the universities, dioceses or monasteries. The others, as soon as they were ordained priests, were eligible to be in charge of a parish. Altogether they formed a large part of the population (about one to every fifty people[1]), so that, with the unordained clergy, the country was 'swarming with clerics'.[2]

The fairly well-to-do students either had a private tutor or went to a small town school before going on to university. The majority of the parish clergy had no such formal education but attached themselves in youth to their local church and learned what they could by observing and helping the priest and receiving some tuition from him. Eventually the novice knew enough to offer himself for examination, so that he might become a clerk (an Old-English word meaning 'priest').

2. MINOR ORDERS

There were four minor orders of priesthood which had all been known since the third century. Even the lowest of these was worth having because it enabled the holder to obtain a benefice. For each one the applicant was briefly interviewed by the archdeacon, representing the bishop. There were questions mainly on his birth (he was not to be

---

[1]This ratio includes both the secular clergy and members of the religious orders.
[2]Jessopp, A. *The Coming of the Friars* (1888), 83, quoted by Moorman, J. R. H. *Church Life in England in the Thirteenth Century* (1945), 55.

illegitimate), age, physique, competence and good character.

As he entered each order the candidate was ordained at a special mass, during which the bishop blessed him for his future work by laying his hands on his head. He received the tonsure (the shaving of the crown of the head) at the first ordination. The lowest of the orders was that of ostiarius, or doorkeeper, a position held by St. Godric at St. Giles' Church, Durham, for some short time between the years 1112 and 1128. Next, the lector was to sing the lessons clearly, the exorcist was to drive out demons and, lastly, the acolyte was to carry the candlestick in procession and assist the priest with the wine and water at mass. Though each minor order had to be taken in turn, the process could be speeded up by taking two at the same time.

With these qualifications the minor clerics had certain posts open to them. They could become accountants or secretaries of wealthy families or business people (the modern use of the term 'clerical work' being derived from their writing activities). A sought-after post was that of parish-clerk, as it was a permanent appointment licensed by the bishop. This clerk was an assistant to the incumbent and was required to do a variety of tasks, both in church and about the parish. On Sundays and festivals he sprinkled holy-water from house to house in return for money or food, and from this duty was sometimes called the 'holy-water carrier.' Parish clerks were generally versatile fellows who could eke out their wages by earning fees for performing useful services. Absolon, in Chaucer's *The Miller's Tale*,[1] could let blood, give a man a hair-cut and shave, or write out a legal document for a land transaction. Sometimes young parish clerks went on to become priests. Robert of Weston, rector of Mareham, Lincolnshire, bequeathed a missal to his clerk, John Penne, in 1389, 'if he wishes to be a priest'.

A clerk in minor orders could still feel a part of everyday life. His religious duties were not heavy and the Church allowed him to marry, as William Langland (c.1330–c.1400), the author of *Piers Plowman*, did. With his wife Kitte and their daughter Kalote he lived in London making a living reciting the words of memorial funeral services and doubtless doing any other clerical jobs that came along. Langland's younger contemporary, the poet Thomas Hoccleve, a clerk in the royal office of the Privy Seal at Westminster, deliberately remained single so that he might obtain a rectory. He married in the end when his hopes for

---

[1] From *The Canterbury Tales* (written c.1387–1400). All other references to Chaucer's characters are from this work.

this had faded. If a man wanted to proceed to major (or holy) orders he had to take a vow of celibacy.

3. A CELIBATE PRIESTHOOD

The idea of a celibate priesthood had been put forward as early as the fourth century so that priests would be free from family ties and able to give all their time to their spiritual tasks. It was not welcomed by the majority of the Western clergy. They knew that Christ had not commanded it and that St. Peter had been a married man. The precept, therefore, was largely ignored and in Anglo-Saxon England clerical marriage continued to be quite common.

The Lateran Council of 1215 made celibacy a definite requirement for the priesthood. The spiritual reason for this was the doctrine of transubstantiation whereby it was believed that, at the mass, the priest held Christ's body and blood in his hands. For this privilege he must be pure, a word the Church held to be synonymous with chaste. There was also a practical reason: a clerical family would naturally be a drain on the income of the married priest and so be a danger to Church property.

The habits of centuries died hard and many priests continued to lead family lives. Attempts were made by bishops to suppress unlawful relationships by threats of suspension and excommunication, but the upper ranks of the clergy were not always guiltless themselves. When William, bishop of St. Andrews (1271–9) told one of his vicars that his 'hearthmate' must go, the lady in question determined to get the better of him. She planted herself in his path and said, 'My lord, I am the vicar's concubine and I am taking these gifts to the bishop's sweetheart who has lately been brought to bed'. This touched the bishop's conscience, so he went away leaving the couple still together.[1]

The wives and families living in the priests' houses may have occasioned grumbling among the lay folk but the reasons were mainly economic. It was feared that, with the additional mouths to feed, the parson would be extra rigorous in collecting his dues. The families themselves were accepted as part of the community. The miller of Trumpington, in Chaucer's *The Reeve's Tale*, was proud to marry the daughter of the parson of the town and she was addressed respectfully by all as 'dame'. The main criticism was kept for brief and temporary

[1] *The Chronicle of Lanercost, 1272–1346*, trans. H. E. Maxwell (1913), 2, 3.

liaisons which were a cause of great scandal and were often reported by the parishioners to the archdeacons on their official visits. Many cases ought to have resulted in deprivation and public penance, but the punishment was more often a money fine and perhaps private penance. As Gerald of Wales, archdeacon of Brecon (c.1147–1223), said, it was hopeless to expect the rule of celibacy to be observed, and it is clear that the Church often managed to wink at the lapses of its ministers.

4. MAJOR ORDERS

Before going on to major orders every ordinand had to have a 'title', that is, a means of support, until he found a parish or other clerical post. This was not always easy to obtain and required an alert mind on the look-out for opportunity. When once achieved, he was able to present himself for examination by the archdeacon. Very little learning was thought sufficient. The Church required large numbers of recruits and could not also have a very strict selection procedure that would exclude many of them. Their reputation for ignorance was well-known throughout Europe. St. Bonaventure in Italy, St. Thomas Aquinas at Paris and Roger Bacon in England, towards the end of the thirteenth century, all wrote complaining of it. Bacon's words were, 'country priests recite the Church services, of which they know little or nothing, like brute beasts', that is, parrot-fashion. Nothing was done to amend this state of affairs, so that in 1509 Dean Colet complained of 'a multitude of unlearned and evil priests.'

The first two of the three major orders were those of sub-deacon and deacon. After the candidates had been ordained they were able to gain practical experience of parish work at a higher level if they intended to become priests. Some did not – often those who were destined for administrative work in a bishop's or the king's service, like Thomas Becket. He remained a deacon till he was forty-three, when he was ordained priest the day before his consecration as archbishop of Canterbury in 1162.

A man who wished to serve in a parish was usually ordained to the priesthood (the third of the major orders) when he was the minimum age of twenty-four, or soon after. Having received the sacrament of ordination, he was then able to administer the five sacraments of baptism, penance, the eucharist, matrimony and extreme unction (confirmation and ordination itself being reserved for the bishop).

Fortunate men were instituted straight away to benefices and then went off to their parishes to be formally inducted by the archdeacon or his delegate. Some of the new priests were wealthy young rectors who were immediately given licences of non-residence so that they could study at university.

5. BENEFIT OF CLERGY

The clergy had one great privilege not possessed by the rest of the people, known as 'benefit of clergy'. This was the right to be tried in the ecclesiastical courts which had been created by William I, following continental precedent. It applied to greater crimes other than treason; for lesser offences they must stand trial in the ordinary courts. Any man who claimed this right was required to prove that he was a clerk, and a reading-test in Latin became the most important method of proof. This usually amounted to reading the first verse of the fifty-first psalm (known as the 'neck verse' because it might save a criminous but largely unlettered clerk's neck).

There is plenty of evidence of clergy being convicted of homicide, assault, rape, burglary and receiving stolen goods. The Church was concerned to be just, but its heaviest punishment was imprisonment and it was widely held to be easy to escape from a bishop's prison. For the crime of murder it could not impose the death penalty, which a layman would have suffered in the king's court. Henry II cared passionately about the injustice of this. In 1160, on learning that a hundred murders had been committed by clerks since his accession six years earlier, he decided that something must be done. His Constitutions of Clarendon (1164) stated that if a Church court degraded a guilty clerk from his orders then he was to be subject to punishment for his crime as a layman. Thomas Becket rejected this, saying that degradation was itself the punishment and that God did not judge twice for the same crime. This idea was an innovation, later taken up by the Church when Becket was murdered. After that the king had to admit failure.

Throughout the Middle Ages the clergy in both minor and major orders took advantage of this right. Besides bona fide clerics there were some who had ceased to have a religious appointment but instead lived as laymen. When justice was hard and a man might be hanged for stealing a horse, people cast envious eyes on a large privileged minority which would never have to face the threat of the death penalty. The system itself encouraged far-seeing folk to enter the ranks of the minor clerics as a kind of insurance in case of unforeseen trouble. Among them were potential criminals, and it was reported to one of the popes in the early sixteenth century that they had sought minor orders deliberately so that they might be able to commit crimes with impunity.

6. THE PARISH AND ITS INCUMBENT

Parishes originated in Anglo-Saxon England when local lords built churches on their estates for the use of themselves, their tenants and serfs. By the end of the thirteenth century there were some 9000 of them with their boundaries known and observed. Each lord considered that he possessed the advowson of his church, that is, the right to appoint the priest. After the Conquest this man was called the rector (ruler) or parson (chief person) of the parish. He was given the benefice, or living, which included the responsibility for the cure of souls (the spiritual welfare of his people). For his maintenance he was entitled to certain land and the right to collect a share of the parishioners' income in produce, as well as their offerings in church.

At first each rector lived in the parish, carrying out his duties and receiving good payment in money and the fruits of the land. This was a satisfactory system but it came to be misused. The lay patrons often gave the benefice to their friends or relations as a means of providing them with financial support. Many of these men took the income of the parish but did not bother to live there because they had higher appointments elsewhere.

The holding of more than one benefice, known as pluralism, was against Church law, but was nevertheless common, for popes readily granted a dispensation (a licence to overlook a rule) in return for a handsome sum of money. It was regarded as perfectly normal and nothing to be ashamed of. Indeed, Thomas Becket, when accused by the bishop of London of having been raised from poverty by the king, claimed that that was not so, for he had held the archdeaconry of Canterbury and 'quite a few other benefices.' An absentee of this sort hired a clerk in holy orders who was glad to get a job and do the work for a very low annual stipend of perhaps a twelfth of the rector's income. This deputy was called either a curate, a parochial chaplain or a parish priest. William Langland, in *Piers Plowman*, referred to 'Parsons and parish-priests', and this phrase noted the difference between the beneficed rector, whether resident or not, and the unbeneficed substitute. There was a clear distinction between the two types of appointment, instanced by the witnesses to a Yorkshire will of 1467 – 'Christopher Conyers, rector of the church of Rudby,' and 'Richard Mansfield, parochial chaplain of the said church'.

One of the parsons who found more congenial employment out of his parish was Thomas Howes, the domestic chaplain of Sir John Fastolf (1378?–1459) of Caister in Norfolk. He acted more as agent and protector of his master's affairs than in any religious capacity. So reliable did he prove that Sir John rewarded him with the living of Castle Combe, in Wiltshire, when it became vacant. This was equivalent to a rise in salary without Sir John having to pay it. Howes received the income of the parish but put in a parochial chaplain to do the work. Some years later he also became rector of three local parishes in Sir John's gift and must have finished up a wealthy man. At the same time William Worcester was employed as Sir John's secretary and gave a life-time of faithful service. When he suggested that he ought to receive more payment for his work Sir John said that if he had been a priest he could have been given a living.

Chaucer's Poor Parson was a rector who resided in his parish, which was large and sparsely populated. His benefice was not one of the wealthiest, but the fact that he was generous to his even poorer parishioners was the cause of his own poverty. It was a rare example that he set and Chaucer thought there was not a better priest anywhere. Certainly one was not to be found in *Piers Plowman*, in which the author wrote about Sloth, who had been a parson for thirty years. In spite of that he could hunt and check the manorial accounts better than he could sing the services or teach his parishioners. With these attributes and failings he was typical of the village clergy.

A lay lord sometimes wished to make a generous gift to a monastery or other religious house without parting with any of his land. In this case he might give away the revenue of his parish, provided that the recipients made arrangements for the church's worship. This was the system of appropriations. The institution then became the rector, collected about two-thirds of the income and appointed a substitute for life called a vicar, who received the other third. By 1535 more than one-third of English churches were appropriated.

In these ways about half of the country's parishes came to be cared for by poor, peasant-born vicars and chaplains with hardly any education. They were often ignorant of the meaning of the little Latin that they managed to articulate and were unable to give their people a proper understanding of the faith. There must have been other worthy priests besides Thomas, vicar of Branscombe in Devon, whose sidesmen said, in 1301, that he 'beareth himself well in all things and preacheth willingly, and visiteth the sick, and doth diligently, all that pertaineth to his priestly office.' Nevertheless, the Hereford visitation (281 parishes) of 1397 points to a greater number with a lower standard – a quarter of the priests leading immoral lives, some haunting taverns and many neglecting their churches. While these men were doing their incompetent best, or less, the absentee rectors ignored their responsibilities, yet willingly took the income produced by the labour of the parishioners.

7. THE PRIEST'S SPIRITUAL WORK

The spiritual work of the rector or his substitute was two-fold: to instruct his parishioners in their faith and to administer the sacraments. He was supposed to see that everyone knew the Paternoster (Lord's Prayer), the Creed, the Ave Maria ('Hail, Mary,' – the words of Gabriel's greeting) and the Ten Commandments, either in Latin or in English. Many never received even this minimum teaching, largely because the majority of the priests themselves were not much wiser than their flocks.

In some ways the priest seemed little different from his people. He might be related to some of them, as was Chaucer's Poor Parson, whose brother was a ploughman and a carter of dung. Like them, he was dependent in great measure on the produce of his land, so that the vicissitudes of the weather were of paramount importance to both him and them alike. In short, his daily life was interwoven with theirs. What set him apart was his celibacy, his consecration at ordination and his power of celebrating the sacraments of the Church. His essential distinguishing quality was demonstrated at mass. The Church taught that when he consecrated the bread and wine it was changed into the body and blood of Christ. This superhuman power of the priest to 'produce the body of Christ' (as John Gower, a contemporary of Chaucer's wrote) placed him, with all his human imperfections, above his more ordinary neighbours.

8. ASSISTANT PARISH CLERGY

Several assistant clergy, an average of about five ordained men, worked in each parish. The most important of these was the chaplain in charge of a chapel of ease, if one had been built to serve a distant part of the parish. There he had a certain measure of independence and received some of the income of that part of the parish for his support. There was often a chantry priest who sang masses for the soul of the founder of the chantry; he had no other responsibilities but might share in the general work of the parish (see chapter 2, section 11e). Those priests who were unable to obtain a permanent position were glad to be hired for parish work in a temporary capacity. Such stipendiary priests received only a very low payment.

9. CLERICAL DRESS

Outside the church there was little to distinguish the clergy from the laity, apart from the tonsure. They were supposed to wear their stoles at all times, even when travelling, so that their calling might be known, but this requirement was rarely observed. Apart from that there was no special kind of dress, although they were expected to wear simple and sober long gowns. In spite of this many went about looking like men of the world, the tonsure being covered by head-gear or even being allowed to disappear altogether. Bishops sent out repeated instructions that they must not be too smart, wear red and green or display swords, all of which were largely ignored. Those who could afford it inclined to fashionable styles and colours, even the forbidden red and green, with gold and silver belts and buttons. One learns of an untonsured deacon dressed in scarlet and wearing rings, of clerics in short tunics with belted swords and of many more who left their finery to others in their wills. The poorest of the parish priests went sedately enough and tried to avoid shabbiness. Sometimes they may have acquired rich gowns as bequests from superiors or kindly parishioners.

During services the clergy wore distinctive clothes called vestments. These had all been items of ordinary wear in the early days of the Church. Kept for special use, they were looked after carefully and so survived longer than outdoor articles. In addition, some of them were costly gifts and some had been worn by saints. These increasingly old-fashioned clothes came to be considered the correct wear for priests in church and when they needed to be renewed they were replaced by garments in the same style.

10. FORMS OF ADDRESS OF THE LOWER CLERGY

In Anglo-Saxon times priests were simply addressed by their names as other people were. Bede, in his *Ecclesiastical History* (completed in 731), and the *Anglo-Saxon Chronicle* referred to them as, for example, 'the priest Cynebil' or 'Gyric the priest'; and 'Aelfsige the priest in Croydon' was a witness to a will.

The Norman-French influence brought in the word 'Sir' as a prefix to the name of a superior's social position, like Sir king, Sir bishop, Sir knight, or Sir clerk. It was also used before Christian names, 'the pope, Sir Adrian', for instance, or 'Sir Herod', as in the fourteenth-century *York Mystery Plays*. This appellation became a permanent part of the title of knights. It was also allowed to the ordinary clergy, in order, presumably, to give them some standing among their fellows. It served to distinguish between the university graduate, known as 'Master', and the humbler, uneducated priest. This difference is shown in a Nottinghamshire will of 1517, to which 'Master Robert Neville, parson of the church of Grove and Sir Thomas Elton his parish priest' were witnesses.

People who lacked respect for a particular priest might refer to him rather familiarly, as 'Sir John,' as did Chaucer in *The Prologue of the Nuns' Priest's Tale*: 'Come near, thou priest, come hither, thou Sir John'. A number of 'Sir Johns' were so ignorant that they gained the nick-name 'Sir John Lack-Latin'. Sir Francis Bigod used the term contemptuously in 1534 when writing of an absentee rector who placed in his parishes 'a Sir John Lack Latin, that can scarce read his porteous [prayer-book].'

The title was still employed in the sixteenth and seventeenth centuries, witness the Welsh parson, Sir Hugh Evans, in Shakespeare's contemporary comedy, *The Merry Wives of Windsor*; and when Viola said, in *Twelfth Night*, that she would 'rather go with sir priest than sir knight', the Elizabethan audience would be well-acquainted with the terminology.

11. PRIESTS' HOUSES

Incumbents were responsible for the building and upkeep of their rectories. These varied, according to the wealth of the benefice, from comparatively modest constructions to sturdier residences which might be as fine as small manor-houses. There are several in existence today, such as the timber-framed parsonage at Dean, Sussex,[1] and the stone-built pele-tower at Elsdon, Northumberland. Where the rector was an absentee he probably let the house, but he would have to see that the chaplain he appointed in his place had a suitable abode. The house called Priesthill or Priesthall at Kentisbeare, Devon, seems to have been built for this purpose. If the church was appropriated the monastery or institution concerned might let the rectory or use it as a holiday home and provide other accommodation for the vicar. Some vicarages were purpose-built, like the fine one at Muchelney, Somerset, which was begun in the fourteenth century. The unbeneficed assistant clergy lived either in lodgings, with the incumbent, or, in some cases, in little dwellings in the churchyards, some of which are still to be seen; the one at the Chapel of Our Lady at Great Horkesley in Essex, built before 1500, adjoins the west end of the church.

Rectories and vicarages were usually sizeable buildings because they had to provide living quarters for several people – possibly the priest's parents, some of his clergy staff and perhaps one or more servants. Every vicar had at least a servant-boy who made his bed and looked after his horse. This lad, referred to by Chaucer, in the Prologue to *The Pardoner's Tale*, as the 'priest's page', was paid such a pittance that he was known as one of the poorest of village-folk. There needed also to be accommodation for visiting church dignitaries, such as the archdeacon, and their followers. Near the house there would be outbuildings, a stable, a brewhouse, a dovecote and the like. Altogether, with barns, paddocks and orchards, the whole site would look rather like a farm. An interesting example of this remains at Ashleworth, Gloucestershire, where the rectory and tithe-barn are close to the church.

The cost of maintaining these buildings was high and absentee rectors and appropriators, as well as poor vicars, did not always bother to spend money on them. Consequently, many, especially flimsy, wooden erections, fell into disrepair and their condition was commented on in archdeacons' tours of inspection: at Shute, Devon, in 1301, the chaplain's house was in such a bad state that its occupant was sleeping in the church. It is the well-built and well-cared-for houses that have survived.

---

[1] A National Trust property.

12. INCOME

a. *The glebe*

In medieval times all the people, rich or poor, needed some land on which to grow the food they ate. The incumbent's was called the glebe. It varied from parish to parish, but was usually about thirty to forty acres. This land might be in one piece near the parsonage or in several strips scattered through the open fields. The parson had to work this land, usually through tenants or hired labour. It forced him into the agricultural life of the area and often into disagreements with his peasant neighbours, the while taking him away from his spiritual work. Many of them found it easier to rent out part or all of the glebe.

b. *Tithes*

As a source of income the tithes were even more important than the glebe, being worth about three times as much. The word means a tenth and the system had its origin in the story of Jacob's ladder in the Book of Genesis, when Jacob promised one tenth of his produce to God in gratitude for his protection. This led to a system of religious taxation by the Hebrews which was later adopted by the Christian Church. At first the payment was only a voluntary offering but by the tenth century it had become a legal obligation. It meant that every man had to give a tenth of his annual produce to his rector. This did not take into account the expenses of production or carting and it is reckoned to have been equivalent to an income-tax of twenty per cent. It involved his corn (the greater tithes) and all other products (the lesser tithes) such as hay, vegetables, fruit, eggs, wool, honey, beeswax, animals and even grass cut by the wayside. Where the rector was an appropriating institution it received the greater tithes and the lesser tithes were paid to the vicar.

A great deal of produce was collected at one time and it was stored in large, specially-built tithe-barns, some of which still survive. One, built in the thirteenth or early fourteenth century at Bredon, Worcestershire,[1] housed the local rector's tithes; and the early fifteenth-century one at Wellingborough, Northamptonshire, was built to store the tithes of the parishes appropriated to the nearby Crowland Abbey. There was often more than the incumbent could use and he sold the surplus, thereby getting involved in hard bargaining with his neighbours. It was difficult for non-residents to gather in their share of the harvest and some of these 'farmed' the tithes, that is, they allowed a man on the spot to collect them

---

[1] A National Trust property.

in exchange for a money payment. If a parishioner was not a worker on the land he had to pay a tenth of his profits, fees or wages.

With the tithe, or its sale-money, the parson had to provide payment for his own assistant clergy, be ready to give hospitality to the bishop or his officers and contribute to the upkeep of the chancel of the church. In early times a quarter of it had been intended for the poor of the parish, but this praise-worthy custom had been abandoned by the thirteenth century. Consequently, when the hard-done-by peasants saw the fruits of their labours piling up in the rector's tithe barn or trundling out of the parish to a distant monastery they felt very resentful about it. All gave unwillingly but, like Chaucer's Ploughman, whose 'tithes paid he full fair and well', they might not mind quite so much if the recipient was of the rare kind who resided in the parish and used the ancient traditional share of this income for the benefit of the local poor. Where the tithes went out of the parish or were for a resident but negligent rector efforts were made to conceal the full amount of goods on which tithes ought to be paid or to fob the parson off with the poorest corn or the weakest lambs. This sort of behaviour is portrayed in the fifteenth-century Towneley play, *The Killing of Abel*. In it Cain grumbles incessantly about his tithes and picks out the worst of his sheaves as his offering: 'this may we best miss.' His words must have evoked an understanding response from most of the audience.

Aware of the universal backsliding in this respect the Church tried to frighten the reluctant payers into submission by pronouncing the curse mentioned in Malachi 3.9. On four Sundays of the year the sentence of excommunication was read out in church to all, as a threat of what would happen to culprits who had committed certain sins including the non- or short-payment of tithes. It was an impressive ceremony, fit 'to strike greater fear in the congregation', and few people would have observed it without guilty consciences. The priest, carrying his book, while his assistants held the cross and a lighted candle, pronounced the dreadful curse in English, to the accompaniment of the tolling bell. He proclaimed, 'Curse them Father and Son and Holy Ghost ... that they have no part of Mass nor Matins nor of none other good prayers that be done in Holy Church ... but that the pains of hell be their meed ... and the life of them be put out of the Book of Life till they come to amendment and satisfaction made.' This said, the priest put out the candle, dashed it down and spat on the ground. The bell continued to toll and the listeners were filled with dread, visualising themselves snuffed out like the candle and imagining the terrors beyond. This was cursing 'with bell, book and candle' and many priests must have revelled in the dramatic situation, while at the same time they looked forward to an improvement in their tithe offerings. Not so Chaucer's Poor Parson: 'Full loth were him to curse for his tithes.' Yet it was his duty to do so and he must have flinched from the wretched business.

If an individual was accused of defaulting he was allowed three warnings before being suspended. Those who persisted probably had genuine doubts as to the incumbent's right in particular cases, or else failed to agree that his excessive claims were correct. The matter then went to the ecclesiastical courts where there was a constant stream of litigation about the settlement of tithes disputes.

c. *Oblations*

In return for the spiritual care of his parishioners the incumbent could collect offerings and fees from all those over eighteen years of age who were independent of the parental home. A vicar or parish-priest received a proportion of these. They had begun as voluntary contributions, became customary and finally were claimed by the clergy as rights. They were paid at Christmas, Easter and two other festivals, which varied from place to place. In addition the people were encouraged but not compelled to give 'mass-pennies' every Sunday, but probably rarely did so. There was also money collected for weddings, churchings and funerals, as well as 'confession-pennies'. Offerings in kind were made at certain times, eggs at Easter, cheese at Whitsuntide, fowls at Christmas and occasionally wax or candles for lighting both church and house. Besides these there would be the contents of an alms box or a box placed before an image. With perquisites for such things as the making of wills all these offerings and oblations together formed a considerable addition to a rector's income.

The total revenue of some parishes constituted a highly satisfactory means of support, especially if augmented by shrewd trading of surplus contributions by business-like rectors. These were the men who were able to leave large sums of money in their wills, together with silver table-ware, jewelled rings and furred robes. At the other end of the scale were the lowly holders of poorly-endowed vicarages and parish priests who lived close to poverty, especially during times of bad harvests.

It was through the local clergy that the Church touched the people. Some of them were humble and hardworking, leading unselfish and caring lives and struggling to bring their flock nearer to God. Too many others made their appearances in visitation records and the literature of the time as lazy, pleasure-loving, ignorant and immoral. They called forth little respect from those whose good example they ought to have been. All of them, rich and poor, worthy and unworthy, educated and untaught, were caught up in a system which promoted self-seeking without associated responsibility, which encouraged the vigorous collection of dues and which tolerated the spiritual care of the weakest being in the hands of the least efficient members of the clerical community.

SELECT BOOK LIST

BENNETT, H. S. *Life on the English Manor* (1937). *The Pastons and their England* (1921).
CHAUCER, Geoffrey. *The Complete Works of Geoffrey Chaucer*, ed. W. W. Skeat (1919).
COULTON, G. G. *Social Life in Britain from the Conquest to the Reformation* (1918). *Medieval Panorama* (1938). *The Medieval Village* (1925).
CUTTS, E. L. *Parish Priests and their People* (1914).
GABEL, L. C. *Benefit of Clergy in England in the Later Middle Ages* (1929).
HARTRIDGE, R. A. R. *A History of Vicarages in the Later Middle Ages* (1930).
HEATH, P. *The English Parish Clergy on the Eve of the Reformation* (1969).
LANGLAND, William. *Piers Plowman*, C-text, ed. D. Pearsall (1978).
MOORMAN, J. R. H. *Church Life in England in the Thirteenth Century* (1945).
PANTIN, W. A. 'Medieval Priests' Houses in South West England', in *Medieval Archaeology* 1 (1957).
PLATT, C. *The Parish Churches of Medieval England* (1981).
RICHARDSON, H. G. 'The Parish Clergy of the Thirteenth and Fourteenth Centuries', in *Transactions of the Royal Historical Society*, Third series, vol. VI (1912).
SMITH, H. M. *Pre-Reformation England* (1938).
THOMPSON, A. Hamilton. *The English Clergy and their Organization in the later Middle Ages* (1947).
WINSTON, R. *Thomas Becket* (1967).
WOODS, W. *England in the Age of Chaucer* (1976).

CHRISTIAN LIFE

1. BIRTH AND BAPTISM

a. *Born into the Church*

As all persons were born subjects of the king so also were they born subjects of the Church. Throughout life they were made aware of its concern for and control over them. The priest told them of the allegiance they owed, the actions that they must perform and the punishments that awaited them in this life and the next should they in any way fail. Medieval people looked on the Church as part of the natural order of things. It was important to them not only for its doctrines but also for the rites it provided as essential accompaniments to the great events of their own lives.

b. *Original sin*

From the moment of birth a child was thought to be in need of the Church's ministrations. This was due to the doctrine of original sin (the idea that, following the fall of Adam, all men were afterwards born sinful) linked with Christ's statement[1] that no one could enter the kingdom of God without being born from water and spirit, which was understood to mean baptism. The Church, therefore, taught that this rite was absolutely necessary for salvation. Without it, people had no chance of going to heaven but would suffer torments in hell. (Thomas Aquinas [c.1225–74], an Italian theologian, thought that they went into 'Limbo' – a place of happiness, but without the vision of God). This was the reason for infant baptism and, until it was performed, the child was not a member of the Church. Henry VIII, in Shakespeare's play of that name, was clear about that when he said of the infant Elizabeth (born

---

[1] John 3.5.

1533),

> I long
> To have this young one made a Christian.
>
> (V, ii)

If a child died before it could be baptised bereaved parents were told that it was useless to pray for God's mercy on its soul. To add to their sorrow the Code of Canon Law of the early thirteenth century stated that the unbaptised should not be given Christian burial in a consecrated churchyard.

By the twelfth century the Church had become more and more concerned with the high mortality rate among infants and the consequent risk to them of being deprived of heaven. Therefore it ordered that all of them had to be baptised as soon as possible, certainly by the eighth day, and immediately if in danger of death; Prince Arthur, son of Henry VII, was baptised on the day of his birth in 1486. In an emergency, when the child seemed likely to die and the priest couldn't be got in time, anyone present was to baptise the child by sprinkling water on it and saying, 'I christen thee, John (or other name), in the name of the Father and of the Son and of the Holy Ghost. Amen'. If the child were still-born the Church taught that it could not be saved and midwives were forbidden to comfort the parents by repeating these words over the dead child.

c. *Godparents*

The new-born child was brought to church by its godparents, with friends and relatives, but not the mother, attending. It was wrapped in a shawl known as the bearing-cloth, the quality of which showed the social status of the parents. In Shakespeare's *The Winter's Tale* the shepherd says that he found the abandoned baby Perdita wearing 'a bearing-cloth for a squire's child' (III, iii).

The godparents (two men and one woman for a boy, two women and one man for a girl) were needed as spokesmen for the infants and guarantors for their Christian upbringing. It was thought that baptism created a new spiritual relationship that was superior to the natural one. This was supposed to be of such strength that godparents were forbidden to marry either each other, their god-children or the widow or widower for whose child they had stood sponsor.

The terms god-son, god-daughter, godmother, godfather and god-sib (i.e. god-related) were known in Anglo-Saxon England. The latter could refer to any godparent and by quick repetition it became 'gossip'. It is used in this sense by Henry VIII in Shakespeare's play when thanking the godparents for their christening gifts to the baby Elizabeth:

My noble gossips, y'have been too prodigal ...

(V, iv)

It was known that some people refused to be godparents because of the expense of buying a christening gift. The Church, in 1288, declared that, apart from the chrisom (see below), presents were not necessary. Nevertheless it remained the custom for gifts to be given. These were generally one or more apostle spoons, twelve in a set, with a figure of an apostle as part of the handle. They were silver from those who could afford it – hence the expression, 'born with a silver spoon in his mouth' – and base metal from the poorer people. When Cranmer, in *Henry VIII*, modestly hesitates on being asked to be Elizabeth's godfather, the king says, 'Come, come, my lord, you'ld spare your spoons' (V, ii), jocularly accusing him of not wanting to buy a christening gift. In fact Cranmer gave a standing cup of gold.

d.   Naming

The child was named by its parents and from time to time during the baptismal ceremony the priest referred to it by this name, which he obtained from the godparents. He himself did not bestow the name, for baptism was not a naming ceremony. However, coming so soon after birth, it seemed to most people that it was. John Paston, alluding to the new-born daughter of the Duke of Norfolk, in 1472, wrote '... my young Lady was christened and named Anne.' The Church encouraged the use of the names of saints and, by the end of the thirteenth century, the name John accounted for a quarter of recorded men's names and others from scripture were in common use. After 1170 Thomas became one of the most popular names, following the martyrdom of Thomas Becket at Canterbury. Women's names were almost entirely replaced by scriptural and other saints' names, Mary being first recorded about 1203.

e.   *The ceremony outside the church*

The first part of the ceremony took place outside the church door or in the porch, to demonstrate that baptism was the gate to a new life. This would be either the north or the south door, whichever was in daily use. Everyone would know of it, like William Webster of Northampton, who left specific instructions that he was 'to be buried in the churchyard of St.

Peter before the christening door.' There, certain rites of initiation were performed. At the beginning the priest made the first of several signs of the cross on the child's forehead with his thumb, saying, 'The sign of our Saviour and Lord Jesus Christ', from which came the more popular term 'christening'. The proceedings were lengthy, rich in symbolism and spoken in Latin except for some instructions to the godparents. When they were finished the priest led the company into the church.

f. *At the font*

The child was undressed at the back of the church, which must have been a cold affliction for a new-born child to endure. The infant William Barantyne, born 31 December, 1481, was undressed by the midwife beside a fire in th belfry before his baptism, but he belonged to a locally influential Oxfordshire family. The majority of parents would be unable to provide such a luxury. When all was ready the little party approached the font.

In the font was water which had been consecrated in an elaborate rite on the eve of Easter. To it had been added oil and chrism (a mixture of oil and balsam) blessed by the bishop on Maundy Thursday. The admixture in the font was considered to be sacred and only to be touched by the priest, the child and, unavoidably, by the godparents. It was not heated except perhaps for the children of important families – warm water is known to have been used at the christening of Princess Elizabeth.

At the font the godparents made the Christian renunciations and promises on the child's behalf. Then the priest dipped the child three times in different positions so that in the course of the dippings it had been completely covered by the water with the exception of the head. When he had finished, the godparents together lifted the child up.

Then the priest anointed the child's head with the 'chrism of salvation', the symbol of the giving of the Holy Spirit. To prevent the unction from being rubbed off, the priest fastened a long, folded white linen band over it, known as the chrisom cloth, which had been provided by the parents. That of Prince Edward Tudor was carried by his four-year old sister, Elizabeth, in the procession for his christening. If the child should die within a month it was buried with this band wrapped round its swaddling clothes, which were normal wear during the first months of life, (presumably imitating the swaddling of Jesus).[1] Several of these swaddled children were depicted on brasses, and where the child

[1] Swaddling was the custom from the Early Middle Ages to the beginning of the nineteenth century.

was aged a month or less the band round it would be its chrisom cloth. An example can be seen at Stoke d'Abernon, Surrey (1516). Such an infant was known as a chrisom child – Shakespeare's inn-hostess in *Henry V* (II, iii), when describing the death of Falstaff, said that he 'went away an it had been any chrisom child'. The head-band was all that remained of the white robes symbolising a sinless life, which the newly-baptised had been accustomed to wearing since the 4th century. After the infant was clothed, a burning candle, brought by the godparents, was put in its hand as a symbol of readiness for the coming of the Lord.

The care given to all the things used in the ceremony led to a superstitious belief in their magical properties. Because of this they were guarded to prevent them being taken to 'baptise' (or make well) a sick animal. Fonts were covered and locked to prevent the consecrated water being removed and used for such purposes, as well as for black magic practices. (Any pre-Reformation font will still show the remains of the iron hinge and the hasp opposite each other on the rim, or their removal scars).

g. *Confirmation and communion following baptism*

If a bishop was present the child was also confirmed as Princess Elizabeth was. For over a thousand years this had been done in the Western Church but it gradually lapsed as bishops became men of public affairs and often absent from their dioceses. The custom was maintained in the Eastern Church by giving priests the right to confirm.

Up to the thirteenth century infants were then communicated, being given a small amount of bread and wine or wine only. Then the doctrine of transubstantiation made the Church uneasy about babies who might innocently treat the 'flesh and blood of Christ' in an irreverent manner. So the practice was discouraged and gradually ceased to be done. The Eastern Church went on giving communion to its infants and has continued to do this up to the present time.

Having provided the chrisom cloth and a candle the parents did not have to pay a fee although sometimes a free-will offering might be expected.

When all was done the newly-baptised child was taken home to its mother, who was given an account of the proceedings, and doubtless celebrations followed.

h. *Churching*

A month after the birth the mother came to church with her midwife for the ceremony called the 'Purification of a woman after child-birth', more commonly known as 'churching'. It was based on the ancient Jewish idea (Leviticus 12. 1–9) that a woman was 'unclean' after child-birth and needed to be 'purified' before she could enter the church again. As the Virgin Mary had acted according to this law of Moses (Luke 2.22) it seemed to the Church very proper that all Christian mothers should do so. The woman was met at the door of the church by the priest who said psalms and prayers of thanksgiving with responses. He then 'cleansed' her with holy water, the while quoting psalm 51 verse 7, 'Take hyssop and sprinkle me, that I may be clean; wash me, that I may become whiter than snow'. The woman then gave an offering and also brought to church the chrisom cloth which had been put upon the new baby at baptism. It had traces of the blessed chrism oil on it so it could not remain at home. It was thereafter put to some devotional use by the priests such as wiping the hands at mass. Finally the priest led the woman by the right hand into church.

2. CONFIRMATION

Confirmation was the custom of bishops laying hands on those who had been baptised, following the practice of the apostles after the resurrection. By this action the gift of the Holy Ghost at baptism was confirmed. The popular name for the ceremony was 'bishoping' and a person confirmed was known as a 'bishop's son (or daughter)'.

Bishops in general seem to have neglected confirmations and often delegated the task to suffragans. When a confirmation was to be held the people were summoned, by means of the local clergy, to bring their children to a certain church. The service itself was short but it might be protracted because there were often large numbers awaiting the laying-on of hands. In 1336 Bishop Grandisson of Exeter confirmed in the village church of St. Buryan, in Cornwall, 'children almost without number from the parish and district round about'.

The children were brought to church by their parents and with a godparent. The latter was not to be one of those chosen at baptism. As with baptismal sponsors, there was considered to be a spiritual affinity constituting a bar to marriage between the godparent, the child and the real parents (if a widow or widower). It was possible at this time to change the Christian name, if desired. As well as the laying-on of hands the sign of the cross was made with chrism on each child's forehead and a chrisom cloth was bound over the anointed place. This had been provided by the parents and it was their duty to bring the child back to the church within a week to have his or her forehead washed over the font by the priest. The cloth was then burned or left to the use of the church. People believed that the cloth itself strengthened them against the assaults of the devil and also against bodily ills.

Very often the confirmation was a more casual affair than this, the children being brought to a bishop as he passed along the road. On a journey a bishop would wear normal travelling attire, but Thomas Cantilupe, bishop of Hereford from 1275 to 1282, always wore a stole when riding through his diocese in case he was stopped by parents and asked to confirm their children.

The lack of urgency in the bestowing of confirmation tended to give lay people the impression that it was of little importance. The Council of Lambeth, held in 1281, was aware that large numbers of people had grown old without ever having received the grace of this sacrament. Such behaviour was 'damnable negligence' and the Council stated that in future, nobody except the dying could be admitted to communion unless they had first been confirmed. Even this exempted people who had been reasonably prevented, a clause which could apply to most and which recognised the practical difficulties.

3. CONFESSION

a. *Obligatory confession after 1215*

The Fourth Lateran Council (1215) ordered all children to communicate for the first time when they attained 'years of discretion' (thought to mean between seven and fourteen). When this age was reached the child was required to confess his or her sins to the parish priest before the communion and subsequently once a year. This obligation was not founded on the teachings of Christ; his stories, such as that of the Prodigal Son, show that in repentance, humility and love a man may deal directly with God. Similarly, the first Letter of John states, 'If we confess our sins, he is just, and may be trusted to forgive our sins and cleanse us from every kind of wrong' (I John, 1.9). Accordingly, repentance and prayer to God were believed sufficient for pardon during the first century and a half. The Letter of James, however, suggests, 'Therefore confess your sins to one another, and pray for one another, and then you will be healed' (James 5.16), and this direction developed in time into voluntary confession to a priest.

In 1215 confession was made obligatory because it was thought that a higher standard of conduct based on Christ's teaching could be inculcated by the practice and that the spread of heresy would be checked. Henceforth everyone had to confess to his or her own parish priest once a year. Failure to do so would result in excommunication. Exceptions were made for those unavoidably away from home who were allowed to make their confession to a priest on the spot. The priests in the small towns and villages of Christendom were thus made into key figures in the new requirement, although at the same time Pope Innocent III declared that they were the chief source of corruption to the people. As they were educationally little better than their parishioners and received hardly any guidance from their superiors it is not surprising that, for most of them, confession did not achieve a deep religious significance.

Confession was now elevated to being a sacrament, the number of which was finally settled at seven (orders, baptism, confirmation, penance or confession, the eucharist, extreme unction and matrimony). It was therefore thought to be a channel of God's grace and not merely a sign of it. As such it was indispensable for forgiveness and consequently for salvation.

b. *An annual rite*

In England confession was generally called by the Anglo-Saxon word 'shrift'. Originally, shriving of penitents guilty of serious sins was done during the three days before Lent began, Shrove Sunday, Monday and Tuesday. When enforced confession for all was introduced it was not possible to do it in those three days and then the rite was spread throughout Lent. Everyone was expected to fast during this penitential season so the day before it began, Shrove Tuesday, became a time of eating and drinking and general merriment. Eggs and dripping (forbidden in Lent) were used up in pancakes thus giving the alternative name to the day of 'Pancake Tuesday'. As absolution left people in a state of grace they were inclined to put off their confession till towards the end of Lent; they did not want to risk falling from that into a state of sin before receiving their Easter communion, for to do that would itself be a sin. In 1406, during a busy session of Parliament, members used the necessity of confession to their own parish priests to plead for a postponement of the proceedings. Henry IV was obliged to allow this and Parliament was adjourned on Saturday, April 3 (the day before Palm Sunday). This gave everyone the minimum of time to get home to perform their spiritual duty.

The priest would announce certain times when he would be in church to listen to his flock, generally at the end of the working day. People would arrive and await their turn, for it was often crowded. If necessary, assistant priests would be taken on in a temporary capacity. The confession was made in the sight of all but out of ear-shot. The priest generally sat at the entrance to the chancel, but some churches had a special seat called the shriving 'stool' (or 'pew' or 'place'). The penitent approached and knelt or sat beside or before him. Women with their heads covered, men with their hats removed, whispered their confidences 'to the ear' of the priest. The relationship between the two was looked on as that of God the Father with his children. This may have been based on the words of the Prodigal Son (Luke 15.21), 'Father, I have sinned, against God and against you; I am no longer fit to be called your son.' According to John Mirk, Prior of Lilleshall in Shropshire, in his *Instructions for Parish Priests* (c.1400), a penitent was to say:

> With sore heart I ask God mercy,
> And thee, father, in God's place.

With this in mind people addressed the priest as 'Father' and he them as 'Son' or 'Daughter'.

Each individual confession, necessarily conducted in English, was a lengthy affair, for opportunity was taken to find out if the Lord's Prayer, the Hail Mary and the Creed were known. Then, with encouragement from the confessor, the telling of sins began. The priest was not only to listen to the stumbling penitent but to ask probing questions about the degree and repetition of sins, those that had been 'forgotten' and even habits that had not been thought sinful. (There was in this a danger that such inquiries might teach sin to the unaware). To some it was a religious experience giving comfort, to others it was a shaming trial. There were those who chose to delay it till near death, in spite of the fear of excommunication and the risk of dying unabsolved.

There were two categories of sins, the worst kind being called mortal – pride, wrath, lechery, sloth, avarice, gluttony and envy. These came to be known as the Seven Deadly Sins. Each required seven years penance in order to be remitted (perhaps fasting on bread and water every Friday and refraining from eating meat on Wednesdays). If they remained unrepented and unatoned they condemned the soul to hell. As an early fourteenth-century poem put it:

There are deadly sins seven
That lets[1] man to come to heaven.

A mural (c.1400) in the church at Ingatestone, Essex, shows the seven sins personified in little scenes painted between the spokes of a wheel, the centre of which is Hell's Mouth; and they are carved on bench-ends at Wiggenhall St. German, Norfolk. Venial sins (such as perjury, tardiness in visiting the sick or speaking ill of people) were not quite so serious, only sending the soul to purgatory. Although it was not officially necessary to confess these, the sinner was expected to do so. There were degrees of sin and, sometimes, mortal sins might be judged as venials and vice versa. This gave some hope but also some anxiety to a sinner, who could never be certain whether his venial sin was really a mortal one.

John Mirk devoted a large part of his book to a searching investigation to be conducted during confession. Firstly, there were questions on the articles of the faith, for example,

Believest also verily
That it is god's own body,
That the priest giveth thee
When thou shalt i-houseled be? [i.e. receive communion].

A negative reply to this would lay the answerer open to a charge of heresy for, since 1215, it was absolutely necessary to believe that the bread and wine at the eucharist were changed into the actual body and blood of Christ. A catechism about the ten commandments followed which managed to include, 'Have you withheld any payment of tithes?' Among inquiries about the seven deadly sins were, 'Have you back-bited your neighbour?' and 'Have you come to church late?'. With venial sins were questions as to the performance of the seven deeds of mercy (feeding the hungry, giving drink to the thirsty, clothing the naked, harbouring the stranger, visiting the sick, ministering to prisoners and burying the dead), then others on everyday faults: 'Have you left the churchyard gate open so that beasts got in?'; 'Have you come by the churchyard and not prayed for the dead?'; 'Have you ever ridden over growing corn?'; 'Have you taught your troublesome children good manners?'

When a man confessed to taking something from or hurting another, the priest instructed him to make restoration or pay for the harm done, otherwise he would not absolve him. Claudius, in Shakespeare's *Hamlet*

---

[1]Prevents, as in the preamble to a British passport.

(III, iii), confesses in prayer to his brother's murder and hopes for pardon; he realises he cannot have this because he still possesses the 'effects' for which he had committed the crime:

My crown, mine own ambition, and my queen.

A confessor, while refusing absolution, tried not to send such a sinner away in despair. After reproof he was given some good work to do in the hope that its performance would lead him to amend his ways.

c.   *The seal of confession*

It would have been next to impossible to get people to confess their sins to a man they saw daily unless they were confident that their disclosures would never be divulged. Keeping inviolate the seal of confession was a most important part of the instructions to priests. If one were questioned in a court of law about a penitent's confession he was to say that he knew nothing whatever as man, meaning that anything he knew, he knew as God. Even so, the priests were only human and there were stories of those who repeated confessions, probably after drinking in the ale-houses; thus did Sir Thomas Folyot, of Garway in Herefordshire, in 1397, whose sidesmen stated that he 'revealed publicly the confessions of Robert Scheppert his parishioner'. People who had reason to be worried about such unworthiness were allowed to find another priest if they could, otherwise to confess only those sins that would not hurt them or others if disclosed.

d.   *Absolution*

When the priest had heard all and convinced himself that the penitent was truly contrite and intended to sin no more he pronounced absolution in the forthright assertion, 'I absolve you from your sins'. This formula was based on an interpretation of scriptual texts, like John 20, 22–3, when Christ said to the assembled disciples after his resurrection, 'If you forgive any man's sins, they stand forgiven; if you pronounce them unforgiven, unforgiven they remain.' The words were considered to be the essential part of the sacrament, actually giving grace. It added enormously to the power of the priesthood, for these words, it was believed, would forgive a man's sins and get him into heaven via purgatory. Without them he was consigned to hell. Colloquially the word absolve became 'assoil' and, when speaking of the departed, a man might add, 'Whom God assoil!'

Besides making the yearly confession, no good Christian wanted to die without first confessing his sins and being absolved. Sudden death was a thing to be feared, there being no opportunity for confession and absolution; he remained an unrepentant sinner and, if his sins were mortal (and no man could be sure that they were not) they would carry him to hell. The murdered king, in *Hamlet*, was given no time to make his 'reckoning' (i.e. the amount of penance to be done to balance the total of his sins) and his ghost returned to say,

> Thus was I...
> ...sent to my account
> With all my imperfections on my head...
>
> (I, v)

(It was to purgatory, held to be a place of punishment and expiation, that he went, where his sins were being 'burnt and purged away' before he could enter heaven). It was to avoid such a contingency that Henry V, on the night before the battle of Agincourt, ordered his men to make their confessions. The Church had a merciful attitude towards the dying supposing that anyone who merely asked for a confessor, or a good church-goer unable to do so, might be absolved. However, a priest who arrived after death could not absolve, as he only had authority over the living.

Having been granted absolution the penitent was then said to be in a 'state of grace'. His sins had been forgiven and he had thus, so far, avoided hell. Before leaving, some payment was made to the confessor and this was a welcome addition to his income.

e. *Penance*

Although the sins were now forgiven, the guilty one had yet to atone for them by suffering some punishment reckoned to be their equivalent. It was expected that after death this would be the fate of everyone in purgatory. Only when the debt of sin had been expiated would the sinner be able to enter heaven. The prospect was alarming, but there was another way: the suffering which was owed could be experienced, either partly or fully, on earth by doing a penance imposed by the priest.

It was remembered that Christ never imposed penance, saying only to the woman accused of adultery, 'You may go; do not sin again (John 8. 3–11).' Consequently penances were deliberately made light and acceptable – saying a number of Paternosters and Aves, fasting or giving alms to the Church for the benefit of the poor. Like confession, they too were private, for other people were not to realise that penance was being performed.

Some public penances were imposed for public sins, 'those scandalous and notorious sins which set the whole town talking'. Robert the Devil, Duke of Normandy, the father of William the Conqueror, was strongly suspected of poisoning his brother, Duke Richard, in 1028. He presumably confessed this and was sent on pilgrimage to Jerusalem in 1035. He travelled barefoot, 'driven by the fear of God', and died at Nicea on the return journey. His great-great-grandson, Henry II of England, admitted that his hasty words may have led to the murder of Thomas Becket in 1170. Four years later part of his penance was to walk barefoot through the streets of Canterbury to be scourged by the monks.

Pilgrimages were not ordered for lesser sins as they could not fail to be noticed and thus the seal of the confessional would be broken, but some people chose this form of penance as a voluntary means of expiation. Others undertook the ascetic practices of undergoing vigils, flagellation or the wearing of a hair shirt. The material of this last was woven from the hair of goats or camels and its normal use in the East was for sacking, tents or bad-weather outer clothing. From early Christian times it had been used for uncomfortable garments worn next to the skin by public penitents. The repenting Purnele (who represented Pride), in *Piers Plowman*, said that she would sew hair-cloth as a lining for her undergarment and Thomas More (1478–1535) always wore a hair shirt.[1]

The fulfilment of penance was, at the least, inconvenient, and the practice of redeeming it for a money payment was common. Both parties gained by it – the wealthy sinners got rid of the nuisance of penance and the priests received the alms. Even death-bed penance, to be performed in purgatory, could be bought off. A noble or prelate, having made his last confession, would have his sins and the years of penance due to them totted up by the priest. In this urgent situation, to redeem them would probably require more ready money than he had available. Instead, it might be suggested that he gave the equivalent value in land to his church or an abbey. This explains why the words 'for the remission of my sins' or 'for the saving of my soul' are included in many such grants. This exchange of wordly wealth for claims on heaven resulted in the transfer of a large part of the lands of Europe to the Church, about one-third of England being in its hands by 1535.

---

[1] Still preserved in a convent at Newton Abbot, Devonshire.

4. MASS

All the parishioners were expected to go to their own parish church to hear mass every Sunday morning after breakfast, usually at nine o'clock, and on another twenty or so major holy days in the year. It was accounted as a serious sin if they did not go and they thereby risked public humiliation: a woman who had done her washing then would have to carry a bundle of it in a future Sunday church procession, clad in the white sheet of a penitent, and suffer two beatings.

Few people had the means of knowing the exact time so the doorkeeper gave warning of the approaching service by ringing the church bell for about half an hour beforehand. As all the people gathered together it was natural for them to greet one another and exchange news and gossip. The devout among them carried beads as an aid to their devotions. On first entering, and again on leaving, they paused at a stoup and crossed themselves with holy water believing that it cleansed them from venial sin.

A well-provided-for church with its colourful walls, gleaming windows and shining altar vessels seen in the fitful candlelight, was a finer place than many had ever been in, especially for the country-folk from their wattle-and-daub houses. To some it may have seemed like going into heaven itself. However, their ultimate destiny was painted on the wall of the chancel arch. This was the picture of the Last Judgement showing the good souls being accepted into heaven while the damned were driven into hell by devils. It forcibly reminded the onlookers of what they as sinners might expect at death. Only the worship of the Church, the prayers of the saints and the mercy of God could help them. They might be aware of the latter as they looked at the great cross on the roodscreen with the form of the crucified Christ on it. Even this was associated with suffering for it illustrated the medieval emphasis on the death of Christ (a past historical event) which obscured the everlasting nature of the resurrection.

The congregation was optimistically expected to kneel all the time, apart from standing at the Gospel and Creed. This imposed a great strain on the worshippers and many of them leaned against walls and pillars instead or even walked about. At first there was no seating at all. Then the lord of the manor provided a pew for himself and his family, and in the fifteenth century some parishes put in others, usually for letting to monied people. Benches were quite often placed along the walls for the frail and elderly. (This is thought to be the origin of the phrase, 'The weakest go to the wall').

The language of the service was Latin and the action was in the chancel, almost out of sight and hearing of the congregation. The people had come to 'hear' mass; it was not the custom for them to partake in it and there was very little for them to do. A few of the wealthier and more pious may have had primers (prayer-books for lay people) suggesting prayers in English that could be said privately at certain points in the service. The rest were encouraged to repeat the Paternoster and Ave. The priest and people, in fact, followed different ways of devotion, the latter being little more than distant spectators. This led to inattentive and even irreverent behaviour, common at all levels of society.

The sanctus hand-bell was rung by the parish clerk to draw the wandering attention of the congregation to the moment when the priest held the consecrated elements high overhead. All had been taught to believe that they were then looking upon 'Christ's own body' and the worshippers knelt in reverence. Only the priest and the assisting clergy received the bread and wine. It was enough for the onlookers to have seen them in order to share the advantages.

Most people did not really understand the doctrine of transubstantiation. If ordinary bread and wine had been changed into Christ's body and blood by the pronouncing of certain words it seemed to suggest that a magic incantation had been pronounced and they looked for marvellous results. Consequently there were stories told of people who said they had seen the host turn into flesh and blood and even into a child. Certainly all had been assured by the priest that, whenever they saw 'God's body', they would have meat and drink for the rest of that day and be in no danger of sudden death or blindness.

The body and blood of Christ were considered to be sacrificed anew on the altar at every mass (the word 'host', used for the consecrated wafer, was derived from the Latin *hostia*, meaning 'a victim'). The benefit which accrued to this act was the remission of sins. This applied to everyone present and also to the dead, for whom prayers were offered, because it would help to loose the bonds of those yet suffering 'the bitter pains of purgatory'. Besides the dead in general it was possible to be more specific. For payment of a fee, or by bequest, one's name, or that of a loved one, could be put on a list called the bede-roll and this was read out at mass on the anniversary of the death.

While the priest and clergy were making their communion the pax-board was presented to the people. This was a small tablet on which was a representation of a crucifix or other religious subject.[1] The parish

---

[1] St. Peter Hungate Church Museum, Norwich, has two of ivory and one of bronze on display.

clerk offered it to each person to kiss, using such suitable words as, 'Christ alone is the Peacemaker, which straightly commands peace between brother and brother'. This ceremony had developed from a time when the faithful had kissed each other before communicating. It was found to be a far from ideal practice and so the pax-board was substituted. In spite of being an emblem of peace it gave rise to its own quarrels for some thought they should kiss it before their neighbours did.

Preaching was not a customary part of Sunday worship but occasionally the priest would turn to his people and give them some explanation of the Creed, the Ten Commandments, the Seven Deadly Sins and other requirements of the faith.

After the communion some bread known as the Holy Bread or Holy Loaf was blessed (not consecrated) by the priest 'so that all who consume it shall receive health of body as well as of soul'. It was provided by certain parishioners in turn and the churchwardens bought baskets to keep it in. When he had cut it up into small portions the priest advanced to the chancel steps and the people went up to kiss his hand and receive a piece. It was thought to be a medicine for the sick as well as a preservative against the plague so it was sometimes taken home for poorly friends or kept as a charm. If any was left after the service the priest was allowed to have it for his own domestic use.

People were encouraged to make a money offering at mass but this was not compulsory and not expected from the poor. Whatever the amount it was always known as a 'mass penny' and was part of the rectorial income. In the lesser villages it would not amount to much but in the larger churches with wealthier congregations it might be a sizeable addition to other oblations.

At the end of the service the priest said the Latin words, '*Ite, missa est,*' meaning, 'Go, (the congregation) is dismissed.' The phrase gave the name 'mass' to the rite and was used for this as early as the fourth century. The polite and reverent worshippers then departed. Others had already gone, after having seen the elevation of the host, for that was all that was needful, they thought, to do them any good. In this rush to get away they behaved 'as though they had seen not Christ, but the Devil', a phrase of St. Bernardino of Siena (1380–1444).

After the service people were free from religious obligations for the rest of the day. Those from outlying parts perhaps brought a packed meal with them and ate it either in the church itself (in bad weather), the churchyard or the church-house, if there was one, the latter being equivalent to the modern parish hall. Evensong in the afternoon was probably poorly attended for, especially in summer, the morning worshippers were then ready for recreation – archery, sports and dancing. The church-wardens might provide refreshments, putting the profits towards church expenses. From this free time on a holy day has come our modern word holiday.

5. MARRIAGE

a. *Betrothal*

When two people agreed to marry they joined hands and promised to take each other as husband and wife. They then exchanged gifts such as a pair of gloves, a belt or rings. This ceremony, with or without witnesses, was known as the troth-plight or hand-fasting. In the eyes of the law this betrothal was recognised as a marriage and was absolutely binding.[1] If, later on, either partner chose to disregard it and marry another the existence of the first contract made the second illegal. It was for this reason that the children of Edward IV (Edward V and his brother and sisters) were removed from the succession by Parliament in 1483 when the news of a secret pre-contract of the king with the Lady Eleanor Butler was revealed by the bishop of Bath and Wells.

Much hung on the actual words spoken. When Margery Paston was betrothed to Richard Calle, her brother's chief bailiff, in 1469, there were no witnesses. Her angry family sent the pair to be examined separately by the bishop of Norwich. Margery repeated what she had said to Richard, and added that 'if those words made it not sure ... she would make it sure ere she went thence'. The bishop's inquiries led him to decide in favour of the pair.

After betrothal some couples might quite properly decide to live together as man and wife. The Church did not approve of this but it supported the promises made and upheld the legality of the marriage. In addition, it tried to insist on a church ceremony as well, for it held that this was a sacrament and conferred grace.

b. *Impediments to marriage*

The priest published the banns on three successive Sundays or holy days.

---

[1] Such hand-fast marriages remained legal in England till 1754, and in Scotland till 1940.

This was necessary in order to avoid marriage with a blood relation[1] or with someone connected through another person's marriage, as well as with a spiritual relative gained at baptism or confirmation. These were the rules of the Church but in the small communities of medieval England it was almost impossible to keep them strictly. Hearing the banns, any members of the congregation who knew of a hindrance to the marriage had to 'say now or never on pain of cursing.'

c. *At the church door*

Weddings took place before noon, as the bride and bridegroom came fasting in preparation for the nuptial mass. Petruchio, going to marry Kate, in Shakespeare's *The Taming of the Shrew*, was aware of this when he said,

> The morning wears, 'tis time we were at church.
>
> (III, iii)

The bride and bridegroom were dressed in their best or new clothes of whatever colours appealed to them. The apparel of the very wealthy would be something specially grand and doubtless kept carefully afterwards. Isabel, Countess of Warwick, by her will of 1439, left her wedding gown to Tewkesbury abbey. It was probably meant to be used in a way similar to that indicated by Sir William Compton in 1523, 'To the Abbey Church of Winchcombe ... my wedding gown of tinsel[1] satin to make a vestment'. It was customary for the bride to wear her hair flowing over her shoulders, the 'new untrimmed bride' referred to by Constance in Shakespeare's *King John* (III, i). On her head there would be either a garland of flowers or a jewelled band. Some parishes possessed ornaments for their brides to hire – a set of jewels was presented to Henley-on-Thames parish church in 1518 for this purpose.

The priest met each couple and their friends outside the church, for the first part of the ceremony was held at the door or in the porch, so that there would be as many witnesses as possible. Chaucer's Wife of Bath had married five husbands at the church-door, the first one when she was only twelve years old. This custom applied to all, even royalty. When King Henry I married Matilda of Scotland at Westminster abbey in 1100 the nobles and lesser people 'were crowding round the King and the maid in front of the doors of the church', to see them 'joined together in

---

[1]This included anyone within the fourth degree of consanguinity, that is, the two people concerned had a common great great grandparent.
[1]Material woven or interwoven with gold or silver thread.

lawful matrimony with the dignity befitting King and Queen.' In the later Middle Ages the convention began to change and there are some instances of weddings taking place inside the building – in 1451 Sir William Plumpton and Joan Wintringham (wearing 'a garment of green checkery' and 'one of a red colour', respectively) were married in Knaresborough parish church, Yorkshire, 'they standing at the door of the chancel of the said church, within the said church'; and in 1501 the ten-year-old Henry, Duke of York (later Henry VIII) led Catherine of Aragon down the length of St. Paul's cathedral to her marriage with his elder brother Prince Arthur.

Much of the service was in Latin, but, as it was essential that the bride and bridegroom should understand what they were promising to do, the most important words were in English. Each was asked, 'Wilt thou have this woman/man to thy wedded wife/husband?' and both, in turn, answered, 'I will.' At that point the woman was 'given' by her father or a friend to the priest, as representing God. The priest's question in the service in use at York makes this clear: 'Who gives me this wife?' He then 'gave' her to the man, as God gave Eve to Adam. After mutual promises to care for each other, a ring and a gift of money were placed on a dish or book, blessed and sprinkled with holy water. The ring was a necessary part of the ceremony – Marion Chamber of Bury St. Edmunds, bequeathed her 'marrying ring' in 1505, describing it as having 'a diamond and a ruby therein'; and in 1530 Mary, daughter of Sir John Nevill, a Yorkshire knight, had a 'wedding ring, gold', for her marriage to Gervys Clifton. Poorer folk made do with rings of baser metal – brass, tin, lead – or even leather or wire. The bridegroom gave the money to his bride and put the ring on the thumb and the first, second and third fingers of the right hand in turn, leaving it on the third, saying, 'With this ring I thee wed and this gold and silver I thee give and with my body I thee worship and with all my worldly cathel[1] I thee endow.' After giving the blessing the priest led the bridal party into the church and the bride and bridegroom to the altar.

d. *Inside the church*

During the nuptial mass that followed, a canopy called a veil or care[2]-cloth was held over the pair. Every church was directed to have one of these by the Council of Exeter in 1287 and it was the churchwardens' duty to provide it. Wealthy people would perhaps supply a more

---
[1] Goods. The word survives as 'chattel.'
[2] Some kind of woven material.

splendid one of their own. 'One piece of Lucca cloth' was used for the canopy of Richard, Earl of Arundel, and Isabella Despenser about 1321. At the end of mass, which the bride and bridegroom and the rest of the congregation 'heard' but did not otherwise take part in, the veil was taken away.

Finally the priest blessed the bride-cup containing bread or cake in wine (known as sops-in-wine) and all the company drank from it, after the priest and the newly-married pair. The cup, sometimes called a mazer, usually belonged to the parish. In 1507 the church of St. John Baptist, at Pilton, Somersetshire, possessed a 'standing mazer to serve for brides at their wedding.' This custom persisted into the seventeenth century and is mentioned in Shakespeare's *The Taming of the Shrew*. That 'mad-brained bridegroom', Petruchio

> quaft off the muscadel[1]
> And threw the sops all in the sexton's face...
>
> (III, ii)

clearly leaving none for anybody else. This festive drink symbolised the beginning of the common life together.

A money offering was made befitting the position and means of the families of the wedded pair.

e. *The wedding-breakfast*

When the party left the church they went to the family home or a local ale-house for the wedding feast. As they had gone to church fasting this first meal of the day was often called the wedding breakfast. Ale had been specially brewed for the occasion and the profits of it were given to the new bride. Thus the event was called the 'bride-ale'. By Shakespeare's time this word had developed into its modern form, for Petruchio's bride, Kate, referred to her 'bridal dinner'. Some families must have found it difficult to meet expenses and occasionally help was given by a richer neighbour; Christopher Mitford, a merchant of Newcastle-upon-Tyne, left money in 1540 for ten poor girls, saying it was 'towards their dinners in the days of their marriages.' There was much eating, drinking and jollity. Open house was kept and attracted such revellers as Perkin the Prentice, of Chaucer's *The Cook's Tale*, for

> At every bride-ale would he sing and hop...

---

[1] A rich, spicy wine.

It was easy for such junketings to get out-of-hand and about 1223 Bishop Richard Poore of Salisbury ordered that marriages should 'be celebrated reverently and with honour, not with laughter or sport, or in taverns or at public potations or feasts'. Similar injunctions continued to be issued from time to time, proving that they were little heeded.

f. *The blessing of the marriage-chamber*

At night the priest arrived to bless the pair in bed. After prayers with responses he sprinkled them with holy water and departed. Oberon, in Shakespeare's *A Midsummer Night's Dream*, echoed this benediction when he said,

> To the best bride-bed will we,
> Which by us shall blessed be;
> And the issue there create
> Ever shall be fortunate.
>
> (V, i)

g. *Divorce*

The Church insisted that marriage was a sacrament and could not be dissolved. Having said that, it also provided the means for stating that an actual union had never been a lawful marriage. Its officials could pronounce that no marriage had existed and so grant an annulment; that is all the word 'divorce' meant at that time.

The many bars to a valid marriage removed a large number of potential spouses, but it was possible to be unaware of some of them or to eliminate them by buying a papal dispensation. If a marriage proved unsuccessful and both parties wished to end it, it was generally easy to discover (or invent) a relationship of one sort or another proving that they ought not to have been married in the first place. It was not difficult to get the needed divorce for, as William Langland wrote in *Piers Plowman*, the Church courts were ready to 'make and unmake matrimony for money', or for 'a mantle of miniver'.

Quite ordinary people appeared as persons divorced or wanting divorces in the records of bishops' or archdeacons' courts. In 1256 Hamon, a cobbler of Caveringham, came before the archbishop of York asking for a divorce from his wife of twenty years so that he could marry Alice Sterling. At Durham, in 1451, John Guy, a dyer, said he had been divorced from Isabella Woodward and therefore his second marriage to Elizabeth Mors was lawful.

The most well-known cases concerned royalty. The marriage of Eleanor of Aquitaine and Louis VII of France in 1137 was annulled, after fifteen years and the birth of two daughters, on the grounds of consanguinity. Two months later Eleanor married Henry, Duke of Normandy, who shortly became Henry II of England. The youngest son of this union, King John, divorced Avice of Gloucester in 1199 following ten years of childless marriage. The reason given was that they were cousins in the third degree, both being great-grandchildren of Henry I, a fact which had been known but more-or-less ignored in 1189. When the eighteen-year-old Henry VIII married Catherine of Aragon in 1509 it was necessary to have a papal dispensation because the bride was his brother Arthur's widow. Years later that was the very reason he advanced for seeking an annulment. He was probably not the only one to be aware, from the beginning of a marriage, of an impediment which might be put forward later as a cause of ending it.

6. PARISH OFFICIALS, EMPLOYEES AND PERFORMERS

a. *Churchwardens*
i. Upkeep of the parish church

The great events of family life gave opportunities for bringing priest and parishioner closer together. They also underlined the fact that the building in which personal ceremonies took place needed preservation. It was usual for the priest to be responsible for the upkeep of the chancel while the maintenance of the nave devolved on the parishioners, who also provided most of the moveables such as ornaments, vestments and liturgical books. Any who refused to contribute were liable to be excommunicated or imprisoned.

The parishioners were represented by some of their number (usually two) called churchwardens – the Rolls of Parliament of 1341 refer to them as 'wardens of the goods of the church.' These important officers were chosen annually at a democratic parish meeting held in the church, at which all men and women had the right to vote. Women were eligible and there was a small minority of them in this position, like Alice Cook and Alice Pyppedon at St. Patrick's, Ingestre, Staffordshire, in 1426, and Beatrice Braye of St. Petrock's, Exeter, in 1428. For perhaps the first time in medieval England lowly but trustworthy men and women with little or no education, chosen only for their good sense and reliability, attained positions in their local communities which used their latent organisational powers.

The duties that these people had been elected to perform were to care for the church building, see to the repair of its contents, renew certain objects and buy additional items, as well as to oversee the behaviour of the clergy. All except the last required money. Fortunate churches possessed lands or houses which had been bequeathed to them and from which they drew a steady rent. Without these assets the money had to be raised by other means.

The churchwardens needed to have some business sense and the ability to arouse and direct the enthusiasm of the parishioners in a variety of ways. Sometimes a stock of sheep or cattle was kept and the milk, wool, cheese and meat sold. Money could be obtained by selling gifts which had been made to the church – a gold ring, a brass pot, a fine gown – or by hiring out bridal jewellery, or the brewing, cooking and baking appliances from the church house. Occasional receipts came from fabric-fund boxes, fees for burial inside the church and collections made on certain holy days both at services and in the street.

In places with little or no regular income the mainstay of the funds was the church-ale. This was a feast for all, usually held in the church house. At times it might be conducted in the church itself, as at St. Lawrence's, Reading, where, in 1506, someone was paid 'for making clean of the church against the day of drinking in the said church'. According to the wealth and needs of the parish one or more church-ales might be held during the year. They took place after mass on such Sundays as Whit, during Lent or at the Feast of the Dedication of the church. The churchwardens provided the ale and the people contributed the food. They were jolly affairs, curious mixtures of religious and secular life. Many enjoyed them as innocent, social occasions although for some the revelry became excessive. Priests would attend but were supposed to be temperate and make an early and sober departure.

Collections were taken and these formed a large part of the revenue of many churches. The money, from this and other sources, was used either for general purposes or for a specific object such as the buying of a new bell. Hard-working wardens, wealthy parishioners and enthusiastic volunteers together provided the means for building and maintaining to the glory of God. Our finest churches stand today as witnesses to their care.

ii. Churchwardens' and sidesmens' reports

Church ales must have been the most agreeable part of the churchwardens' duties. The most unpleasant was the obligation to report on the moral shortcomings of the clergy in their parish. In this they were assisted by four other elected parishioners called sidesmen (a contracted form of 'synodsmen') who attended synods as witnesses in support of the churchwardens' statements. These were held annually at the visitation of each parish, which was generally made by the archdeacon. Then the affairs of the church and parish were investigated in minute detail by going through a prepared questionnaire. The answers were written down in visitation records, several of which have survived, noting faults for future correction. They show that, while many churches were in a good state of repair, being well-provided with vestments, bridal canopies and so on, others had leaking roofs, broken windows, torn service books and even lacked a chalice.

There were also searching questions about the private lives of the clergy which the wardens and sidesmen were obliged to answer. This was a very important aspect of a visitation inquiry, for any liaisons of the priest had an economic as well as a moral implication. The Hereford records of 1397 show about 22 per cent of the parish clergy living with a 'hearth-mate' or behaving promiscuously. For faults of this sort varying penances were awarded. A first offender might be sent on a visit to a shrine, there to give a money offering and to return with a certificate of proof. Suspension from celebrating divine service was an infliction that involved the wrong-doer's money as he was obliged to pay for a chaplain to do so instead. Repeated offences attracted public humiliation like walking round the market place carrying wax or a cope to be donated to the church. If all else failed there might be a spell in the bishop's prison. The ultimate penalties of deprivation and degradation were rarely given.

When everything had been dealt with the little party of priests and parishioners returned to their homes. There was doubtless some bad feeling if any of the parish clergy had been presented by the churchwardens and sidesmen but, after a few days, they probably learned to take a philosophical view of it, knowing that it was one of the perils of their calling.

iii. Peter's Pence

The churchwardens had to collect Peter's Pence, a tax payable to the pope. At first it had been a voluntary donation but by the twelfth century it was looked on as an obligation and the national sum had become fixed at about £40,000. Each householder, except the very poorest, was charged one penny (a day's pay for a ploughman before 1350) on his hearth, or house, and the tax was sometimes called hearthpenny or smoke-farthings. It was the custom in some places to carry the parish levy to the cathedral in procession during Whitsun week, hence it was also known as Whitsun farthings or Pentecostals. This method of collection produced more than the required sum and the bishops pocketed the surplus.

In their dealings with the popes the English kings at times threatened to withhold the payment of Peter's Pence. Edward I did refuse to pay in 1366 and for a number of years afterwards. This apart, it was handed over fairly regularly.

b. *The sexton*

The sexton (a corruption of 'sacristan') was a useful odd-job man. One of his tasks was mentioned in 1463: John Baret, of Bury St. Edmunds, anticipating his funeral knell, left money in his will for the 'Sexton of the church to have ... for his ringing and his meat.' Another was recorded at Cratfield, Suffolk, where, in 1490, the churchwardens paid the sexton his wages for his help with four church ales. Shakespeare, in *Hamlet* (c.1601) refers to a third, for the man digging Ophelia's grave said he had 'been sexton here, man and boy, thirty years (V, i).' This minor official needed to live near the church and St. Edmund's, Salisbury, provided him with a room over the south porch.

c. *The nightwatchman*

Churches were repositories of useful and valuable objects, many of which were bought with money raised by the efforts of the parishioners, who therefore took good care to guard them. Where priests or other staff lived in the vestry or rooms over the porch their presence acted as a deterrent to would-be burglars, but otherwise it was sensible to have a nightwatchman. The churchwardens of St. Leonard's, Hythe, in Kent, paid Thomas the Bedesman for this duty, and in 1480, as an extra payment, he was given a gown 'for lying in the church.' If alarmed, he would have been able to rouse the neighbourhood by ringing the church bells.

d. *The ringers*

If the church had a number of bells a team of volunteer ringers rang on special occasions like Corpus Christi Day or during Whitsun week. In addition to a small money payment for their efforts they also received some sustenance – 'calves heads for the ringers' was the customary dish at St. Dunstan's, Canterbury.

Besides ringing on ecclesiastical festivals, it was required that the bells be rung if ever the king or queen entered or left the parish. This was a means of announcing the approach of royalty, thus providing a reception by the populace and a chance for them to see their sovereign. This practice was first mentioned in churchwardens' accounts in 1444 when Queen Margaret, wife of Henry VI, visited Saffron Walden. Then the men were paid for 'ringing when the queen was here.' Bells were also rung for a bishop so that his flock could come and obtain his blessing as he passed by and perhaps receive confirmation. Archdeacons, too, claimed this right when making a visitation.

Certain special occasions were observed by bell-ringing – a coronation, the birth of an heir-apparent and victorious battles.

The bells themselves had been consecrated and christened by a bishop or his suffragan and it was believed that they were powerful against evil spirits. Since the latter were thought to be the cause of thunder and lightning the bells were rung to dispel storms. This was common practice at St. Mary's, Sandwich, where, in 1464, the wardens gave 'bread and drink for ringers in the great thundering'.

As well as the ringers some parishes had a bellman. He may have tolled for services but also carried a hand-bell round the parish calling attention to church proclamations and funerals.

e. *Travelling workmen and artists*

The only way of lighting the church was by candles and so the candlemakers (or wax-chandlers) were much in demand. It seems that they travelled about from place to place being sure of a waiting market for their wares. At Cowfold, in Sussex, between the years 1471 and 1485, the churchwardens supplied the necessary wax, paid the wages of the men and also provided board and lodging for the master workman. Every church tried to keep a stock of wax ready for the visiting candlemaker. It was a costly part of ecclesiastical requirements, constantly being depleted. For this reason many penances involved carrying a given weight of wax in procession to be handed over for church use.

The store of service books needed making, renewing or mending now and again. This was a task for itinerant craftsmen. At the beginning of the fifteenth century the wardens of St. Augustine's church, Hedon, Yorkshire, bought parchment to make a book. Then a scribe, Adam Skelton, copied the words into it and John Payntor illustrated it. They must have started early in the day when the light was good for they were allowed breakfast money.

A wealthy parish, or one installing expensive new furnishings, needed the services of painters, carvers, silversmiths and gilders. Sometimes there were skilled local craftsmen to call on, otherwise artists were brought in from farther afield.

f. *Miscellaneous occupations*

Payments were made for other tasks when the need arose. Women would always be wanted to make and wash surplices and mend vestments, as well as to polish brass utensils, and this would give a little extra money to a needy household. The graveyard would quickly become overgrown in the summer and a local man would be asked to tidy it up as was John Frye, of St. Edmund's, Salisbury, at the end of the fifteenth century. He was paid for 'cutting down of the nettles and weeds in the churchyard'.

g. *Church plays*

Mystery plays, telling the bible story, were written and performed at several important cities – Chester, Coventry, Newcastle and York, among others. Beginning in the churches with the priests, they had moved out beyond the confines of those buildings and been taken over by the people. They reached their full development after 1311 when the festival of Corpus Christi was established, this being the usual day for presenting the sequence. The actors were the members of crafts gilds – the ship-wrights, goldsmiths, thatchers and so on. The whole cycle took a day to perform at York, starting at half past four in the morning, and three days at Chester. These full-scale performances attracted great crowds including royalty.

There were also many minor church plays put on occasionally in town and country parishes. Besides providing instruction and entertainment they also brought in money for the church funds. The authors were probably members of the local clergy. St. Lawrence's, Reading, performed its play about the three kings (called the 'King Play') on May Day, 1499, and thereafter at Whitsuntide. St. Margaret's, Westminster, had a similar play and in 1483 the wardens paid someone to hang the Bethlehem star from the rood loft. Like these, some plays were acted inside the churches, others in a suitable open space out-of-doors. That of St. Peter and St. Paul, Bassingbourn, Cambridgeshire, was performed in a croft near the church. A stage was often erected and the wardens at Reading paid 'the labourers in the Forbury for setting up the poles for the scaffold' in 1507.

'Players' clothing' of one sort and another is noted in wardens' accounts from 1460. Cloth for a doublet and hose, canvas for caps, material 'to make Eve a coat' and dyed flax for wigs were bought at Reading in 1507. Sometimes a church did not possess any or enough costumes, and, like the wardens of St. Margaret's, Southwark, in 1460, were obliged to obtain what they needed by 'hiring of the Garments'. For those churches with a tradition of performing plays it would have been an investment to have their own wardrobe. Some useful person was then paid for 'keeping the players' clothes', as was done at St. Andrew's, Ashburton, Devon, 1519–20.

A great deal of spare-time work went into the rehearsal and public performances of a play and it deserved a wider audience than its own immediate parish. To ensure this, a messenger was sent round the neighbouring villages to announce the play. It was the only kind of stage entertainment many people were ever likely to see and they streamed in to watch the drama unfold. In this way twenty-seven villages supported the play of 'the holy martyr Saint George' at Bassingbourn in 1511. Conversely the little companies (sometimes called 'Games') quite often went out to their audiences. New Romney's play on the Passion and Resurrection was taken to several small towns and villages in Kent and Sussex between 1399 and 1508, with exchange visits being paid. Thus it was possible for people in a district possessing a number of companies to see more plays than the one belonging to their own home-ground.

The actors, who were devoting their holidays to entertaining the audiences, were sustained with refreshments, usually bread and ale. These were given to Lopham Game and Garboldisham Game when they visited Harling, Norfolk, in 1457, and the same were provided for the Kenninghall Players in 1467.

'Gatherings,' or collections, were made among the onlookers and, when all expenses had been dealt with, the profits went to the church fund in general or for a particular item. In 1505 Henry VII, having presumably viewed a performance, donated money to the 'Players of Kingston toward the building of the church steeple'.

Besides the religious plays, May Day and Whitsuntide saw summer festivities organised by many wardens. To them came the maypole dancers, the morris men, minstrels, the hobby horse and Robin Hood with his followers performing a 'May play'. These were popular entertainers and the resulting 'gathering' was usually a handsome contribution that kept the accounts in a healthy state.

The plays and other parish entertainments linked priest and people in the same purpose and most of them gave the results of their labours to the large building in their midst unquestioningly. A few, perhaps, wondered why their contributions had to be spent on such costly items as a gilded tabernacle to contain an image of the Virgin Mary, a coat of cloth of gold for a statue of St. Mary Magdalene or a silver chalice which they themselves would never touch and only see from afar off.

h. *Organists and singers*

Until the middle of the fifteenth century the sung parts of the mass simply consisted of a duologue in plainsong chanted in Latin by the priest and the parish clerk. Then most large parishes wanted the services to be enriched by part-singing as practised in the cathedrals. More singers and an organist were needed for this and they were accommodated in a gallery specially built on top of the screen at the chancel entrance. As this happened to be beneath the great rood it came to be known as the rood-loft. From this vantage point the occupants could see and hear the priest and know when it was time for their own participation and the moments for leading the responses of the congregation.

The parish clerk was usually the chief musician assisted by the other staff in minor orders. Men and boys of the parish volunteered to join the newly-formed choir and one of them might eventually become the choir master. Those with the best voices and the greatest ability could advance to semi-professional status and were wanted by many churches to augment their own choirs at certain times. St. Mary-at-Hill, London, hired 'a child that sang a treble to help the choir in Christmas holidays', in 1493; and solo men were taken on in subsequent years. While the highly-trained singers were paid a fee, the volunteers usually received a token payment. All were likely to be rewarded with refreshments, like the 'wine for singers on our church holy days' provided by the wardens of St. Andrew Hubbard, London, in 1496.

Promising choir-boys were taught to play the organ and this accomplishment later enabled them to take positions as church organists. Such situations were was often of a casual nature for special occasions, but some fortunate players were able to gain regular employment, like John Fychelle, at St. Margaret's, Southwark, in 1457.

Serving in a humbler capacity an old man might earn a few pence by blowing the organ. Three almsmen took this job in turns at St. Mary-at-Hill in 1525 working a week at a time.

Although in the smaller and more remote churches the chanting of priest and clerk was the only music ever heard, the new polyphonic style widened the experience of many priests and parishioners. The words were still in Latin yet the people's help was wanted and they felt more like participators and less like onlookers only.

i. *The parish meeting*

Everyone who was paid for work done for the church, or whose voluntary efforts earned money which was presented to the funds, was mentioned in the churchwardens' accounts, either anonymously, by group or sometimes by name. These accounts were drawn up at the parish meeting held in the church at the end of the wardens' term of office. Receipts and expenses were listed and entered on a roll of parchment by a clerk, probably one of the parish clergy, who received a fee for doing so. Many of these accounts survive, the oldest known being those of St. Michael, Bath, which began in 1349. The language used was either Latin or English but towards the middle of the fifteenth century English became the more dominant. After being shown to auditors the wardens presented the accounts to the meeting for approval. They were given to the archdeacon at his next visitation together with an inventory of the church goods. Successors for the next period were elected and the outgoing wardens handed over custody of the church funds and property.

There was no parish council, so when responsible people were wanted for a particular purpose, a group was chosen to superintend that matter only. For instance, when the annual accounts of St. Mary-at-Hill were presented in 1526, a bequest of £200 was 'put into the church chest in presence of 12 persons of the parish.' From this kind of requirement a sort of parochial council, which could be called on when needed, came into being in a few parishes early in the sixteenth century.

When all was settled the meeting closed with some form of celebration which probably took place in the nave. At St. Edmund's, Salisbury, it was on Maundy Thursday; in 1461 24 gallons of good ale were bought for the purpose and this custom continued to the end of Henry VIII's reign. Besides this, a meal was provided for the auditors and wardens on Easter Day when the main dish was a calf's head. It was necessary to wait until then for this delicacy as meat was not eaten during Lent.[1] This modest meal was a reasonable recompense for the constant hard work throughout the term of office.

---

[1] For exception to this rule see Chapter Three, section 2.

7. SUPERSTITIONS

Merely being alive in the Middle Ages could be a struggle and a hardship. Everyone was liable to suffer ill-health, pain, disability, petty afflictions, sudden disaster, early deaths of children and their own premature demise. Very little practical help was obtainable. Medical advice, such as it was, could only be had by the wealthy, and the solving of day-to-day problems was beset by ignorance. Most of these ills, according to the Church, were due to the Devil, who was an ever-present force to be reckoned with. Only the Church possessed the supernatural power to oppose him and its countermeasures were available to the faithful. If a man thought that he had clapped eyes on a devil, possibly in assumed human or animal form, he should at once make the sign of the cross and the wicked fiend would immediately be repelled.

There were also witches to beware of, although 'wise women' and 'cunning men' were helpful to their customers, often giving herbal and medical advice. The ones to be feared were the more sophisticated sorcerers who deemed themselves to have special faculties for telling the future, curing one man by giving his illness to another and causing the deaths of their clients' enemies. People viewed a supposed 'black' witch (mainly, but not exclusively, a woman) with fear and were only too ready to attribute their calamities to her. This sometimes led to harmless, lonely, old women, goaded by mocking louts into making threats of revenge, being accused of witchcraft if these seemed to come true.

In the later Middle Ages the Church theologians reached the conviction that witches possessed their occult powers because they had made pacts with the Devil and that therefore they deserved to die. As a result the Inquisition treatise, *Malleus Maleficarum* ('Hammer of Witches'), of 1486 encouraged the persecution of witches because they were devil-worshippers, whether they had performed acts hurtful to neighbours or not. It was not proceeded with in England due, seemingly, to apathy about the matter among both the hierarchy and the people. If witches were prosecuted in the English church courts – and the practice of magic was an ecclesiastical offence – it was because they were thought to have brought harm to others, such as forcing a leg to break or preventing butter from setting. It was difficult to prove that mishaps were caused by witchcraft so the defendant might be discharged and punishments, if awarded, were mainly trivial. Where sentence of death by hanging or burning was imposed it was usually because the witchcraft had a political or treasonable motive, such as compassing the death of the king.

There was a variety of remedies which could be employed without recourse to professional help. The easiest was the frequent repetition of the Ave, Creed and Paternoster. The moments it took to say the latter prayer became a common estimate of time. John Northwood, writing to John, Viscount Beaumont, in 1448, describing an event, wrote, 'All this was done, as men say, in a Paternoster while'. Strings of beads known as rosaries or paternosters helped in counting the number of times these prayers were said.

Some people went about armed against the assaults of the Devil and preserved, they hoped, from lightning, fire, drowning and the like by wearing a talisman round the neck or wrist. It might be as simple as a piece of paper or a medal, with verses from the gospels or the sign of the cross thereon. The most popular was the agnus dei, a wax medallion with the figure of a lamb bearing a cross, representative of the 'Lamb of God.' In the thirteenth century one was fastened to St. Alban's abbey during a thunderstorm but it did not save the building from being struck by lightning. A devout and anxious Christian might have many such amulets hanging about his person. He put it down to their efficiency when he escaped afflictions and blamed his own lack of faith if they failed to protect him.

Fasting on certain holy days was resorted to by some. In the fifteenth century it was believed that sudden death could be avoided by fasting throughout the year on the day of the week on which the feast of the Annunciation happened to occur; and fasting on St. Mark's day gained one protection against fire – a blessing indeed for those who lived in timber-framed houses.

The water of holy wells was thought to have curative powers. These springs had been used in the magical rites of the old heathen religion and had been adopted by the Christian Church, being then associated with the names of saints and so becoming 'holy'.

Certain observances required the professional assistance of a priest. Only he could exorcise the salt and water, together forming 'holy water', to which the Devil was known to be allergic. When the clerk carried it round the parish, people asked him to sprinkle it on themselves, their houses, fields and animals; the sick desired to drink it and it could even be poured down the throat of a bewitched cow. All were glad to make an offering, for it would keep them safe from evil spirits and disease.

If a demon had actually taken possession of someone, shown by a strangeness of behaviour (perhaps a severe type of schizophrenia), the Church had an awesome remedy for the condition. In a formal and dramatic ceremony the exorcist commanded the evil spirit to depart in the name of God and the Church. This was based on the words of the risen Christ to his disciples, 'Faith will bring with it these miracles: believers will cast out devils in my name' (Mark 16.17). There was a general feeling that exorcism could succeed. Where it failed it was put down to the sufferer's sins or lack of faith in the beholders.

In an age when all food eaten had to be grown, plant-pests were more than a nuisance, they were a threat to life itself. Since it was held that all beasts were divinely subject to man, priests would first admonish them, and other misbehaving animals – rats, eels in a lake, sparrows in a church –, and if they refused to heed this censure they were then formally cursed. The Church maintained that this procedure would destroy them.

The belief in the supernatural change in the host led people to think that its presence could produce a material miracle. Advantages might be expected from merely seeing it and the priests were ready to consecrate the bread at special masses on behalf of the sick, for good weather or for avoidance of the plague. Such additional celebrations were paid for by the individual or community hoping to benefit. In 1516 the people of Colchester gave a piece of land to the prior of Holy Cross when the monks celebrated mass 'for the further prosperity of the town'. At Easter a communicant with a particular need would try not to swallow the communion bread but take it away for a magical purpose – to cure a sick member of his family, to fertilise the fields or simply to carry it about with him for good luck. The Church deplored such practices, but they were a direct consequence of its own efforts to exalt the divine power attributed to the consecrated elements.

When large-scale disasters like the plague, poor harvests and bad weather struck, all the people of the parish united in their entreaties. The usual response of the priest was to arrange a public procession. Carrying the host, cross, banners and bells to drive away the evil spirits responsible for the adversities, the procession wound about the streets and fields with stops for intercessary prayers and expressions of repentance. It was believed that these actions could induce God to alter the laws of the natural world.

Probably the more senior, intellectual and spiritual members of the hierarchy and priesthood did not themselves believe in the superstitions that accrued to the worship of the Church. An enlightened man like

Chaucer's Poor Parson, who was not persuaded of the efficacy of the Church's magic, would yet accept it in the hope that a successful outcome would bring the performer to an increase in faith.

It was thought to be unlucky for a traveller to meet a hare, a woman with flowing tresses, a blind or lame man or even a monk. One of the last-mentioned was met by a certain Master William of the household of the archbishop of Canterbury when he set out one day to join the entourage of his lord. The monk himself, aware that this would bring bad luck on Master William, advised him to return. William, however, was not inclined to linger and rode on. He had not gone far before his horse, with him still on it, fell into a pit full of deep water and he was rescued only with difficulty. One of his companions, after pondering on the incident, wrote to Peter of Blois, archdeacon of Bath (c.1135–c.1204), about such unlucky meetings and other superstitions. The archdeacon, who was a relative of the bishop of Winchester and also of the king, replied that a good Christian should leave the future to God and ignore false notions of what was lucky or unlucky. He concluded, 'My own opinion is that Master William would have been equally in danger of drowning if no monk had met him!' If one highly-placed churchman in the twelfth century was able to arrive at such a judgement so were others. The Church as a whole could have taught such Christian common sense but did not choose to do so.

8. SAINTS AND PILGRIMAGES

a. *Pilgrimage*

The Church took over the biblical view that illness was caused by the sin of the sufferer (cf. John 9. 1–3). This being so it taught that, as penitence could bring about forgiveness of the sin, it could also cure the illness caused by the sin. The means of obtaining this desired end was prayer to the saints, those men and women who had led obviously holy lives on earth and had gone straight to heaven at death. There they acted as intercessors between a stern God and fearful humanity.

Following the example of Christ and his disciples the early saints had laid hands on the sick. By prayer and perhaps some sympathetic power or hypnotic influence they had effected 'faith cures'. After their deaths it was felt that they might continue to do so from their heavenly home if appealed to. Since their earthly bodies had accomplished cures it was thought that power still resided in their earthly remains or in objects that had touched them. For that reason it became the custom to place them in raised shrines for veneration and healing purposes. These were so popular that churches without saints wanted their own relics (whether only a rib, some fingers or a tooth) and a large European market developed in them. This was supplied by professional relic-merchants who were not too scrupulous about the authenticity of their goods, so that it was possible to see the head of John the Baptist in three different places. Small shrines, or reliquaries, were made to contain the lesser relics. These were generally little coffers but some were in the shape of the part of the body concerned.

Although the soul of the saint was assumed to be in heaven yet he was considered to reside physically in his shrine. A thirteenth-century stained glass window in Canterbury cathedral shows Thomas Becket climbing out of his shrine so that he could appear to a sleeping monk. As the saint had a local habitation it was necessary to journey to it in order to make one's petition. So the idea of pilgrimage evolved.

At first the holders of relics had a genuine desire to use these possessions to assist people in need. Those who had been helped often gave voluntary offerings in thanksgiving and, because of these, certain monasteries and churches became richer. Others cast envious eyes on them and sought to obtain crowd-pulling relics for themselves. Monks had 'visions' telling them where 'saints' ' bodies would be found. They might even stoop to stealing from an existing shrine, as Elfred Weston stole Bede's bones from Jarrow, in 1022, taking them to the already prosperous monastery at Durham. Even the wealthy monasteries wanted more and more relics to attract more and more pilgrims. The gifts and money that the latter gave came to be looked on as a necessary donation and payment was actually demanded in return for a cure.

All during the Middle Ages pilgrimage was an integral part of everyone's life in spite of the contrary opinions of two notable early scholars, Gregory of Nyssa (c.330–c.395) and Jerome (c.342–c.420). A Christian could worship 'in spirit and in truth' anywhere, they wrote, and gained nothing by seeing wooden relics of the cross or Christ's tomb. It was not a view that commended itself to any other religious leader, in their own day or after. The Church promoted pilgrimage and used it as a means of attracting money and as a punishment to be meted out.

The Holy Land itself was the ultimate goal. When it fell into heathen hands the Crusades were fought to free it once more for pilgrims. Next in importance was Rome, claiming to possess the bodies of Saints Peter and Paul. Other major shrines attracting people from all over Europe were

Thomas Becket's at Canterbury and the supposed St. James the Apostle's at Compostella in Spain. (The French abbeys near Limoges and Arles took advantage of the numbers of pilgrims drawn to the latter destination – they furthered the cult of their own almost-imaginary saints, Leonard and Giles, respectively, to the benefit of their own prosperity[1]). In every country there were hundreds of lesser shrines of national or local fame which were visited in the pilgrimage seasons, mainly Easter week, Whitsuntide and after harvest-time. In England people went to the shrines of Saints Etheldreda at Ely, Edmund at Bury St. Edmunds, Alban at St. Albans, Swithin at Winchester and many others. There were also certain unusual and spurious objects which drew crowds of largely unquestioning believers – part of Christ's manger at Wimborne minster, Dorset, his blood at Hailes abbey, Gloucestershire, wood from the True Cross at Bromholm, Norfolk, and so on.

b. *The making of a saint*

A man or woman who had led a life of service to God and humanity might at death be termed a saint by common accord. Miracles at the tomb would confirm this. St. Cuthbert (c.634–87) was such a person. Priors and bishops concerned would encourage a local belief in sainthood by placing the body in an elevated tomb for veneration. This was accepted practice till the twelfth century. Then the creating of a saint became a matter for papal consent. The first English saint to be thus formally given the title was King Edward the Confessor (d.1066) who was canonised in 1161 by Pope Alexander III. The acquisition of a saint seemed very desirable to bishops and cathedrals for they basked in the reflected glory of the holy man or woman and gained financially by the offerings of pilgrims. For these motives many candidates were put forward for sainthood.

One of these was Thomas Cantilupe, bishop of Hereford (d.1282). A high-born, worldly man with political ambitions, no-one had noticed his sanctity during his life-time. His friend and successor, Richard Swinfield, however, made determined efforts to have him pronounced a saint, ignoring the fact that he had been excommunicated by the archbishop of Canterbury. It was a lengthy and expensive process

[1]Sumption, J. *Pilgrimage* (1975), 116–7.

involving inquiries into posthumous miracles, letters and journeys to Rome and Avignon, the bringing of pressure to bear on the pope by the kings of England and France and payment to everyone involved. At length, in 1320, the papal permission was given and Hereford had its own saint. By then the number of pilgrims who had been going there since 1287 had already begun to decline.

Fewer and fewer requests for canonisation were granted, partly from a proper desire to be careful about awarding such an honour, and sometimes due to strained relations between the papal and English courts. After half-a-dozen English saints had been officially elevated in the thirteenth century there were only Cantilupe in the fourteenth and two in the fifteenth centuries out of at least eleven put forward. The last of these was Osmund, bishop of Salisbury, who died in 1099. He was canonised in 1457 after at least £140,000 had been spent in the process at the papal court. The great amount of money needed to obtain canonisation meant that only important people like bishops and royalty or members of religious orders, who had the backing of wealthy communities, became official saints in the church calendar. The names of the good but lowly remained unknown except in their own localities.

c. *The cult of the Virgin Mary*

In the twelfth century there was a movement to give more honour to the Virgin Mary. She was always described as being loving and merciful and was acknowledged to possess supreme influence as intercessor. The words of St. Bernard, abbot of Clairvaux (c.1090–1153), expressed the principle of intercession: 'She will listen to thee, the Son will listen to her, The Father to Him.' The appeal of this gentle yet powerful figure was such that her cult spread throughout Christendom. People referred to her with affection as 'Our Lady', an appellation first recorded about 1175. Veneration was allowed to her exceeding that paid to other saints. The prayer, 'Ave Maria', became common in the twelfth century, and bishops like Grosseteste of Lincoln (c.1175–1253) insisted on all the faithful in their dioceses knowing it.

The Church created doctrine about Mary which was not based on the New Testament. At the Council of Ephesus in 431 she was given the formal title 'Theotokos' (i.e. 'Mother of God') and was therefore said to have been the only human being born free from original sin. Several eminent theologians of the twelfth and thirteenth centuries – Saints Bernard, Albert, Bonaventure and Thomas Aquinas – disputed this but they were over-ruled and the Feast of her Conception was officially approved in Rome in 1476.[1] Her perpetual virginity was taught from the fifth century, Christ's brothers and sisters mentioned in Mark 6.3 being explained away as step-brothers and step-sisters or cousins. Belief that she was taken up into heaven, body and soul, was formulated in the sixth century[2] and the Feast of the Assumption was everywhere observed from the eighth century onwards.

Churches and monasteries wishing to attract pilgrims turned to Mary whose holiness was beyond dispute and who was not in need of papal canonisation. The ease with which they could do this was probably responsible in some measure for the increasing reverence for Mary.

As the Church had earlier adopted the belief in Mary's physical assumption it was not possible to have a shrine for her body. This did not matter too much for any church could put up a painted statue of the Virgin to attract pilgrims. These were venerated as relics themselves and they also performed 'miracles'. People looked on the statue as a local saint and referred to it as 'St. Mary of Lincoln', 'Our Lady of Doncaster' or of many another place. Individuals often had a favourite, considering one 'St. Mary' better than the next. One reason for the popularity of Marian shrines was that the pilgrim had not far to go to reach one, an important factor to someone who did not want to leave work, home and family for very long.

The most famous of all Marian shrines in England was that at Walsingham, in Norfolk. It had its beginnings in the early part of the twelfth century as the result of the activities of a devout lady, Richelde of Fervaques. Perhaps impressed by the accounts of Nazareth by her crusader son, Geoffrey, she built a supposed replica of the house in which Mary had heard Gabriel's announcement. (A ballad printed about 1496 states that she was directed to do this by a vision of the Virgin). Geoffrey transferred it to the care of a priory of Austin canons which he founded about 1153. It possessed a phial said to contain the Virgin's milk (chalk dust from Bethlehem in water) probably brought back by a returning crusader. In the Holy House was placed a statue of the Virgin which became famous as 'Our Lady of Walsingham'. This shrine became so well-known that by about 1400 it rivalled that of Becket at Canterbury. Indeed, it ranked among the most famous in Europe.

---

[1] It became a day of obligation for the Roman Catholic Church in 1708 and the dogma of the Immaculate Conception was defined in 1854.
[2] This was not defined until 1950 by Pope Pius XII.

d. *The journey*

A pilgrim went sensibly and plainly clad, wearing strong boots and carrying a stout staff with an iron point, a leather scrip (haversack) and a water-bottle – all gear that any medieval foot-traveller would have. The effigy of one can be seen in St. Helen's Church, Ashby-de-la-Zouch, Leicestershire.

Any journey could be a hazardous business, for pilgrims as for anybody else. When making an overseas visit there was always the possibility that they might not return, so those with money and land to leave made their wills first. Before setting out they liked to hear mass at their own church when an intercessary prayer was said for them: 'that they may reach their destination in safety... that no enemy may attack them on the road ... [that they may be protected] from the perils of fast rivers, thieves, or wild beasts.' These fears were justified. Apart from the very poor, they would carry money with them for their expenses and were thus a target for robbers. The good Scots baker, William of Perth, a man of substance able to give every tenth loaf he baked to the poor, stayed a night at St. Andrew's monastery in Rochester on his way to the Holy Land in 1201. He was stabbed to death just outside the town the next morning, presumably for his money. Such events prompted those going on pilgrimage to band together for security.

By the fourteenth century inn-keepers in London had learned to use this desire for company by arranging tours to Canterbury for those able to spend money on them. Chaucer met his group at the Tabard Inn, Southwark, and Harry Bailey, the host, guided them, providing horses (with 'Canterbury bells' jingling on their bridles) and arranging lodging for the week of their outward and return journey. Pilgrims going abroad were venturing into the unknown, and sea captains in Venice smoothed their path and filled their own pockets by offering them an organised tour to the Holy Land.

The places visited depended on the time and money available. In general, it was the clerics and wealthy people who went overseas to Compostella or Rome, taking about sixteen weeks. Chaucer's Wife of Bath had been to both. In Rome she might have seen the supposed table of the Last Supper, hay said to be from the manger at Bethlehem or anything else that was mentioned in the Gospels. She had also been three times to Jerusalem, each journey taking about a year. She clearly enjoyed her pilgrimages, treating them as holidays, and she was not alone in this. The majority of people had to content themselves with a visit to a nearer shrine from which they would be able to return in a few days or weeks.

On the way both rich and poor could stay at conveniently-situated monasteries or hospitals (almshouses), making a suitable offering for their bed and breakfast on their departure. Those who could afford it might choose to stay at inns, as Chaucer's company did. At the pilgrimage centre itself there would be more hospitals and inns. Besides these some individuals took poor pilgrims freely into their houses. The very poor would not have been able to make their journey without begging or relying on the Christian charity of others. If a sick person was unable to make the journey himself a deputy might go instead, as Margaret Paston did in 1443. She went to nearby Walsingham to pray for her husband, John, then very ill in London.

e. *At the shrine*

At the shrine the pilgrims may have first gone through some form of preparation, possibly including fasting. When they approached the holy place at last, they knelt to make their prayer of supplication or thanks. Afterwards they gave their offering, the most common being a coin or a candle. The wealthy gave correspondingly more. Margaret Paston's mother promised to give a wax image of her son-in-law the same weight as himself. This was the gift of a well-to-do family. A king would present gold rings and bracelets, a necklace of gems to adorn the statue of Mary or a sumptuous cloth to cover a shrine, all of which would be on show at important festivals if not permanently. On a feast day the pilgrims would hear mass and then most of them would depart.

Those who had come hoping for a cure stayed behind. They had probably been to a doctor or a local wise woman first or tried home-made medicines or herbal treatment. Now they lay before the tomb, reliquary or statue whereon they placed their hopes, waiting for something to happen. After spending one or more nights there, some awoke declaring a cure although few cures were instantaneous. Others needed to be in closer touch with the saint. Some tombs had niches in the outer stone covering so that a diseased or injured limb might be inserted. The shrines of Edward the Confessor at Westminster abbey and St. Candida at Whitchurch Canonicorum, Dorset, have such cavities. (They are the only two structures still containing the bones of their saints). Certain sufferers were given treatment with objects that had been in contact with the relics or the tomb – dust, stones or scraps of paper which they applied to their bodies.

After a stay of one or more days, weeks or even months the pilgrims, if they had not died there, returned to their homes cured, partly cured or not cured at all. The latter were still hopeful for it was accepted as normal that recovery could take time and be effected afterwards, perhaps with the help of water from a holy well bought to continue the treatment. If the cure did not happen they might pay a second visit or try a different shrine. Those whose cure was completed at home sent an offering or took it with them on a return pilgrimage of thanksgiving. This was often a wax model of the part that had been cured.

All pilgrims carried a souvenir home with them, usually a small object made of lead. In Canterbury they bought badges stamped with an impression of St. Thomas. At Walsingham they might choose a miniature flask as a reminder of the healing water of the two wells there. From the Holy Land pilgrims carried palm leaves and were ever after called 'palmers', sometimes keeping the word as a permanent surname. From Compostella they brought cockle shell badges. All of the small mementoes were greatly valued and sewn onto hats or cloaks to let everyone know where they had been. They were sometimes treated as magic charms which might themselves have miraculous powers.

At each monastery and cathedral shrine one of the monks acted as registrar and entered details of each cure in a register. He liked to have witnesses and with their help set down the pilgrim's illness and the circumstances of the cure, carefully recording the truth as he saw it. In every case, whatever the complaint was, the cure was attributed to the saint concerned and called a miracle. There is no doubt that cures there were, although today we would have a different explanation for them.

f. *Illness and causes of cures*

Bad weather, poor harvests and the want of fresh food in winter meant that people often suffered from malnutrition and had little strength to resist disease. Many of them looked on illness as part of the normal way of life. If they went on pilgrimage in the spring, summer and early autumn they would almost certainly experience a change for the better and this partial improvement was welcomed as a complete cure by both the sufferers and the shrine-keepers.

Fresh air, exercise, a more nourishing diet, warmer weather and the relaxed sense of holiday all contributed to a feeling of well-being. The healing influence of time, also, allowed for natural recovery. Some needed exercise and this they got as they travelled, others required rest which they received at journey's end or at a hospital on the way. Additionally, although the Church frowned on the practice of medicine by the clergy, there were some monastic libraries with medical books, and monks who had read them were willing to give practical help to sick pilgrims. As a result some of the travellers might well be cured already when they reached the shrine but the glory was still awarded to their chosen saint. Sufferers from psychogenic illness, where the condition of the mind induced paralysis, convulsions, etc., although there was nothing physically wrong, might be shocked into health by the anticipation of wonders and the emotional atmosphere at a shrine.

Certain ailments were not susceptible to the methods and treatment available at shrines and the registrar did not bother to write down information about these failures. The unfortunate sufferer who was able to try again very often went to a different shrine next time. If he was cured there, the registrar was careful to note down the previous lack of success at the rival establishment. If he was still not cured but not too disheartened he went on to another shrine. William, the monk historian of Malmesbury (c.1090–c.1143) wrote of a blind man who went to eighty-seven shrines seeking a cure for his blindness.

The actual preparation and effort involved in going to a shrine seem themselves to have helped in the healing process. There was very little else that medieval people could do. The study of medicine in Europe was limited by being deprived of the public participation of the intelligent men of the Church. The blood-letting, unpalatable concoctions and primitive surgery of the lay doctors might easily make a man worse and were unlikely to make him better. A visit to a shrine, with the possibility of a consequent faith-healing, was infinitely to be preferred.

9. INDULGENCES

a. *Prospect of purgatory*

Nobody ever felt free of the terrifying prospect of purgatory. A state of grace only lasted till the next sins were committed, and these remained unabsolved till after the following Lenten confession. The Church dealt with the heavy burden of apprehension, at the same time enriching its own coffers, by the use of indulgences. These were grants which excused the sinner from some or all of the punishment awaiting him in purgatory. The idea was first thought of by Pope Urban II in 1095 to encourage men to join the Crusades. Participation, he said, would be counted as total penance and would secure immediate entry into heaven.

Urban's successors in the twelfth and thirteenth centuries gave partial indulgences to those who, after confession, visited and contributed to the expenses of certain churches in Rome. These lessened the amount of penance owed by a stated number of days or years. Gerald of Wales availed himself of this in 1195 when be heard 395 masses in forty churches and thereby reduced his purgatorial sentence by ninety-two years.

Bishops were empowered by the popes to bestow indulgences which removed a limited amount of after-death penance, generally of forty days. They issued them liberally as a means of attracting contributions to funds of churches and hospitals, towards the building of bridges and to other commendable objects. Alms-giving was emphasised for, in theory, this was the virtue that was rewarded by an indulgence. Archbishop Melton of York (d. 1340) stated this clearly: 'Give, therefore, alms that all worlds may be yours, for the giving of alms frees from death, purges sins, and leads the way to eternal life.'

b. *The Roman jubilees*

In 1300, and again in 1350, jubilees were held in Rome at which plenary indulgences (i.e. those abolishing the full amount of penance acquired) were issued to pilgrims who visited the major Roman churches and made offerings there. Lest anyone thought that freedom from the penalties of sin and consequent entry into heaven could be bought, the conception of the 'treasury of merit' was introduced. This stated that the debt of punishment due for sins was not cancelled, but paid instead from a vast store of 'merits' accumulated during their lives by Christ, the Blessed Virgin and the saints.

The two jubilees were so popular and so financially rewarding that their recurrence became fixed in the Church's time-table. More were held in 1390 and (thirty-three years later) in 1423 (in honour of Christ's years on earth), 1400, 1450 and thereafter every twenty-five years up to the present time.

The jubilee of 1450 attracted more pilgrims than ever, 40,000 on most days of the year being the official estimate, with as many as a million at Easter. John Capgrave, an Augustinian friar of Lynn was one of them. He saw all that there was to see, including the heads of St. Peter and St. Paul, and joined in the Easter processions. When he returned home he wrote a guide-book for the benefit of future English pilgrims describing the relics that could be seen. At the end of that year the advantages were made available to those who had not been able to go to Rome. They could then buy the indulgence for half the cost of the journey to the papal capital. This transaction accorded well with Pope Boniface VIII's phrase, 'this happy commerce'.

Among the many relics to be seen at Rome was one that gained a mention in English literature. This was the veil of St. Veronica – a cloth which, so it was said, had been offered by a woman of Jerusalem to Christ on his way to crucifixion; he had used it to wipe his face and returned it with the impression of his features upon it. The incident is not found in the New Testament but the cloth has been venerated at St. Peter's since 1297. In England it was commonly known as the vernicle and its story was included in the *York Mystery Plays*. Pilgrims to Rome liked to buy a badge showing a representation of it and Chaucer's Pardoner had one sewn on his cap. It is depicted in the Ellesmere manuscript, a fifteenth-century illustrated copy of *The Canterbury Tales*.

Finding accommodation was always a problem and towards the end of the fourteenth century some national hostels were provided. In 1362 John Shepherd, an English rosary-seller, sold his house in Rome to a group of his countrymen 'for the benefit of the poor, infirm, needy and wretched people coming from England to the city, and for their convenience and utility.' John and his wife Alice stayed in the house as paid wardens. It became the English Hospital of the Holy Trinity and St. Thomas. A second such hospital, that of the Holy Trinity and St. Edmund, King and Martyr, was founded in 1396 by a wealthy London merchant.

c. *The Canterbury jubilees*

Three other places were allowed by the popes to have jubilees on special occasions, Compostella, Lyons and Canterbury. The first one to be held in the latter place was in 1320, one hundred and fifty years after the death of Becket, and three more were held at fifty year intervals. Among the large crowds who went to claim the jubilee indulgence of 1370 was the poet, Geoffrey Chaucer, and he returned to write his *Canterbury Tales*. In 1420 the pope refused to grant a jubilee indulgence but the prior of Canterbury, after consulting four doctors of theology, declared one and the jubilee was held. For 1470 a jubilee indulgence was again requested because, said the monks, many English people were too old or infirm to make the journey to Rome and this time the request was agreed to.

The privilege of getting such an indulgence was one that had to be paid for as the popes used their issue to augment the papal revenue. By the end of the fifteenth century it cost several thousand pounds plus a large share (usually a third) of the takings. The price tended to increase and when the monks of Canterbury applied for their usual jubilee indulgence in 1520, and were told its cost, they could no longer afford it. Cardinal Campeggio told their agent in Rome, ' ... it is not possible that the pope will grant you this for no money or favour.'

d.   A private indulgence

In 1399 Thomas Arundel, archbishop of Canterbury, returned to England with Henry, Duke of Lancaster, in rebellion against King Richard II. A French squire who was with the king in Ireland at the time wrote his account of what happened. Those who brought the news of the landing said that the archbishop had been preaching from the pulpit, dangling a plenary indulgence from the pope, with the words, 'I have therefore obtained of the holy father ... that those who shall forthwith bring aid this day, shall, every one of them, have remission of all sins .... Behold the sealed bull that the Pope of renowned Rome hath sent me, my good friends, on behalf of you all. Agree then to help him [Duke Henry] to subdue his enemies, and you shall for this be placed after death, with those who are in Paradise.' This offer, said the messengers, induced the listeners to support the duke against the king. It seemed a little strange to the writer of the story that the pope should support a rebel against his lawful sovereign (although a previous pope had interfered in the affairs of the kingdom on behalf of William the Norman against the legally elected Harold) and he wondered if Arundel had forged the indulgence. The story was unsupported and may have been the result of a misunderstanding, yet it gives an idea of the words used to persuade people of the power of an indulgence.

e.   Pardoners

All kinds of religious institutions bought indulgences from the pope or their own bishop for passing on to others. The keepers of shrines wanted them as another attraction for pilgrims. Hospitals, churches, monasteries and cathedrals used them to get money for their building funds or for the care of the sick and poor. To promote them it was necessary to advertise. The men who did this were called questors or, more popularly, pardoners. Of them Pope Clement V said at the Council of Vienne (1311–12): 'Their sole concern is to communicate to the people the indulgences confided to them and to humbly request alms.' In practice the pardoners saw their role only in terms of making financial gain.

In 1308 the Chapter of Beverley minster began the building of its new nave. In order to gather in funds for this construction a chief questor was appointed, Elyas of Lumby, who himself was empowered to employ assistants. He was a citizen of Beverley doing the job for a living. From his hoped-for collections he was allowed expenses for himself, his horse and his servant, and also a robe 'with tabard'. He had permission to work in the dioceses of York, Durham, Carlisle and Lincoln, an area covering a tract of land from the Scottish border to the Thames. Chaucer's Pardoner, too, was as much-travelled, being well-known from Berwick to Ware. On appointment a questor was given copies of the indulgences, impressive-looking parchment documents with the pope's bull and the seal of the issuing house. He also carried a letter showing his appointment. In each diocese and archdeaconry he entered, the questor went to various officials to receive letters of recommendation to the clergy. Then, armed with these credentials, he was free to speak in any church.

Priests allowed a questor in only on sufferance for they risked excommunication if they refused one admission. The questor went during a Sunday or a feast-day mass and generally gave his message after the reading of the gospel. Opening his bag full of indulgences he displayed them from the pulpit. Then he discoursed in dramatic and persuasive fashion on their virtues and proclaimed that, on receipt of a contribution, he could forgive his hearers' sins, remit their penance and free relatives and friends from purgatory and even from hell itself. As an added incentive he produced his relics, whether genuine or false. (Those of Chaucer's Pardoner were pig's bones). There for all to see was a piece of St. Peter's sail, a phial containing the blood of Christ or a feather from Gabriel's wing. Most listeners were overcome and willingly came forward to touch the relics, to kneel and kiss the pope's bull and then make an offering. Lack of ready money did not matter, for the pardoner graciously accepted payment in kind – silver brooches, spoons or rings, wheat and even animals. Chaucer's Pardoner got more money in a day doing this than the parish priest got in two months. If the priest had powerful friends and raised strong objections the pardoner would bribe him with a share of the proceeds. Langland's Pardoner was ready to 'parten the silver' like this. The pardoner then solemnly swept up his haul and departed, probably making for the nearest tavern, a tendency mentioned in many records.

The job of collecting money and dispensing indulgences attracted salesmen who were more concerned with making a profit than the care of people's souls. Then, far from their masters, it was only too easy for them to dip their fingers into the takings. A common method of dealing with this problem was to farm out the collection rights to groups of professional questors who paid a substantial sum to the employing religious house and then used the indulgences entirely for their own benefit.

The Church had created pardoners and approved of them in principle, but the very nature of their occupation laid it open to abuse. From time to time voices were raised in warning and efforts made to correct faults in the system. John Grandisson, bishop of Exeter from 1327 to 1369, censured the behaviour of questors who 'travel at will through our diocese seducing the simple untaught people, and so much as in them lies, deceive their very souls.' In 1369 Pope Urban V described questors as men who 'go into church on some holy day at the hour when people are accustomed to give offerings, and... make their own collections, speaking until it is no longer possible to celebrate mass'. Church councils repeatedly expressed the same opinions without achieving any improvement. The pardoner was an indestructible figure while the fear of purgatory and the belief that penance could be remitted for money was taught.

10. SANCTUARY

Any wrong-doer risked imprisonment, mutilation, hanging or fining if he were arrested and taken to court, but if he (and occasionally, she) were able to reach a church he could claim the ancient privilege of sanctuary. By this he could stay there undisturbed, protected by the frith (or peace) of the Church. This was available to all except those guilty of heresy, treason and witchcraft. Some thousand people a year from all walks of life took advantage of this benefit, from the highest in the land to the poorest man who was seen to steal a few herrings for his hungry family.

In most cases the fugitive needed to reach the consecrated land of the churchyard although he felt safer when the church door closed behind him. At Durham he called for assistance from inside by sounding the great sanctuary knocker. Some places – Hexham, Beverley and Ripon – had a sanctuary-area that extended for about a mile and a half round the church, marked by crosses on the approach roads. Within this territory there were degrees of safety, the punishments for taking a man out of sanctuary becoming greater as he drew nearer to the church. At Hexham and Beverley the final security was attained by sitting on the frithstool which was placed near the altar. (Both of these stone Saxon chairs survive).

William of Lay, a regular offender, was closely pursued to the church of St. Philip and St. James, Bristol, in 1279. Almost there, he flung himself forward into the churchyard but his feet were outside it. He was taken to the castle and immediately beheaded. The bishop of Worcester declared that the sanctuary had been violated and meted out penance to all those involved. They had to exhume the body of William and re-bury it in the churchyard from which he had been dragged. Then they were compelled to process to the church on four market days to be publicly whipped by the priests. The constable of the castle who bore most responsibility was obliged to erect a stone cross and feed a hundred poor there every year. Stiff penalties like these preserved the rights of sanctuary so that few dared to infringe them.

A sanctuary might stand between the provoked innocent and the doubtful verdict of the law. In 1256, when Alice, daughter of Ivo, was assaulted by Richard, son of Gamel, at Langley in Northumberland, she hit him so hard with a stick that he died. Afraid of the consequences she fled to the sanctuary at Hexham. Convinced of her innocence she allowed her case to go before a jury which found that she had acted in self-defence. Upon sureties being given by her father she was therefore free to go. The frithstool had saved Alice from possible arrest and also, perhaps, from swift physical retaliation by the dead man's relatives.

Hot tempers or accidents might lead to manslaughter, so to be on the safe side, the perpetrator of the unlooked-for mishap would fly to a church for refuge, preferably as distant as possible from the scene of the deed. There, too, went hardened criminals – those who committed robbery with violence and did not stop at murder – if they feared apprehension. Occasionally, also, gaol-breakers made a successful bid for sanctuary. For all of these the reception was the same – confession of the crime to a coroner, protection and sustenance for up to forty days and the choice of having the case taken to court or agreeing on oath to banishment from the country. The latter was known as 'abjuring the realm' and was a custom found only in England. Dreading long incarceration in a town gaol and feeling uncertain as to the outcome of their case, most sanctuary-men chose it as the lesser of two evils.

Banishment for life was not an attractive alternative and, after having had a breather in sanctuary, some of the wilder sort were ready to make a break for it. To prevent this happening it was the duty of the men of the village or township to keep watch round the church. For this reason those running for sanctuary tried to get to a monastery where the grounds were larger and the guard thinner on the ground. Should the miscreant manage to creep out at night and escape, then the local community was forced to pay a fine.

Abjurors were assigned a port (not necessarily the nearest) to which they must walk on the first stage of their journey overseas. Many of these men were ruffians who would seize every chance to return to their old ways, notwithstanding their vows. When three highway robbers abjured the realm at Amesbury church, Wiltshire, the sensible coroner sent one to Portsmouth, another to Plymouth and the third to Bristol.

Keeping to the king's highway, the solitary figures could be recognised by the white cross they carried and sometimes by the wearing of sackcloth. They were thus shown to be under the care of the Church so that none dare touch them. If they should attempt to escape exile by venturing off the main road they would risk retribution from their enemies or local watchdogs. This happened to John of Ditchford, a robber, who took refuge in Wootton church, Northamptonshire, in 1322. Afterwards, on his way to take ship at Dover, he ran over the fields towards the woods. By so doing he put himself outside the protection of the law and therefore lost his sanctuary rights. The hue and cry was raised and the men of Wootton pursued, caught and beheaded him, a perfectly legal way to treat an outlaw. The incident was reported to the coroner who ordered the head to be carried to the king's castle at Northampton. The reward for this was £50, the same as that given for the killing of a wolf.

When at last the coast was reached the abjuror went on board the first outgoing ship and left his native shores forever. There is no record of what happened to such people subsequently. They probably received subsistence at monasteries for a while, but in the end there was little else for them to do other than to live on their wits or to carry on with their former lawless practices. Doubtless some of them returned to England for there was no official means of knowing them again. Not until the reign of Henry VIII was an abjuror branded on the thumb as a means of identification.

Besides the temporary immunity from arrest offered by every church, certain places could give sanctuary for life. Their rights rested on the holding of a royal charter, whether actual or forged. The most famous of these were Beverley in the north and St. Martin le Grand and Westminster in London. To Beverley came malefactors from all over England and, under certain conditions, they were allowed to dwell in the town and even to follow their own trades. St. Martin le Grand, a college of secular canons, became notorious as a centre of the London underworld. From it felons issued forth at night to thieve and rob and then returned to the safeguard of its walls in the morning.

Besides being a haunt of law-breakers Westminster abbey was also the resort of men who had offended the sovereign. Kings and abbots had many arguments touching their conflicting rights over them, which the abbots invariably won. In 1377, during the minority of Richard II, two knights escaped from imprisonment in the Tower and reached the sanctuary of Westminster, where they remained for some months. In 1378 royal officials with armed men arrived to remove them. One was arrested without difficulty, but the other, Sir Robert Hawley, was attending mass with the monks. The soldiers went into the chancel to get him but he made a fight of it and, after being chased round the choir, was eventually cornered and stabbed to death. His body was then dragged down the aisle and flung out of the door. The horror and condemnation of the Church at this outrage was shown by giving the body honourable burial in the south transept (Poets' Corner). It lies beneath a blue stone (which once held a brass showing a knight in armour) still to be seen on the floor there. Naturally excommunications and severe penances followed although the king and his family (who were ultimately responsible) were exempted.

During the Wars of the Roses the Westminster sanctuary was full of the supporters of Yorkists and Lancastrians by turn as each party experienced defeat. They were expected to support themselves and one of the Paston family servants complained that those who brought in food for sale were overcharging. In the circumstances they had no choice but to pay. There were times when the royal family itself sought sanctuary, using the door which linked the palace with the abbey. Elizabeth, queen of Edward IV, went there with her three young daughters in 1470 when the victorious Lancastrians entered London. While she was there the future Edward V was born and at his baptism the abbot was one of the godfathers.

From Saxon times the laws of sanctuary had enabled the Church to put a shield between hapless wretches and rough justice but by the later Middle Ages they had become greatly abused. Righteous anger was felt by honest townsfolk, creditors, victims and their families, as well as officers of the law who saw the guilty cock a snook at them from behind the boundaries of a superior authority. State and Church were always at odds over the matter and in the fifteenth century a few limitations were successfully imposed by the Crown working through the judges. By the sixteenth century only the Church and the criminal classes wanted to keep the privilege. Everyone else would have agreed with Sir Thomas More when he wrote, 'In good faith, if they [i.e. sanctuaries] were now to begin, I would not be he that should be about to make them'. The presence of turbulent sanctuary men must have made life difficult for priests and monks, but the sacred right was never given up because it demonstrated that the Church was more powerful than the law of the land. Only after the Church itself had been subjugated to the Crown in Parliament were sanctuaries (with the exception of churches and churchyards[1] – and these no longer for serious felonies) abolished by an Act of 1540.

11. RITES FOR THE SICK AND THE DEAD

a. *Visitation of the sick*

A ministry to the sick was based upon the example of Christ and the charge he gave to his disciples 'to cure every kind of ailment and disease' (Matthew 10.1). The successors of the apostles included spiritual care of the sick among their functions and as a result of their daily visits, prayers and anointings, recovery was commonly expected. A change of outlook was adopted at the beginning of the thirteenth century when the visitation of the sick changed to become a preparation for death. As such, medieval people tended to shrink from it until there was no hope of recovery.

It was the parish priest's duty to be always ready to attend a death-bed and, on receiving an urgent call, he would hasten to the side of the dying person. As he went the sound of the church bell might have been heard if the relatives of the dying could afford the fee for the ringer. This was known as the passing or forthfare bell and it tolled while the soul was passing from the body, calling on those who heard it to pray for that soul. The priest travelled on foot or on horseback in a dignified manner wearing his surplice and stole and saying the seven penitential psalms. In his hands was a receptacle called a pyx which contained the blessed sacrament. Before him went the parish clerk carrying a lantern and ringing a bell. It was the responsibility of the parish to provide these objects: St. Benet's, Cambridge, owned a gilt cup in 1396 which had

---

[1] This lingered on till 1623.

been given by Dame Alice Chaumberlyn so that the 'Corpus Christi may be carried to sick parishioners'; Jeffery of Drayton, of Great Yarmouth, bequeathed money, about 1374, for 'the support of the light of Corpus Christi, to be carried to the town for visiting the sick'; and St. Mary's Church at Sandwich possessed 'a bell of silver, to be borne with the sacrament', in 1483.

The intention of this ceremonial was to draw the attention of onlookers to the fact that the host was being conveyed through their midst. As this was believed to be actually 'God's body' everyone was supposed to kneel down and adore it whatever the state of the ground. There must have been some careless folk who were occasionally tempted to ignore the requirement. A cautionary illustrated story in the *Nuremberg Chronicle* of 1493 told of what happened to such a party of merrymakers. The wooden footbridge on which they were standing gave way and they were drowned after the priest and his boy had crossed in safety. It was a tale to warn others to conform. Conversely, those who respectfully followed the little procession might gain a ten-days indulgence from their bishop. The sight of the host was generally welcomed for, according to the Church's teaching, it brought practical benefits for that day: enough to eat and drink, God's forgiveness of idle oaths, eyesight preserved and safety from sudden death. Pious watchers offered devotions to the host, such as: 'Hail flesh of Christ, which has suffered for me!' The bread carried was part of that consecrated during the previous Sunday's mass. It had then been 'reserved,' that is, kept for the visitation of the sick, either in an aumbry or recess in the wall (Thame church, Oxfordshire, had 'an aumbry for the Lord's Body'), a tabernacle on the altar or (the more usual English practice) a pyx hanging over the altar.

On arriving at the bedside the priest first saw to the practical matter of the disposal of the sick person's property, for it was the Church's prerogative to supervise will-making whether in writing or by word of mouth. For doing this the priest received a satisfactory remuneration. This right of the Church meant that it was almost impossible to avoid making bequests to clergy and religious institutions and failure to do so might be labelled as heresy.

No-one could share out their goods exactly as they wished. First claim on the property of a manorial worker belonged to the lord of the manor. He took a heriot – the best beast or chattel – and the rector took a mortuary (or corpse-present) – the second-best beast or chattel. The excuse for the latter was that since everyone hated paying tithes they must at some time in their lives have paid less or of poorer quality than they ought. To save their souls from the sin of keeping something back that was owed to God it had to be made up at the end. This was expressed in wills by some such phrase as, 'for my tithes and offerings forgotten and not paid'. In 1450 Sir Thomas Cumberworth of Somerby, Lincolnshire, gave 'my blessed Lord God for my mortuary ... my best horse with my best saddle and the harness thereto'. A horse given in this way would follow the corpse in the funeral procession (a custom surviving in some state funerals). A woman might give her 'best mantle furred' or her 'best gown'. These were better-off people who took pride in a handsome gift.

The less-fortunate might have their livelihood wrenched away. Bishop Hugh of Lincoln (d.1200) took a poor widow's only animal, an ox, as a heriot on one of his manors. She begged him to restore it and he consented, saying to his disapproving steward, 'This woman had but two work-fellows; death hath robbed her of the better, and shall we rob her of the other?' Gerald of Wales recorded this story as an example of unusual charity. Stephen Langton, archbishop of Canterbury from 1207 to 1228, in his Provincial Constitutions, limited the taking of an animal to those who had left at least three beasts. This was ignored by Evesham abbey, rector of the church at Abbots Salford in Warwickshire: on the death of a poor fellow, Richard Herberd, in 1271, the abbey took an overtunic as the mortuary and also claimed a half-share in his only animal, a cow (the other half going to the lord of the manor as his heriot). A mortuary was taken from every individual, even the poorest: from 'Ashley's wife', 'a stranger woman who died in the parish', 'John Kyng's maid-servant', 'a poor fellow at the barber's' and 'Maurice the labourer', who were among those mentioned in two Oxford parishes between 1487 and 1527. If there was no animal, then it would be a sum of money, a garment or other object, whichever was easiest to come by or to sell.

Besides the mortuaries people were encouraged to donate additional gifts to the clergy and churches as a means of shortening the pains of purgatory. As well as money the richer testators gave such costly articles as candle-sticks, chandeliers, copes and silver-gilt cups. For the same reason it was also reckoned to be worthwhile to bestow money, clothes or food on the poor. John Toker, a vintner of London, directed in 1428, that his clothing should be sold and the money received given to 'poor folk lying bed-ridd,' for 'the health of [his] soul.' Money was sometimes left to supply doles of food for the needy on the anniversary of the death or on certain special days: in 1462 Sampon Meurrell provided for bread to be given to the poor every Sunday at Tideswell church, Derbyshire. Such loaves were placed on the tomb of the donor and issued after mass to those gathered around it. The recipients then knelt and together offered a prayer for the soul of their benefactor.

b. *The rites for the dying*

The matter of the will and mortuary being settled the priest then began the final rites, asking questions in English and saying his own prayers in Latin. If the sick person was so ill that he could not speak, but yet managed to give some sign that he wished for the sacraments, the ceremony was to go on, it being assumed that he possessed the correct spiritual attitude.

First the priest sat down near the dying man and heard his last confession. This was meant to be a very intimate exchange between man or woman and priest, other people perhaps being in the room but out of ear-shot. The dying person spoke for as short or long a time as he needed or had the strength for. If he was too ill to talk the priest simply charged him to ask for God's mercy with a humble heart. When he had come to an end the priest absolved him of all his sins and did not give any penance.

Then came the anointing with olive oil. In the early Church this was thought to have a healing effect but in the thirteenth century the ecclesiastical authorities had come to believe that it was a preparation for death, having a purifying power and therefore conferring remission of sins.

When this was completed the priest asked the sick man whether he believed that the consecrated bread was the body and blood of our Lord Jesus Christ. On receiving an affirmative answer the priest proceeded to communicate him with the reserved host. This last communion was known as the Viaticum – 'provision for the last journey' – it being looked on as an assurance of resurrection to eternal life. The dying person had now made all his preparations and could contemplate death with equanimity; the last rites of the Church had guaranteed him eventual entry into heaven via purgatory and the priest could depart. Anyone who refused them – and Mirk wrote of 'he that ... despiseth it' – was 'damned' and could expect to go to hell.

Since all trace of bodily healing had been removed from the sacrament it only remained for the sick one to die. There was some anxiety about being thought dead when only deeply unconscious, and a general fear of being buried alive. Sir Thomas Cumberworth expressed this in his will, 'I will my body be still, my mouth open, unheled [i.e. uncovered], twenty-four hours'. The most famous example in literature of a premature burial is, of course, that of Juliet in Shakespeare's *Romeo and*

Juliet.

c. *The funeral*

The body was washed soon after death, then closely wrapped and sewn up in a cere-cloth (winding sheet or shroud). This was made of white (undyed) linen dipped in or smeared with melted wax to make it waterproof. (Royalty, the nobility and churchmen did not have a cere-cloth but were robed in stately or priestly array). Then the body was placed in the parish coffin, a plain oblong box which had been brought from the church. According to contemporary illustrations it might have either a flat or a coved lid. People in the upper ranks of society would have their own coffins. Some people liked to have candles about the body before it was taken to the church. This desire is stated in the will of the London widow, Margarete Asshcombe, in 1434: 'Also I will have ... two tapers to stand at my head while my body resteth in my house of dwelling'.

In the early centuries of the Church death was looked on as a step forward to a better life and therefore to be celebrated with joy, but when the doctrine of purgatory was taught in the thirteenth century, with its expectation of extreme physical suffering, death became something to be dreaded. As well as experiencing bereavement friends and relatives were worried about the fate of their loved ones and the torments they would even then be enduring. The priest had told them about these and the terrifying scenes of the Last Judgement painted over the chancel arch did not let them forget. Mindful of these, all thought of joy drained out of the funeral rites to be replaced by sombre behaviour and prayers on behalf of the dead.

The procession that formed up at the house of the deceased was subdued and doleful. For a family of some wealth and local standing the whole of the church staff would be there – the holy-water carrier, the cross-bearer, acolytes with lighted candles, a thurifer swinging incense, the sexton ringing a hand-bell to bid passers-by say a prayer for the dead person's soul and the clerks singing the penitential psalms. After them the coffined corpse would be carried, either on the shoulders of friends or lying on a bier. The coffin often supported a hearse, a gabled structure, over which was draped a large cloth or pall decorated with a cross. In 1511 St. Mary's, Cambridge, possessed a 'covering of tapestry work for the hearse' and also a 'green coverlet for the said hearse'. Wealthy families and companies preferred to use their own more splendid ones. Dunstable priory, Bedfordshire, still possesses an early sixteenth-century pall made of red brocaded Florentine velvet with a fringed satin border which probably belonged to the gild of St. John the Baptist. Alongside the bearers of the coffin walked some poor men, and occasionally women, carrying torches. For this duty they received some form of payment – a black, white or grey gown to wear at the funeral, a little money and perhaps a meal afterwards.

The mourners themselves followed the coffin wearing voluminous black mourning gowns and concealing hoods. These are mentioned in Shakespeare's *King Henry the Sixth, Part Two* (II, iv) when Humphrey of Gloucester and his men enter 'in mourning cloaks'.[1] Black had become customary wear during the fourteenth century, at least among those who could afford the extra expense. Edward III even ordered his court into black when mourning for King John II of France in 1364. It was probably worn for some time by close relatives and friends – Palamon, in Chaucer's *The Knight's Tale*, wore black at Arcite's funeral and, much later, was still mourning for him 'in his black clothes'. The very poor wore what they had. Perhaps there were suitable gowns in the family gained by walking in a better-off person's funeral or kindly neighbours may have lent them.

On reaching the churchyard the procession awaited the arrival of the priest. Where there was a lych-gate with its coffin table it would provide a support for the coffin and a resting-place and shelter for the bearers. The priest began the funeral service there before leading the mourners into the church. The coffin was set down on a low base so that the pall reached the ground on either side. The usual position was at the east end of the nave before the rood-screen but churchmen were placed in the chancel. Some parishes had a hearse (different from the one placed on top of the coffin). This was a wooden enclosure, with iron sockets for candles, inside which the coffin was laid on its stand. If there was no candled hearse one or more great tapers in large holders stood on the floor near the coffin. The cost of candles and the hire of candle-sticks were beyond the means of the poor, and charitable people sometimes made bequests for their provision to the needy. These lights burning about a coffin signified that the pain due to sin must be expiated by the cleansing fires of purgatory. The more candles provided the greater the soul's chance of salvation. There were so many at John Paston's funeral mass at Bromholm priory in 1466 that a glazier 'had to remove two panes of glass so that the mourners should not be suffocated.'

---

[1] Strictly speaking, these were late-sixteenth century replacements of the medieval mourning gowns.

Altogether there were three funeral services. The first was in the evening after which the corpse was left in church overnight with the tapers burning round it. Next morning matins, known as the 'dirge', was chanted and then the requiem mass, during which the deceased person was mentioned by name in some of the prayers. The 'mass penny' was offered (the actual amount varying according to the worldly wealth of the donor) and then the friends carried the coffin to the churchyard followed by the mourners.

Psalms were sung while the grave was dug by the sexton, hired labourers or friends. From contemporary illustrations graves seem to have been about three or four feet deep and wider than modern ones, thus giving room for Hamlet, in Shakespeare's play of that name, to fight Laertes in that of Ophelia. The grave was blessed, censed and sprinkled, before the shrouded corpse was taken out of the coffin and placed in it. Then, after prayers for forgiveness had been spoken, it was filled up. It seems unlikely that this lengthy two-day rite was performed for the very poor or for those whose homes were in a distant part of the parish. Probably in such cases only the requiem mass was said. There is a touching record in the *Bursar's Yearly Account* of Lincoln College, Oxford, of the death from the plague of the servant-lad of the rector of the college in 1507. It condenses the care given to the dying boy and the rites after his death into a few evocative phrases: 'For watching-candles for the poor child; for his shroud and making his pit [grave]; for ringing and the mass-penny; to a woman that kept him two nights and two days; for treacle [medicine]'. The total cost paid by the bursar was about £20.

The site of the grave was marked by a wooden cross with a gabled cover. This was not a very permanent erection and after the deaths of friends and relatives the precise position of a grave was forgotten. It often happened that when digging a new grave the bones of former occupants came to light as is shown in illustrations of the time. It would not have been surprising to the first audiences of *Hamlet* that the grave-digger should dig up a skull while making Ophelia's grave. These disinterred bones were gathered up and put in a charnel house – a building in the churchyard or a vault beneath the church. From time to time this was cleared out and the bones buried together in a pit in the churchyard.

Burial in the churchyard was the right of all faithful Christians. Only the excommunicated and suicides were denied the privilege. The body of Ophelia (who presumably had drowned herself) should, according to the priest, 'in ground unsanctified have lodged'. Her close connection with the royal family obtained a grave in the churchyard for her body but no requiem mass was sung.

People of some importance often chose to be buried inside the church. The most imposing and expensive type of tomb was a large stone or marble box-shape above ground level that may well have been prepared in the deceased's life-time. The body, still in the coffin, was put into this and later an effigy was placed on top. Lesser people were buried below the floor of the church with a gravestone or brass plate laid over. Churchwardens would not refuse requests for burial within the church because that privilege had to be paid for and so their funds benefited.[1]

These memorials to the dead are still to be seen in our cathedrals and parish churches. They were displays of earthly state but their inscriptions were often earnest pleas for heavenly assistance – 'Jesu mercy, Lady help' – or they implored passers-by, in Latin, French or English to pray:

> That my pains lessened may be
> With one Paternoster and one Ave.

At the end of the funeral a tomb inside a church was left with wax tapers burning near it. King Henry IV, in an effort to assuage the guilt he felt for taking the crown from Richard II, paid for four tapers to burn night and day about his predecessor's tomb in Westminster abbey 'while the world endureth'. This seemed desirable in order to remind people to pray that the soul of the departed might soon be brought out of darkness and into the light of heaven.

When all was done the mourners were invited to a funeral dinner by the bereaved family either in their home or at an inn. In most cases this would have been a meal for immediate friends and relations. Those of the grander sort, who wanted as many people as possible to go to their funerals in order to gain more prayers for their souls, included everyone who attended. This provision was looked on as a work of mercy on behalf of the dead as well as a kindness towards the living.

d. *Memorial observances*

Even when the corpse had been buried the funeral rites were not yet over. The thought of the pains then being suffered in purgatory dominated the worship of the Church and the living were expected to do all that they could to alleviate them. The poor could only offer up a

---

[1] With certain exceptions, based on ancient rights, burial in churches built before September 1848 was forbidden by the Burial Acts and the Public Health Acts of the nineteenth century. It was totally forbidden in churches built after that date.

prayer on behalf of the departed soul as they passed through the graveyard or during mass when the priest prayed for all the faithful departed. Royalty, the nobility, bishops and merchants could do more. Masses were said for the soul of the dead person, usually on the third, seventh and thirtieth days after the interment, for which fees were paid. The ceremonies were very like the funeral all over again, with the three services, poor men carrying torches, candles round the grave (if inside the church), a dole of money to the poor and a dinner for friends who were there. The last of these days was known as the 'month's mind' (remembrance) and it ended the funeral rites. An enormous amount of money could be spent on these occasions and few questioned it. Thomas Ryche, a member of an important Oxfordshire family, was unusual in directing, by his will of 1471, that no month-mind should be kept for him and that the money saved should be given to the poor.

The anniversary of the death, known as the obit, or, more popularly, the year's mind or year-day, was kept a year later and often subsequently. As many people as possible were wanted at the services and money was left to pay the local bellmen to announce the details. John Baret of Bury St. Edmunds, in 1463, instructed that they should 'go yearly about the town at my year-day for my soul'. The ceremonial was as grand and the outlay was almost as great as for the funeral itself. The high and mighty expected these occasions to be repeated forever. Lesser mortals specified in their wills the number of years they were to go on and left money accordingly. Afterwards it was usual to provide food for all who had attended, whether it was a great banquet at the obit of a rich abbot or 'bread, ale and cheese' for 'the ringers and other that will come' at the year's mind of a more ordinary individual.

As new obits were added to those already kept at a particular church, and especially in towns where there were several or many churches, the number of obits held during a year proliferated. Attending them and taking part in the processions and services was regarded as a duty by relatives, friends and associates and it was possible to have too many to go to. Towards the end of the fifteenth century any London goldsmith who fulfilled the obligation to attend all the obits of former colleagues could lose one working day in every twelve. The poor profited by this increase and droves of them must have received money, new gowns and free meals. One suspects that many went from church to church for the purpose, almost making it their means of subsistence. The lower classes could not afford to pay for anniversaries but yet considered them to be desirable. The villagers of Croscombe in Somerset paid for one obit on behalf of all deceased members of the parish by contributing to a common fund; as each mass was held to have a marketable value the share in its benefits was known to be very small but felt to be better than none.

e. *Chantries*
i. The multiplication of masses
The belief that many masses said on behalf of the soul of a dead person helped that soul by shortening its term in purgatory was firmly held in all ranks of the Church. It followed that if a yearly mass was advantageous a daily one was even more so. This mechanical view led to the multiplication of masses so that thousands were said for one person's soul. Thomas Walwayn of Much Marcle, Herefordshire, for example, in 1415, wished to have ten thousand masses said for his soul 'with all haste'. To sing mass for an individual in return for a money payment was selling the sacraments, a practice officially frowned on by the authorities but encouraged by their example.

The institution of repeated masses for the repose of souls after death was called a chantry because of the chanting of the service. Chantries began to be important in the thirteenth century and the first one recorded is that of Bishop Hugh of Wells at Lincoln cathedral, about 1235. At the same time the rule was made that, with certain exceptions, priests should not celebrate more than one mass a day, so the requirement for an additional daily mass involved creating a post for a chantry priest. His payment was provided by the founder whose family usually kept the right of appointment. Many founders were thoughtful of people who had to set out on their travels early in the morning and who liked to hear mass before doing so as a guard against the day's mishaps; they specifically provided for their masses to be sung 'every morning before sun-rising for such travellers by the way.' The first mass of the day was known as the morrow-mass and might be sung as early as four or five o'clock. When it was over the chantry-priest was finished for the day although he might assist with parish work and some (about nine per cent) were responsible for a small, casually-run school for a few boys.

To support a man in this way was expensive, so many chantries were for a limited term only, usually anything from one to ten years. John Toker desired to have a priest 'to sing and read for his soul' for three years in St. Mildred's Church, Bread Street. He also expressed a wish to have 'a discreet and an able priest', and similar concern is apparent in many other wills. Only men who were honest, true, virtuous and of good behaviour were wanted, 'and none other', which rather suggests that there were some 'others'.

ii. Perpetual chantries

Extremely wealthy people were able to found perpetual chantries, that is, masses to be said for their souls forever. Besides the stipend for the priest, all things necessary for the conduct of the mass were given – vessels for the altar, service books, candles, vestments and sometimes more besides. To provide continuing funds for this, lavish endowments were made in money, tenements and lands. So much land was given to the church in this way that the Crown became involved because, as a result, it was losing its normal dues. Religious institutions never died so their lands were not liable for death duties, nor did they pay marriage or other fees. Such lands were said to pass into the mortmain (French, 'dead hand') of the Church. Edward I and his Parliament checked this by passing the Statute of Mortmain in 1279. After that no land could pass into mortmain without the king's licence which might be obtained only by paying a substantial sum of money.

The majority of chantries were simply a matter of a priest saying a daily mass at a named altar in a particular church. The opulent upper-classes went further, erecting purpose-built chapels, about seventy of which still survive. Vast sums were expended on the building and beautifying of these chantry chapels by royalty, the nobility and high-ranking ecclesiastics in the greater churches and cathedrals, by lords of the manor in their local churches and by successful merchants in large town churches. Henry VII's was a completely new addition to the east end of Westminster abbey, and there were other such annexes as the Beauchamp chapel at St. Mary's, Warwick. Some were miniature buildings placed between pillars like Bishop Audley's at Salisbury cathedral.

Not all chantries were on behalf of the founder. Some were made in expiation of a crime for the soul of the victim. Henry V did this in remorse for his father's taking of the crown from Richard II in 1399 and the consequent death, almost certainly murder, of Richard. Reflecting on this before the battle of Agincourt in 1415, he says, in Shakespeare's play, *Henry V*:

>   and I have built
> Two chantries, where the sad and solemn priests
> Sing still for Richard's soul.
>
>   (IV, i)

These chantries were at Shene abbey and Syon nunnery.

Founders of chantries usually included one or more relatives for whom the chaplain was to pray, perhaps also the king and queen and possibly some others, together with 'all the faithful departed'. Only a few showed particular consideration for the poor and friendless: William of Brocklesby (diocese of Lincoln), in his chantry foundation of 1343, included 'the souls labouring in purgatory who have no one especially appointed to pray for them'.

iii. Soul-masses and the Black Death

The appalling mortality during the Black Death and the recurrences of the following twenty years were caused, said the Church authorities, by the anger of Christ with the sins of men. With sudden death daily expected, and 'willing to be prepared for a sudden change' (as a burgess of Great Yarmouth put it in his will of 1349), the desire for soul-masses increased. Some of the parish clergy obtained licences from their bishops to celebrate them in their own churches in order to satisfy this need and also to augment their own incomes. The deaths of at least a third of their parishioners, with the resultant lack of oblations and tithes, caused some rectors and vicars within reach of London to leave their parishes in the hope of becoming chantry-priests there and being well-paid for celebrating masses. In the Prologue to *The Canterbury Tales*, Chaucer refers to such a one who:

> Left his sheep encumbered in the mire,
> And ran to London, unto Saint Paul's,
> To seek him a chantry for souls.

By the end of the fourteenth century there were more than seventy perpetual chantries in Old St. Paul's, as well as over a hundred obits and other requiem masses. The numerous chantry priests were notorious for resorting to taverns after they had said their morning masses.

Failing the obtaining of a chantry, there were still casual masses to be sung, as mentioned in *Piers Plowman*:

> Parsons and parish priests complain to the bishop
> That their parishes are poor since the pestilence time
> Asking leave and licence to live in London
> And sing there for simony, for silver is sweet.

Langland was critical of such behaviour because the simony mentioned was the singing of mass in return for money and against canon law.

iv. Chantry colleges

In the fourteenth and fifteenth centuries the idea developed of founding chantry colleges. The word 'college' (from the Latin *collegium*) meant 'a gathering together' and up to this time had been used to denote churches known as collegiate, like Beverley in Yorkshire or Crediton in Devon, where the governing body was an association of priests. Their duties were to recite the canonical hours as well as to provide for the cure of souls in their parish. With the increasing popularity of chantries and the consequent numbers of chantry priests the word was applied also to groups of the latter who were formally combined into an official organisation.

A contributory factor was the attempt of founders to provide a fitting environment for, and some control over, their soul-priests, many of whom had the reputation of haunting taverns or loitering about when their morning's mass was finished. John Gifford, a wealthy cleric, when raising Cotterstock church, Northamptonshire, to collegiate rank in 1339, was careful to state that the college priests were to be 'lettered, of honest report, chaste, sober and quiet, abstaining altogether from junketings, drunkenness, wanton ways, strife and brawling, and all such things as detract from and confound the devotion proper to so high a service'. In these colleges rules were laid down about attendance in church and other duties, and a house was provided so that the priests might live a decorous life in common. A few of these chantry houses have survived – at Trent in Dorset, Terrington St. John's, Norfolk and elsewhere.

The most famous of these establishments were the schools given by certain public-spirited people as part of their chantry institutions. Eton College was founded by Henry VI in 1440 for a provost, ten priests, twenty-five beadsmen and twenty-five poor scholars, whose duties were to pray for the king and the souls of his ancestors. The scholars were to be taught by only 'one master or teacher in grammar'. Similarly, the early colleges of Oxford and Cambridge, whilst fundamentally places of learning, were also chantry foundations. In time these bodies became famous for their teaching and continued to exist when other chantries did not. Hence the word 'college' has come to mean an educational institution only.

v. Chantries in hospital chapels

Another way of obtaining prayers was to build a hospital, like Richard

Whittington's almshouse in Highgate, known indiscriminately as God's House, the Maison Dieu, the Domus Dei, the Bedehouse or the Spital House, and which always included a chapel. There the chantry priests said masses for the founder and the residents also were present to add their prayers of intercession. Inmates of hospitals were often called beadsmen and beadswomen; a bead (or bede) was an Old English word for a prayer and it had come to mean particularly a prayer of intercession for souls. Many founders liked to have their chantries in hospital chapels because the guaranteed daily attendance of the permanent inhabitants was thought to ensure the regular repetition of the masses, whereas chantry priests in a parish church might prove to be unreliable.

vi.   Religious gilds

The great attention paid to intercessory masses by people of means was obvious to all and the humbler folk were just as eager to lessen the pains of purgatory. In the mid-fourteenth century two parishioners of Tydd St. Giles, Cambridgeshire, associated with others to pay for a chantry chaplain 'because they two alone were insufficient to do this'. Such religious groups or parish gilds, sometimes called brotherhoods or fraternities, grew in popularity, and in the fifteenth century, especially after the Black Death, almost every church had one or more. They varied in size and importance: there was the little company of four men and four women who, in 1379, could afford to provide only a candle to burn during the daily mass at the church of St. Nicholas, Great Yarmouth; and there were the more prosperous ones in the towns and thriving villages which were able to add their own chantry chapels to the parish churches, possess distinctive livery, form impressive processions at funerals and obits, meet in fine gild-halls, assist poor members, mend bridges and much besides. Bearing in mind their primary intercessory function the brethren dedicated their gilds to those saints thought to be especially powerful or to objects connected with the Passion of Christ, one frequently adopted being that of Corpus Christi.

The Gild of the Holy Cross at Stratford-on-Avon obtained its licence in 1269. It was even then wealthy enough to build its own chapel, quite separate from the parish church. This was rebuilt in the fifteenth century and the painting of the Last Judgement over the chancel arch (still to be seen) reminded members of the reason why they were there. The gild employed a number of chaplains who were so well-rewarded that priests were ready to pay in order to obtain the position. This is reminiscent of Chaucer's description of a vicar or rector who resigned his benefice in order to obtain a more lucrative and less strenuous 'brotherhood'. The gild achieved an influential position in the town and many people wanted to join it, even royalty, for George, Duke of Clarence, and his family became members in 1477. The funds were used for the support of a grammar school and almshouses. The size and central position of the chapel, the gild hall and the almshouses together, give some idea of the important part the gild played in the life of this small medieval town.

vii.   Numbers of intercessory institutions

By 1535 there were probably at least about four thousand chantries (including the larger gilds, non-university colleges and hospitals) in England and Wales employing one or more priests in a full-time capacity. In addition there were the less-frequent masses of the poorer gilds and the many obits of individuals. During the years since their inception some chantries had declined because of lack of proper endowments and other reasons. Certain obits, too, had ceased to be kept after running their allotted terms of years. Altogether these memorial observances must have numbered many thousands, and the fact that all sorts and conditions of men were willing to spend money on them is evidence of the general apprehensive belief in the flames of purgatory.

The Church felt itself to have the power to guide the lives and souls of its people from the moment of birth to the time of death and even beyond that. Every aspect of life was affected by the all-pervading influence of this omnipotent institution which claimed to interpret God's wishes to the laity. The attitude of the lay people themselves towards it tended to be like that of erring school-children to authority, forgetting it when their misdeeds were not seen, being fearful of its judgement when retribution caught up with them. Understanding but little and, at first, questioning hardly at all, they were entirely dependent for the means of grace and the hope of glory on the one Church, which itself only dimly comprehended heaven while having much to say of hell.

12.   THE JEWS

Among the Christian population of medieval Europe groups of dispersed members of the Jewish race had an uncertain existence. They were almost always treated with hostility because, from Constantine's reign onwards, the blame for the Crucifixion had been laid on their whole nation by the Church.[1] This doctrine ignored the fact that there could have been no Crucifixion if the Roman Pontius Pilate had not permitted it, but remembered only the crowd's cry, 'His blood be on us, and on our children.' The Jewishness of the twelve apostles and of the family of Jesus was deliberately overlooked so that the ordinary lay person hardly realised it. According to Sir Thomas More, an English lady he knew was shocked on learning that Mary was a Jewess and vowed to love her the less thereafter because of it.

The two religions were mutually exclusive of each other, for the older one denied the divinity of Jesus, while the other claimed it as a fundamental belief. There was nothing about the medieval Church that the Jews could respect and they were particularly contemptuous of the worship of images and the too-easy acceptance of so-called miracles. The Church looked on the Jews as slaves and its superior attitude was personified by the statues often carved on either side of the entrance to great churches. The one representing the Church was a crowned figure carrying a banner in triumph; that representing the Synagogue was a blindfolded, drooping form whose crown had fallen off, leaning on a breaking staff and holding the tablets of the ten commandments. The best-preserved of these can be seen beside the chapter-room doorway of Rochester cathedral.[2]

Once possessing the same rights as other citizens of the Roman empire, the Jews, by the Middle Ages, were not allowed to own land, to carry arms or to trade (because they were debarred from membership of the quasi-religious craft-gilds). This reduced them to such an inferior social degree that they became merely the chattels of their overlord. To make a living there was little else for them to do other than to lend money at interest, a practice thought by the church to be sinful and forbidden to Christians.

The first Jews in England were brought over by William I, doubtless to act as his financial agents. They settled in London and eventually in some twenty other towns also, preferably where there was a royal castle to which they could retreat if danger threatened. They paid taxes according to the need of the king, who also took a third of a deceased Jew's estate, so it was a matter of good economics for the king to look after his Jews. Their numbers rose to between 4,000 and 5,000 in the mid-thirteenth century. Each group had its synagogue, and houses were

[1] This remained the teaching of the Roman Catholic Church till 1965 when the Second Vatican Council declared that the Jewish people as a whole were no longer to be considered responsible for the Crucifixion.
[2] There are similar sculptures on the twelfth-century font at Southrop, Gloucestershire.

built conveniently near it and the market-place. This arrangement can be understood from the plan of Norwich where the synagogue was to the east of the Haymarket. The area was generally called the Jewry. The name survives in several places, as at Jewry Street, Winchester, Old Jewry, London and Jury Street, Warwick. The houses of the wealthiest Jews were often of stone, which gave greater protection from fire and human foes than the more common timber-framed constructions. One of these, the Jew's House at Lincoln, survives, and the home of Jurnet the Jew at Norwich (now called the Music House) remains in part. Certain other stone houses in Lincoln and Bury St. Edmunds may have been in Jewish ownership.

The Jews differed from the indigenous population in appearance, language (like the Normans, they were French-speaking), way of life, religious beliefs and rituals. Even so, they made a recognised contribution to local trade, a fact remembered by the citizens of Lincoln two hundred years after they had left. When all went smoothly the two groups could live together in harmony. During the Barons' War in the reign of Henry III, when the Jews were afraid that they might be a prey to lawlessness, many Christians were willing to take care of the valuables of their Jewish neighbours. Not all the dealings between Jews and Christians were cases of hard-hearted lending to desperate borrowers and mutual respect existed between honest men of both communities. In 1238, for instance, Copin, a Jew of Oxford on whom suspicion had fallen, was exonerated by a jury of twelve Christian fellow-townsmen who testified on his behalf. He had, they said, been brought up among them from infancy, and bore himself ever leally [faithfully] in all manner of lealty'.

The main business of the Jews was money-lending and the most proficient of them were among the wealthiest men in the kingdom. When Aaron of Lincoln died in 1186 a special department of the Exchequer had to be set up to deal with his enormous assets. There were, of course, lesser money-lenders and pawn-brokers as well as agents, clerks and members of household staffs. Professional people included the rabbis and other synagogue officials, teachers (most Jews were literate) and doctors, whose ability was so respected that they were eagerly consulted by their Christian neighbours.

As money-lenders the Jews performed a service that was welcomed by those in need of ready money, whether they were newly-made knights wanting a suit of armour or ambitious abbots with major building projects on hand. The usual rate of interest was twopence in the pound per week, which soon mounted up to a considerable sum. Also, at the time of the deal, a pledge was handed over – jewellery, fine clothing, monastic linen or estates – to be returned when the debt was honoured. Transactions were entered on documents, drawn up in duplicate and kept in a local office under the control of Jewish and Christian officials who were responsible to the Exchequer of the Jews at Westminster. This organisation enabled the king to assess the financial condition of the Jews and to decide his consequent taxation of them.

Trouble arose when the day of settlement loomed and an improvident debtor was unable to pay. Most resigned themselves forlornly to the inevitable loss of their pledge which the financier then sold for his own profit. When land came onto the market in this way there were plenty of careful landlords waiting to buy. Monastic houses often disguised such a purchase as a pious benefaction of the unfortunate loser. The more violent clients sometimes resolved on killing their creditor, as Sir Simon de Novers (or his henchmen) killed Eleazar, a Jew of Norwich, in 1146. In spite of this, they would not have escaped completely for, at death, the debts owing to Jews became the property of the king. This new creditor, however, might be inclined to settle for less than the full amount.

Christians were least likely to look tolerantly on the Jews during Lent when all their ceremonies reminded them of the Crucifixion. It was at this emotive time, Easter Eve, 1144, that the partly-clothed body of a twelve-year-old boy was found in a wood outside Norwich. The victim of what was almost certainly a sex-murder was an apprentice of the town called William. As he had last been seen on the previous Tuesday entering the house of a Jew the distraught mother jumped to the conclusion that her son had been killed by the Jews. Although there was no evidence for this many people added their voices to hers. The excitement might have died down but for the fact that the dead boy's uncle, Godwin the priest, repeated the accusation during a diocesan synod held shortly after Easter. The Jews were summoned and came with the sheriff, who eventually removed them to the castle for safety. If Godwin was correct the boy could be looked on as a saint and martyr, dying for his Christian faith. In spite of many sceptics the boy's body was buried in the monks' cemetery. After miracles were thought to have been performed there, in 1151 a shrine was erected for 'St.' William in the cathedral itself. It really expressed the need for the offerings of pilgrims as well as hatred of the strangers within the gates.

The story became well-known, as Norwich monks and also the bishop travelled in England and on the continent, and similar versions were spawned. In the same century it was used to explain other unsolved child-murders at Gloucester, Bury St. Edmunds, Bristol, Orleans and Blois. The most serious consequences for English Jews followed the discovery of the body of the boy Hugh at Lincoln in 1255. At the order of the king the supposed murderer was hanged and ninety-two others were arrested, eighteen of whom were executed. 'Little St. Hugh' attained more than local fame for, a hundred years later, his story was told anew by Chaucer's Prioress. The remains of his shrine can still be seen in the south transept of Lincoln cathedral.[1]

The death of William of Norwich, whose body was said to have been crucified in mockery of the death of Jesus, originated the charge of ritual murder thenceforth made repeatedly against the Jews. Later it was alleged that such atrocities were committed in order to obtain human blood for Passover rites. The popes rejected this libel and never formally canonised any of the child-victims. Unfortunately the condemnatory attitude of the Church towards the Jews in general created an attitude among the ignorant populace and lower clergy receptive of the vilest slanders. Papal protests regarding specific accusations of ritual murder were issued too late to save the Jews from baseless calumny and violent death.[2]

Four of these murders had occurred in England before 1189, when the new king, Richard I, was making preparations for the Third Crusade. As with the two previous crusades from the continent the idea of going to the Holy Land to war against the infidel brought smouldering prejudice to the fore and a desire to punish those unbelievers already within reach. On coronation day itself a deputation of Jews bearing gifts to the king was attacked at Westminster, when several members of it were killed and the London Jewry was set on fire. Then, during Lent, 1190, when crusading detachments were assembling in many provincial towns, a series of massacres took place. Starting at Lynn, the example was copied in Norwich, Stamford, Bury St. Edmunds, Lincoln, York and some other places.

[1] Now bearing a notice with the words, 'Such stories do not redound to the credit of Christendom and so we pray, "Remember not, Lord, our offences nor the offences of our forefathers."'

[2] Accusations continued to be made throughout and beyond the medieval period – some hundred and fifty are recorded – with resulting terror for the Jews. The charge was raised again in Nazi Germany in 1934 when there were protests from the civilised world. In a letter to *THE Times* the Archbishop of Canterbury referred to 'legends and lies about the alleged custom of ritual murder by the Jews which have been over and over again exposed.'

The Medieval Church in England
ILLUSTRATIONS

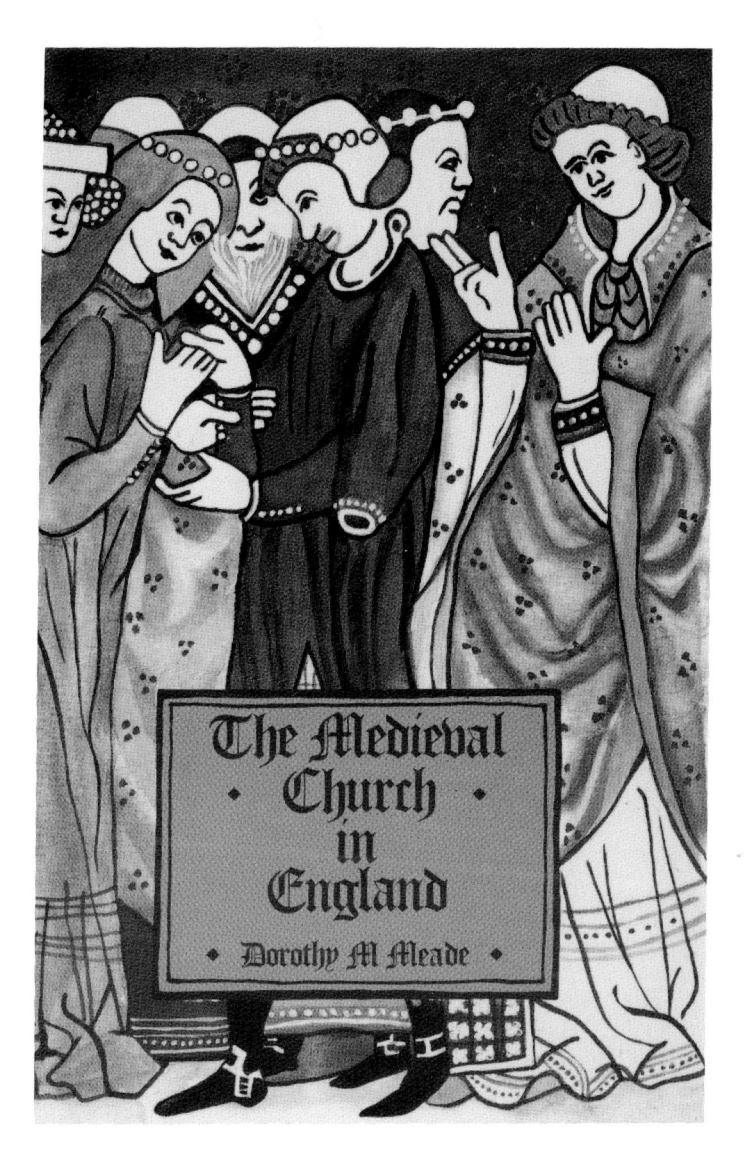

1. *Frontispiece*

   Marriage at the church door, early fourteenth century. The priest, in mass vestments, watches the bridegroom performing the ring ceremony.

2. Brass of Thomas Wardysworth, vicar of Betchworth, Surrey (d. 1533). He is holding a chalice with the host to indicate his priesthood.

3. Ashleworth, Gloucestershire. The church (twelfth-century, extended in the fifteenth century) was appropriated to Bristol abbey in 1154. The abbatial authorities built the rectory c.1460 and added the tithe-barn later.

4. Brass of Elyn Bray, a chrisom child (d.1516), in St. Mary's church, Stoke d'Abernon, Surrey.

5. The Last Judgement. Painting (c.1500) over the chancel arch in the church of St. Thomas, Salisbury. At the rising of the dead, the blessed (on the left) are ushered into heaven by angels, while the damned are driven into Hell Mouth (on the right) by devils.

6. A fifteenth-century ivory pax-board (Flemish), circulated during mass for the kiss of peace. It shows St. Martin of Tours cutting his cloak in order to share it with a beggar. Ashmolean Museum, Oxford.

7. Public penance. The monks of Canterbury whipping Henry II at Becket's tomb. This fifteenth-century depiction, on a roof boss in the cloisters of Norwich cathedral, was a reminder that the powers of the Church were superior to those of kings.

8. The vigil (first of the three funeral services), showing the pall-covered coffin lying beneath a gabled hearse, attended by poor men (carrying tapers) and mourners. The smaller pictures (in clockwise order beginning top left) show: the doctor attending the dying man; confession; communion; anointing; burial – the sexton putting the shrouded corpse into the grave (crosses mark three other graves).

9. The chantry chapel of Bishop Edmund Audley (d.1524) in Salisbury cathedral.

10. Cobham college, Kent, founded in 1362 by Sir John de Cobham, for a master and four priests to say masses for the souls of himself and his ancestors. Adapted as almshouses in 1598.

11. Statue of 'the Synagogue' (early fourteenth-century, head restored in early nineteenth century), doorway to Chapter Room, Rochester cathedral. The condition of the statue has deteriorated since this photograph was taken, c.1912.

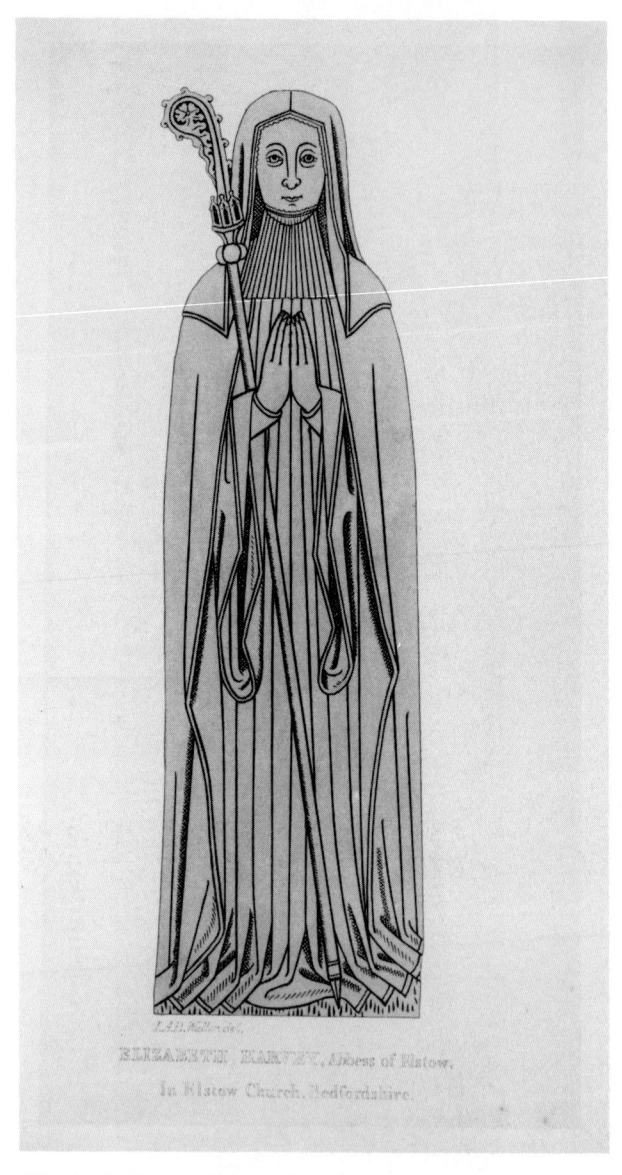

Elizabeth Herwy, abbess of Elstow (d. 1527), drawn from the brass in the church at Elstow, Bedfordshire, the former Benedictine nunnery.

13. Blackfriars, Newcastle-upon-Tyne, c.1789. The ground-floor refectory (now a restaurant) was in the south range (left). The west range contained the guest-hall. The whole complex (including the east range) has been restored for use as a craft centre.

14. Maplestead, Essex. The round church built by the Knights Hospitaller, c.1340.

The most dreadful deeds of all occurred at York. They were committed by certain local gentry led by Richard Malebisse (the 'Evil Beast'), intent on getting rid of their Jewish creditors. At the beginning of March they looted and burned the house of a wealthy Jewish family and killed its occupants, upon which the rest of the Jews took refuge in the castle. The constable seemed to them to be untrustworthy and, after he had gone out, they refused to re-admit him. He then called in the sheriff of Yorkshire who besieged the castle. This action encouraged the marauders, joined by the wilder youth of the town, in thinking that the king would approve of their behaviour. A few days later, when siege engines were brought up, it became clear that the Jews could hold out no longer. Refusing to accept death at the hands of their enemies, on Friday, 16 March the majority obeyed the call of Rabbi Yomtob to follow Hebrew tradition and take their own lives. The next morning, the day before Palm Sunday, a few fearful survivors agreed to accept Christian baptism, but even they were butchered as they emerged from the castle. Altogether there were about one hundred and fifty deaths.

Elated with their success the conspirators went straight to York minster where the Jews had deposited their bonds for safe keeping. They compelled the clergy to hand over the documents, which they then set on fire on the floor of the church, thus destroying the evidence of their debts. (It was after this event that the system of offices for the registering and storing of bonds was set up). This action showed the basic reason for the outbreak, although the religious element served to inflame anti-semitic passions. The monastic chronicler, William of Newburgh, while disapproving of the Jews, could not condone the behaviour of their Christian tormentors. 'A blacker page in English history than this I do not know', is the comment of a later historian.[1]

An attack on the Jews was equivalent to an attack on the king whose revenues were affected. Outraged at the news Richard I, then in Normandy, sent his Justiciar to make enquiries and to punish offenders. The constable and sheriff were immediately dismissed from office, while the leaders were fined and suffered the partial confiscation of their estates. (These were later restored). A severer punishment would have been very unpopular and a few years later William of Newburgh wrote

---

[1] W. Rye (1887), quoted by Dobson, R. B., *The Jews of Medieval York and the Massacre of March 1190* (1974), 37 and n. 119. On 1 November 1978 a ceremony of reconciliation took place at the foot of Clifford's Tower. In the presence of the Lord Mayor of York a tablet commemorating the Jews who died was unveiled by the Chief Rabbi and the Archbishop of York.

that 'even unto this day no man hath been sentenced to death for that slaughter of the Jews'. One hundred hostages were taken from among the York citizens although they all maintained that they had not been involved. They were heavily fined because they had failed to keep the peace in their city.

From time to time efforts were made to bring the Jews to Christianity. A convert faced ostracism from his fellows, was obliged to give up most of his wealth to the king and, as a Christian, was not allowed to make a living by money-lending. Apostate Jews, therefore, were probably not doing well financially and risked being expelled from the country. Other renegades turned informers and, of necessity, embraced the Christian faith. The most pitiful succumbed to the threats of a blood-thirsty mob and only saved their lives by agreeing to be baptised. At baptism the Jewish converts were given Christian names and, to distinguish them from others of the same name, were usually referred to as 'the Jew' or 'the convert' (actually the Old French *convers*). These have survived as the rare modern surnames 'Jew' and 'Converse'. During the assault at Westminster the wealthy Benedict of York was badly wounded and agreed to receive baptism in a nearby church. The next day he recanted although he knew his behaviour would be deemed unforgivable by his fellows. The unfortunate Benedict set off for the north but died of his wounds at Northampton, where neither the Christians nor the Jews would consent to bury his body in their cemeteries. A few months later it was the attack on his house and family that sparked off the York riot.

Some converts welcomed the freer life outside the Jewry and obtained positions so far denied them – one was knighted by Henry III – but for most, life was hard and they were often dependent on charity. Recognising this, Henry III provided a hostel for them in London in 1232, known as the *Domus Conversorum* – the 'House of the Converts.'[1] The number of inmates fluctuated according to the general treatment of the Jews and the financial state of individuals. In the later part of the reign of Edward I almost a hundred were living there.

If any man ever thought of renouncing his Christian faith for Judaism there were enough obstacles to make him change his mind and only two are known, with any certainty, to have taken this solemn step.[2] They risked loss of property and even life itself and gained membership of an unfree, foreign, circumcised and persecuted minority. Probably only the

---

[1] On the site of the Record Office in the modern Chancery Lane.
[2] Possibly also two Cistercian monks mentioned by Gerald of Wales (1146–1223).

desire of a Christian to marry a Jewess would lead to apostasy. To prevent this happening the Fourth Lateran Council, 1215, ordered that Jews should wear a badge so that Christians should be forewarned and a romantic relationship would not develop. (Henry III was willing to dispense with it in return for a money payment). A few years later an English deacon, having fallen in love with a Jewess, became a convert to the Jewish religion. He was brought before a council of the southern province summoned by the archbishop of Canterbury, which was held at Osney abbey, Oxford, in 1222. There he was condemned as a heretic, publicly degraded outside the abbey church and handed over to the sheriff of Oxford who immediately saw to his burning.[1]

Fifty-three years later in London, Robert of Reading, a Dominican friar who had studied Hebrew texts, chose to become a Jew, taking a Jewish name, Haggai, and also a Jewish wife. He is not known to have suffered as a result but Jewish chroniclers saw his conversion as a cause of further repressive measures taken in 1275 and the years following.

After the massacres of 1190 the position of the Jews slowly returned to something like normality. New settlers came, even to York, where, by 1221, the community had become the richest in the country. In spite of this the thirteenth century was a time of lessening prosperity, for Henry III and Edward I fleeced the Jews continually, enforcing payment by threats, arrests, tortures, forfeitures and hangings. By this time the old prohibition against usury had been steadily disregarded and there were now great Italian banking-houses with London representatives as well as individual Christian money-lenders. Because of this Edward I no longer valued the Jews. In 1289 his urgent need for money led him to expel all the Jews from his duchy of Gascony, after first seizing their property, and in 1290 he treated the English Jews in the same way.

Given only a few months to prepare, the Jews were told that they must be out of England by All Saints' Day (1 November). They lost their houses and bonds, which escheated to the king, but were allowed to take their portable property with them. In the autumn this wronged people (then totalling about 2,500), without any rights in law, rejected by their 'owner' and castigated by the Church, embarked unhappily for the continent, not knowing whether they would find a more hospitable refuge under a less hostile ruler. In fact, this was only a stage on their long wanderings, for the example of the English king was eventually

---

[1] In the fifteenth-century barn at Osney there is a memorial plaque to the deacon, although he has been confused with the later Robert of Reading.

followed by several other European sovereigns.

Perhaps, in 'the Island'[1] they had left behind, there were for a while a few compassionate Christians like Thomas Wykes, whose humane outlook can be learned from the chronicle of Osney abbey: 'And though the Jews were not of our religion, ... we ought to love them because they are men and have been created in the image of God'. But in the centuries that followed, the unyielding attitude of the Church remained dominant. It continued to remind its flock of the 'perfidious Jews' on Good Friday and promoted the shrines of 'St. William' and the other 'crucified' boys. As a result the memory that remained preserved all the intolerance that had been too-easily aroused, and the Jews were remembered with dread as epitomes of evil, fearsome creatures to frighten children with.

After 1290 no Jew, other than converts, doctors (whose skills were appreciated) and a few refugees from the Spanish Inquisition (expelled by Henry VII when Prince Arthur married Catherine of Aragon) set foot in England again till the sixteenth century.[2]

SELECT BOOK LIST

Works used in most sections:
BENNETT, H. S. Both works cited.
CHAUCER, Geoffrey. *Op. cit.*
COULTON, G. G. *Medieval Panorama* (1938), *The Medieval Village* (1925).
COX, Charles, J. *Churchwarden's Accounts* (1913).
CUNNINGTON, P. and LUCAS, C. *Costume for Births, Marriages and Deaths* (1972).
CUTTS, E. L. *Op. cit.*
DEANESLY, Margaret. *A History of the Mediaeval Church* (1925).
GASQUET, F. A. *Parish Life in Mediaeval England* (1906).
KINGSFORD, H. S. *Illustrations of the Occasional Offices of the Church in the Middle Ages from Contemporary Sources* (Alcuin Club Collections, No. XXIV, 1921).
MANNING, B. L. *The People's Faith in the time of Wyclif* (1919).
MOORMAN, J. R. H. *Op. cit.*
PLATT, C. *Op. cit.*
ROCK, D. *The Church of our Fathers*, ed. G. W. Hart and W. J. Frere, 4 vols. (1903–4).
SMITH, H. Maynard. *Op. cit.*
SOUTHERN, R. W. *Western Society and the Church in the Middle Ages* (1970).
THOMAS, Keith. *Religion and the Decline of Magic* (1971).
WOODS, W. *Op. cit.*

[1] The name for England in medieval Hebrew usage.
[2] They were officially allowed to return in the time of Oliver Cromwell.

1) Birth and Baptism
BAILEY, D. S. *Sponsors at Baptism and Confirmation* (1952).
COULTON, G. G. 'Infant Perdition in the Middle Ages' (*Medieval Studies*, No. 16, 1922).
FISHER, J. D. C. *Christian Initiation: Baptism in the Medieval West* (1965).
OSBORN, R. R. *Forbid them not* (1972).
PAGE-PHILLIPS, John. *Children on Brasses* (1970).
PEARSON, A. Harford. *The Sarum Missal done into English* (1884, second edition revised).
STONE, D. *Holy Baptism* (1899).
WHITAKER, E. C. *The Baptismal Liturgy* (1965).

2) Confirmation
BAILEY, D. S. *Op. cit.*
MACLEAN, A. J. and OLLARD, S. L. Chapters in *Confirmation* by various writers. Vol. I (1926).

3) Confession
BLOOMFIELD, M. W. *The Seven Deadly Sins* (1952).
LANGLAND, William. *Op. cit.*
LEA, H. C. *A History of Auricular Confession and Indulgences in the Latin Church* (1896). Vols. I and II.
TENTLER, T. N. *Sin and Confession on the Eve of the Reformation* (1977).

4) Mass
DUGMORE, C. W. *The Mass and the English Reformers* (1958).
HEATH, P. *Op. cit.*

5) Marriage
CLARKE, W. K. L. (ed.) and HARRIS, C. (Assistant). *Liturgy and Worship* (1932).
DUBY, G. *Medieval Marriage* (trans. by E. Forster from the French, 1978).
POWER, E. *Medieval Women* (1975).

6) Parish officials, employees and performers
CHAMBERS, E. K. *The Medieval Stage*, Vols. I and II (1903).
HARRISON, F. L. *Music in Medieval Britain* (1958)
JENSEN, O. 'The 'Denarius Sancti Petri' in England', in *Transactions of the Royal Historical Society*, New series Vol. XV (1901).
MASON, Emma. 'The role of the English parishioner, 1100–1500', in *Journal of Ecclesiastical History*, Vol. 27 (1976).
TEMPERLEY, N. *The Music of the English Parish Church* (1979).

7) Superstitions
KITTREDGE, G. L. *Witchcraft in Old and New England* (1929; reprinted 1956).

8) Saints and pilgrimages
ADAIR, J. *The Pilgrims' Way* (1978).
BONSER, W. *The Medical Background of Anglo-Saxon England* (1963).
CLAY, R. M. *The Medieval Hospitals of England* (1909, reprinted 1966).
DICKINSON, J. C. *The Shrine of Our Lady of Walsingham* (1956).

FINUCANE, R. C. *Miracles and Pilgrims* (1977).
HALL, D. J. *English Medieval Pilgrimage* (1966).
JUSSERAND, J. J. *English Wayfaring Life in the Middle Ages*, trans. L. Toulmin Smith (1891).
SUMPTION, J. *Pilgrimage* (1975).
WALL, J. C. *The Shrines of British Saints* (1905).

9) Indulgences
JUSSERAND, J. J. *Op. cit.*
KELLOG, A. L. and HASELMAYER, L. A. 'Chaucer's Satire of the Pardoner', in *Publications of the Modern Language Association of America*. Vol. 66 (1951).
LANGLAND, William. *Op. cit.*
LEA, H. C. *Op. cit.* Vol. III.
SUMPTION, J. *Op. cit.*
TREVELYAN, G. M. *England in the Age of Wycliffe* (1899).

10) Sanctuary
COX, J. C. *The Sanctuaries and Sanctuary Seekers of Medieval England* (1911).
McCALL, A. *The Medieval Underworld* (1979).
SMITH, D. *The Sanctuary at Durham* (1971).
THORNLEY, I. D. 'The Destruction of Sanctuary', in *Tudor Studies presented to A. F. Pollard*, ed. R. W. Seton-Watson (1924).

11) Rites for the sick and the dead
BOASE, T. S. R. *Death in the Middle Ages* (1972).
CLARKE, W. K. L. (ed.) and HARRIS, C. (Assistant). *Op. cit.*
COOK, G. H. *Medieval Chantries and Chantry Chapels* (1947; rev. edition 1963).
COOK, G. H. *English Collegiate Churches* (1959).
COULTON, G. G. 'Priests and People before the Reformation' (*Medieval Studies*, No. 8, 1907).
Fifty (The) Earliest English Wills in the Court of Probate, London, ed. F. J. Furnivall (Early English Text Society, original series 78, 1882).
FREESTONE, W. H. *The Sacrament Reserved* (Alcuin Club Collections, No. XXI, 1917).
KREIDER, A. *The English Chantries: the Road to Dissolution* (1979).
Lincoln Diocese Documents, ed. A. Clark (Early English Text Society, original series 149, 1914).
WESTLAKE, H. F. *The Parish Gilds of Mediaeval England* (1919).
Wills and Inventories from the registers of the Commissary of Bury St. Edmund's and the Archdeacon of Sudbury, 1370–1650, selected and edited by S. Tymms (Camden Society, 1st. series 49, 1850).

12) The Jews
ANDERSON, M. D. *A Saint at Stake* (1964).
DOBSON, R. B. *The Jews of Medieval York and the Massacre of March 1190* (Borthwick Papers, No. 45, 1974).
HILL, J. W. F. *Medieval Lincoln* (1948).
JESSOP, A. and JAMES, M. R. (ed.) *The Life and Miracles of St. William of Norwich* (1896).

LIPMAN, V. D. *The Jews of Medieval Norwich* (Jewish Historical Society of England, 1967).
MAITLAND, F. W. *Canon Law in the Church of England* (1898).
McCALL, A. *Op. cit.*
RICHARDSON, H. G. *The English Jewry under Angevin Kings* (1960).
ROTH, C. *A History of the Jews in England* (1941).
ROTH, C. *The Jews of Medieval Oxford* (Oxford Historical Society, New Series, Vol. IX, 1951).
ROTH, C. (ed.) *The Ritual Murder Libel and the Jew* (about 1935).

THE CHURCH'S YEAR

1. THE DEVELOPMENT OF THE ECCLESIASTICAL CALENDAR

The ecclesiastical calendar which was observed throughout the Church in the Middle Ages developed gradually from local celebrations in certain churches. At first there was only 'the Lord's Day' (called Sunday by converted sun-worshippers) when groups of early Christians met together to eat bread and drink wine, according to the last instructions of Jesus. Then acts of remembrance at Jerusalem and Rome – during Lent, Pascha (Easter), Pentecost, Christmas and Epiphany – were repeated in other places. Soon the commemoration of the major events in the life of Jesus formed the framework of the Christian year and others were added later.

The apostles and other New Testament figures were given particular days when their relics, or supposed relics, were discovered. Because of a deficiency in this respect there were initially no feasts of the Virgin Mary, the Annunciation and Purification having begun in connection with the Life of Christ. The Visitation and other Marian feasts – of her Conception, Nativity and Assumption – were originally observed in the Eastern Church and brought to Rome at some time after 700.

There had been no mention of the actual cross since the day of the Crucifixion. Its 're-discovery' is a matter of something ordinary worked on by imagination to produce a pretty legend which was soon accepted as historical fact. Some wood was dug up during the excavations for the emperor Constantine's Church of the Holy Sepulchre (c.325–35). After some three hundred years the sudden appearance of the cross would have been seen as a mark of God's favour towards Constantine and his dynasty, but there was no contemporary statement to that effect. Some twenty years later the wood was described as being that of the cross and slivers of it were sold to pilgrims. By 395 the discovery of the cross was attributed to the emperor's mother, Helena (who had visited the site), although no mention is made of this in the detailed biography of the empress by Bishop Eusebius of Caesarea (d.340). As a result of the 'miraculous' find two days in honour of the Cross entered the Church's calendar – the Invention (i.e. the finding) and the Exaltation (the veneration of the remains).

In post-apostolic times holy men and women who had lived exemplary lives or who had died for the faith were given places in the calendar as saints and martyrs. The first one to be acknowledged in this way in England was St. Alban, who was beheaded during the Roman occupation at the town which now bears his name.

As well as days of celebration there were also penitential days which required partial abstinence from food. Christ had given no rules on the subject and he and his disciples did not observe the twice-weekly fasts of the Pharisees. Because he himself had fasted in the wilderness and had suggested that his disciples would do so when he was taken away from them the custom was approved by the first Christians. Friday became the recognised fast day and was later said to have been chosen because it had been the day of the Crucifixion. In England the longest period of fasting was called Lent, from the Anglo-Saxon word for spring, the season in which it occurred.

In time there were enough religious commemorations in the year to name a majority of the days and this almanac permeated life at all levels. Monastic annalists, and clerks in royal and noble houses, had calendars to hand and used the holy days to date their records, charters and correspondence. Matthew Paris (c.1199–1259), chronicler of St. Albans abbey, in his *English History*, mentions events happening 'on St. Valentine's day', 'near about the festival of the Finding of the Holy Cross', and 'in the first fortnight of Lent', to notice but a few. Like the clergy, the ordinary folk, who knew little more of the time than the march of the seasons, referred to local incidents or personal events in the same way. Twelve jurymen who were called to establish the age of Walter Fitz Wauter, a local heir, at Braintree, Essex, in 1423, gave evidence of the date of the young man's birth (Tuesday 22 June 1400) by connecting it with their own experiences on the same or a near holy day. Among them, Robert Normandy said that he had married Rose, the servant of the child's mother, the week previous to the birth, on the feast of Holy Trinity; Richard atte Hoo recalled that on the Monday before the feast of St. Alban (the day before the birth) John Waryn had hanged himself;

John Borham of Sandon remembered that he had broken his arm while playing football on the feast of St. Alban; John Marler said that the rector of the parish church of Woodham Walter had baptised the newly-born Walter there on the same day; and Walter Tabenham stated that his own father had died two days later on the feast of the Nativity of St. John the Baptist.

The Jews had reckoned each day from sunset to sunset and the first Jewish Christians followed this ancient custom till it was displaced by the Roman idea of the day beginning at midnight. Even then the old notion survived in the 'eves' of Christian festivals, the eve being considered as part of the festival itself.

In the Roman Empire time had been reckoned in years and months since the Julian calendar had been introduced in 45 B.C. by Julius Caesar. Varying systems of names or numbers were applied to the years at different times and in different countries and this was sometimes confusing. In 525 Dionysius Exiguus, a monk living in Rome, compiled a table for calculating the date of Easter. In so doing he numbered his list of years from the birth of Christ. This method was introduced into England by Wilfrid (soon to be Bishop of Ripon) at the Synod of Whitby in 664. This clear and satisfactory scheme was used by Bede when writing his *Ecclesiastical History*. Henceforward it was commonly employed for the dating of English official documents, each numbered year being referred to as 'from the Incarnation' and later as 'the Year of Grace.' It spread to the continent with Anglo-Saxon missionaries in the eighth century and eventually to Rome, where it was adopted by the papal chancery in 1048.

Although the Roman civil year began on 1 January, the Church preferred that the year should begin on one of its major festivals. Bede chose Christmas Day and this was accepted throughout western Europe for many centuries. It gave way to the feast of the Annunciation, 25 March, probably because of increased devotions to the Virgin Mary. This new starting-point was in common use in England in the late twelfth century (remaining so till 1752), where it was popularly known as Lady Day. It began both the civil and ecclesiastical years, although 1 January was still called New Year's Day.

2. THE CELEBRATION OF HOLY DAYS

At the Conversion of England in 597 a cycle of established heathen festivals, related to the hopes and achievements of the agricultural seasons, was taken over by the Church which invented a Christian reason for its existence. Because of this, holy days were of both religious and pragmatic significance for they were linked to the routine of the husbandman's year. As toilers on the land formed about nine-tenths of the population, and the lives of the remaining tenth were naturally bound up with them, every person was very much aware of holy days and what should be done on them.

There were two sorts – penitential days, which required fasting, and feast days, which were celebrated with joy. Ideally, everyone ought to have stopped work and attended mass on all major ones – a matter of fifty or more a year besides Sundays. As the calls of the land and the needs of the towns made this impractical the number which were actually observed by the population at large amounted only to some fifteen or twenty.

Fast-days were intended to strengthen a person's spiritual life by lessening earthly pleasures, but they were not popular or even sensible and, by the late Middle Ages, means were found to relax the rules. To the original permitted single meal were added breakfast and a light evening repast, and this was approved even in the monasteries. The main difference was a change of diet, for fasting also meant abstaining from meat and meat-products – milk, eggs, butter and cheese. Days without these were generally known as 'fish days' (for fish usually replaced meat then), as opposed to 'flesh days' when they were allowed.[1] About one-third of the days of the year were fish days – every Friday, the forty days of Lent, ember days, rogation days and vigils (the days before certain important festivals). Surviving menus, accounts and letters show that they were punctiliously observed and that the contents of larders were stored with these in mind.

The prohibition against meat meant that the catching and selling of fish were of great importance to the economy of the country. English fishing-boats went as far as Iceland and there was a thriving import and export industry with the continent. Fairs and markets were established specially for fish, and fish-mongers became wealthy merchants. Fresh fish were, of course, most desired and large estates kept them in their fishponds. Fish brought from distant fishing-grounds were preserved in two ways: one by splitting and drying (stock-fish), and the other by

---

[1] 'Fasting' and 'abstinence' were then interchangeable terms. The Roman Catholic Church distinguished between then in 1781.

storing in salt (salt-fish).

Kings, nobles and bishops could enjoy Lenten fare by having a great variety of fish – salmon, sturgeon, trout, oysters and mussels – so that their meals amounted to feasts of a different sort. Lesser people, who had to survive on a dried- or salt-fish diet, must have found it very monotonous, like the poor scholar, who, in the fifteenth century, wrote, 'Thou will not believe how weary I am of fish, and how much I desire that flesh will come in again, for I have eat none other but salt-fish this Lent ... .'

Sundays were never fast days and even on those which came in Lent, meat products could be eaten. In parts of the country simnel[1] cakes made of dried fruit were special Lenten fare. These may have been made before the season began to use up surplus dairy-produce. (Pancakes were made on Shrove Tuesday for the same reason – see Chapter Two, 3f). They became specially connected with the fourth Sunday in Lent, known as Mid-Lent Sunday, perhaps because the Gospel of the day was about a biblical feast – the feeding of the five thousand.[2]

Butchers were not entirely put out of business. Erasmus noticed that veal, kid and lamb were on sale in Italian markets during Lent, so it was likely that such trading occurred in other Christian countries also. It was fortunate that Lent came at the end of winter when meat was generally scarce anyway. When the grass stopped growing in November large numbers of cattle were killed because there was not enough fodder to keep them all alive till spring. Their meat was salted to preserve it, but after four or five months it ceased to be appetising.

When Pascha was introduced into England it coincided with an existing spring festival called Easter (after the goddess Eostre) and took its name. Its date was determined by the Paschal full-moon of the Jewish lunar calendar and varied between 22 March and 25 April. Lent, therefore, always started towards the end of the ecclesiastical calendar, but everything about it pointed to Easter. It began on Ash Wednesday, when the previous year's palm leaves were burned in church and the consecrated ashes were strewn on the heads of the people to symbolise the defilement of sin.

To show that sin prevented the realisation of heavenly joy a linen curtain, the Lenten veil, was stretched across the church between the

---

[1] From Old French *simenel*, itself derived from the Latin *simila*, meaning fine wheat flour.
[2] This developed into the seventeenth-century custom of giving a simnel cake to one's mother on that Sunday, mentioned in Robert Herrick's poem, *Hesperides*, in 1648. Mid-Lent Sunday was first recorded as 'Mothering Day' by Richard Symonds in 1644.

chancel and the nave hiding the altar from view. This was a large item and was probably made of smaller pieces, like chrysom cloths, sewn together. The curtain was temporarily drawn back on Sundays in Lent and finally on Maundy Thursday. Adding to the atmosphere of heaven withdrawn, crucifixes and images were shrouded, chrysom cloths being useful for this purpose also. Exceptions might be made for popular statues if they were likely to bring in money. It was in these mournful surroundings that the Lenten confessions were made (see Chapter Two, 3f).

The climax of all this was Holy Week. It began on Palm Sunday with a great procession round the outside of the church, re-enacting the entry of Christ into Jerusalem. The clergy carried a shrine containing the blessed sacrament and it was treated as Christ by the people who carried 'palms' – branches of box, yew or willow blessed by the priest. During the mass that followed the palms were given in to be kept till the next year's Ash Wednesday.

Maundy Thursday received its name from the anthem *Mandatum Novum* ('I give you a new commandment') which was sung at the washing of the feet of the poor, a rite imitating the action of Christ at the Last Supper. It was performed in cathedrals and abbeys by the rulers of Church and State, although what started as an act of humility became a ceremony clothed in splendour. To have their feet washed, even by the high and mighty, could not have appealed very much to the poor and doubtless it was for this reason that they were rewarded with gifts of money, food or clothing. After mass, ornaments and cloths were removed from the altars, which were washed that night. Spring was in the air and the people probably did some cleaning at home as well, the priests reminding them that, before Sunday, they 'should in like wise cleanse the house of their souls.' They smartened themselves up also, cutting their hair and trimming their beards, 'to make them honest against Easter day.'

On Good (i.e. holy) Friday everyone was expected to go to church where a crucifix was laid on the altar steps and proclaimed as 'the wood of the Cross.' The people approached on their knees to adore and kiss it, this action being known as 'creeping to the cross.' The veneration was originally intended for Christ, but the words and the actions encouraged people to worship the object before them. Afterwards mass was celebrated using a host consecrated on the previous day. Then the crucifix and another host from the Maundy Thursday mass were placed in the Easter sepulchre (a temporary or permanent receptacle in the chancel), as Christ's body had been placed in the tomb, and a lighted taper was left burning near it till Easter morning.

The next day was Easter Eve or Holy Saturday. In spite of the latter name its most vivid event, the blessing of the new fire, had been inherited from a heathen spring-time festival in honour of the sun. The Church explained this custom as symbolising the Resurrection and Christian priests made the new fire and lit the tall paschal candle with it. At some time during that day the images were uncovered to be ready for the coming celebrations.

The great day of Easter was welcomed by everyone. At last the depressing emphasis on sin was over and all were permitted to be joyful as they thought on the risen Christ. The prospect of better things to eat, also, hurried folk to church on Easter Sunday morning when, like Langland, they heard the bells:

> Men rang to the resurrection and with that I awaked
> And called [to] Kytte my wife and Kalote my daughter,
> Arise, and go reverence God's resurrection....

Probably before the congregation arrived the priests took the host from the sepulchre and put it in the usual place for the reserved sacrament. Then they removed the hidden crucifix and placed it on a side altar. When the people came they crept to it again, as on Good Friday. As they went they carried with them their compulsory Easter offering to the priest – money, perhaps, or eggs – and put it in a basin beside the cross. Afterwards, in cathedrals and churches with large staffs, the monks or priests represented the women finding the empty tomb and possibly other incidents of the Resurrection story.

The Easter Day mass was very special for all lay folk because it was the one day in the year when they took communion themselves. For this reason they came fasting, as King John, present in Lincoln cathedral at Easter, 1213, and wanting his dinner, reminded the rather long-winded Bishop Hugh. There had been a time when everyone received the bread and wine each Sunday. A change came about with the declaration of the doctrine of transubstantiation in 1215. It was then thought that in handing the wine (the blood of Christ) to the people there was a risk of it being spilt, an irreverent deed that could not be tolerated. So from that time the chalice was withheld from the laity and they received communion in one kind only. Even for that a cloth was stretched before them in case the consecrated bread should be dropped.

When the mass was ended everyone, like King John, went eagerly to enjoy a good meal. The Lenten fast was over and fish could be almost forgotten. Some parishioners may have joined together in sharing a parish breakfast of bacon and eggs, as did those of Nettleham in Lincolnshire. Many lords gave feasts for their manorial servants to which the villagers took contributions of eggs. Great magnates, like Bishop Swinfield of Hereford in 1290, fed their friends with roast ox and various other kinds of meat.

Permission to eat eggs again must have been a particular pleasure at Easter, and hard-boiled eggs, which had been coloured by using natural plant-dyes, were a favourite gift. This practice had been inherited from the pagan spring festival; then they had been looked on as emblems of continuing life but Christians saw them as symbols of the Resurrection. It was a custom observed by royalty also, for in 1290 Edward I gave four hundred and fifty eggs, 'stained' by boiling or covered with gold leaf, to members of his household. In Scotland and northern England they were known as 'pace-eggs', a corruption of the word Pascha (an adjective evidently put in by the Church to give a Christian connotation).

The week following Easter Sunday was a week away from work when general merry-making was the rule. For people who had to labour hard in order to grow the food to keep themselves alive it must have been a joyous respite from toil.

It was important that parish boundaries should be known so that tithes and dues were paid to the right parson. In the week before Ascension Thursday all the parishioners processed round the parish boundary with the blessed sacrament, cross, banners, bells and lights. There were stops for prayers of supplication, reading the gospel at certain prominent trees – 'Gospel oaks' –, blessing of the crops and painful reminders (with attendant rewards) to small boys – being thrown into ponds or bumped against trees or rocks – so that they would remember the boundary marks. Ascension Day itself was a major feast of the Church and the people attended mass in the morning to give thanks for the Lord's ascension into heaven. Some churches had a play, like that performed by the Holy Trinity gild, at Sleaford, Lincolnshire, in 1480. The rest of the day was a happy holiday, given over to may-pole dancing and other summer pursuits.

The second great religious feast of the year to bring with it a week's holiday was that of Whit. Officially it was Pentecost, but the Old-English term, remembering former white-clad adult candidates for baptism, exceeded it in popularity, so that Whit Sunday gave the name Whitsun or Whitsuntide to the whole of the following week. After mass the parishioners shared in a church ale. They may have chosen a Whit king and queen who, throughout the week, would preside over dancing, entertainment by morris men, shooting at the butts and other social events. It was one of the most enjoyable weeks of the year, for the food was fresh and the weather could be expected to grace outdoor pursuits.

Corpus Christi, on the second Thursday after Whit Sunday, celebrated the institution of Holy Communion as a joyful occasion, unlike the similar but sorrowful Maundy Thursday. It was a day of colourful pageantry, when reverence was paid to the blessed sacrament as it was carried at the head of a parish procession. In large towns the trade gilds joined in with their banners. This became the day when the great cycles of mystery plays were performed, the first recorded being that of Chester in 1328. It seems likely that they developed from already-existing Christmas and Easter plays which were gradually added to and then acted by the different gilds. Although the subjects, drawn from the Old and New Testament stories, were religious the actors often managed to put in comic episodes and the onlookers found the plays full of interest.

The day of St. Peter ad Vincula (St. Peter-in-chains) on 1 August was important to country folk because it marked the end of the hay-harvest and the beginning of the corn harvest. Just before that time most of them would be running short of flour and longing for the new wheat. They called the day Lammas (Old-English *hlaf-mass*, that is, 'loaf-feast'), for they took loaves made from the first gathering of wheat to church, where they were blessed. Then they used pieces of them as charms.

From Lammas to Michaelmas on 29 September (the Feast of St. Michael and All Angels) men worked hard to bring in the harvest, and so ended the husbandman's year. It was then that many parishes held their 'wake-day' – the day of the saint to whom the church was dedicated. Although these were spread throughout the year, many celebrations were moved nearer to Michaelmas time when a holiday could be enjoyed in the knowledge that the work was finished for the time being. The wake was a vigil kept in church during the eve, and the day itself started with a mass in honour of the patron saint. Very often neighbouring villages came in procession to take part and afterwards there was a 'wake ale' with sports, games, dancing and other community pleasures.

The agricultural cycle started straight away with ploughing and the sowing of the winter corn, a task to be finished by All Hallows (1 November). Then the cattle were driven from the summer pastures to spend the winter in byres. It was an anxious time, for the winter's meat-supply depended on this operation. Pre-Christian men believed that evil spirits, recruited from the dead, were abroad, so they held a great festival to appease them. The Christian Church changed this into a feast in honour of All Saints (or All Hallows), while appointing the following day, 2 November, All Souls, to commemorate the dead. A little more than a week later, on St. Martin's Day (11 November), the slaughter began of those cattle that could not be fed through the winter, the meat being salted. Medieval folk then looked forward to the third great religious holiday of the year.

Christmas lasted for twelve days because the winter sowing had been completed and the time for the spring sowing had not arrived. Kings, lords and people made the most of it. William I chose to be crowned on Christmas Day, 1066, and thereafter had solemn and splendid 'crown wearings' on that day, as well as at Easter and Whitsuntide, a custom continued by his successors. It was a day of religious significance that all people could understand and share in. Nothing was demanded of them except the normal duty of going to mass. There might even be the enjoyment, at or around Christmas or Epiphany, of seeing a dramatic representation of the story – a play about the wise men was regularly put on at Great Yarmouth from 1462 to 1512.

After the Christmas morning mass everyone went home for their Christmas dinner. Simnel cakes were often made at this time and also plum puddings. The latter were made with dried plums and still keep the same name, although the English fruit has been displaced by foreign currants, raisins and sultanas.

At some time during the fortnight those who lived on manors went to their lord's hall for a grand community dinner, taking with them a contribution of ale, loaves or fowls. When all was eaten the guests could take part in the singing and dancing of carols, join in noisy games and perhaps watch a mummers' play.

There were other holy days during the Christmas season, Holy Innocents Day, on 28 December, being the most notable in attracting a unique observance. As a commemoration of the children killed by Herod a boy was chosen as 'bishop', and others were his attendants. Dressed in expensive vestments, he took part in processions, preached a sermon, sang part of the mass, attended banquets, gave gifts and received oblations. This 'Feast of Boys', or 'Childermas', was very popular and took place in cathedrals and royal chapels, as well as many parish churches. In spite of the interest in the occasion the day of the week on which it fell was considered to be unlucky all during the following year and this belief nearly changed the date of a coronation. The advisers of Edward IV pointed out to him that the previous Holy Innocents' Day had fallen on a Sunday, which was the day chosen for his coronation, 28 June, 1461. The matter was taken seriously and there was talk of the crowning being put off till the Monday. In the end Edward decided to ignore the superstition and went ahead with the arrangements as planned.

The Christmas season was not considered to be finally over till 1 February, when the holly, ivy and mistletoe, which had decorated churches and houses, were taken down. The next day was the feast of the Presentation of the Lord in the Temple, when Simeon's description of the child as 'a light that will be a revelation to the heathen' was recalled. This happened about the time when ploughing started again. A heathen heat-festival had once helped the plough along and the Church fused the two celebrations together by bringing the people into church with their pagan torches or candles. These were blessed, lit and carried in procession through the streets, before all returned to the church for mass. The visual effect of all this gave the popular name Candlemas to the day.

Lent started soon after Candlemas and, when Lady Day came again, the Church's year went forward as of old, intertwined with the inexorable demands of the soil.

SELECT BOOK LIST

BENNETT, H. S. *Life on the English Manor* (1937).
CHAMBERS, E. K. *Op. cit.*
CHENEY, C. R. (ed.) *Handbook of Dates for Students of English History* (1945).
CLARKE, W. K. L. (ed.) and HARRIS, C. (Asst.) *Op. cit.*
COULTON, G. G. *Medieval Panorama* (1939).
CRAIG, H. *English Religious Drama of the Middle Ages* (1955).
DIX, Gregory. *The Shape of the Liturgy* (1943).
DRUMMOND, J. C. and WILBRAHAM, A. *The Englishman's Food: A History of Five Centuries of English Diet* (1957).
GASQUET, F. A. *Op. cit.*
HOLE, Christine. *British Folk Customs*. (1976).
HOMANS, G. G. *English Villagers of the Thirteenth Century* (1941).
HUNT, E. D. *Holy Land Pilgrimage in the Later Roman Empire, A.D. 312–460* (1982).
McARTHUR, A. Allan. *The Evolution of the Christian Year* (1953).
OWEN, D. M. *Church and Society in Medieval Lincolnshire* (1971).
POOLE, R. L. *Medieval Reckonings of Time* (1921). *Studies in Chronology and History* (1934).
POWER, E. and POSTAN, M. M. (ed.) *English Trade in the Fifteenth Century*

(1933).
PULLAR, P. *Consuming Passions. A History of English Food and Appetite* (1970).
ROCK, D. *Op. cit.* Vol. IV.
SMITH, H. Maynard. *Op. cit.*
SPICER, D. G. *Yearbook of English Festivals* (1954).
WILLIAMS, A. *The Drama of Medieval England* (1961).
WOOD-LEIGH, K. L. *A Small Household of the Fifteenth Century* (1956).

BISHOPS AND ARCHBISHOPS

1. DIOCESES, PROVINCES AND CATHEDRALS

Every parish was part of a larger area called a diocese. In England the dioceses were based on the old Anglo-Saxon kingdoms or their sub-divisions. By the time of the Norman Conquest there were fifteen, with Ely being added in 1109 and Carlisle in 1133. These seventeen, plus the four Welsh ones, remained unchanged for the next four centuries.[1] Each was ruled by a bishop (this word being an Old English corruption of the Greek *episcopus*, meaning overseer, shepherd or elder).

The dioceses were grouped into two provinces at whose head were the archbishops of Canterbury and York. As a result of the establishment of the first archbishopric in the south and the historical progress of the Conversion they were unequally divided. Fourteen in the southern part of the country, plus the four Welsh ones, belonged to the province of Canterbury, one of the largest in Christendom; the three in the north (York, Durham and Carlisle) belonged to the province of York, one of the smallest. After the Conquest, the former's metropolitan claimed precedence but the latter's maintained his own equality. This rivalry was settled by Pope Innocent VI (1352–62), who gave the title 'Primate of England' to the archbishop of York, although the southern archbishop was to have precedence with the title 'Primate of All England'; also, each was allowed to have his cross carried before him in the other's province. Only after this recognition did archbishops of York consent to accept translation to Canterbury as promotion, Thomas Arundel being the first to do so in 1396.

An Anglo-Saxon bishop had a special seat, the cathedra, in which he

---

[1]Canterbury, Rochester, Winchester, Worcester, Norwich, Ely, Carlisle, Durham, Chichester, Salisbury, Exeter, Lincoln, London, Hereford, Lichfield, York, Bath and Wells. The Welsh dioceses were Llandaff, St. David's, St. Asaph and Bangor.

sat to teach his people about the faith and to superintend their community life. If he moved his centre of government to a different place he took his chair, his symbol of authority, with him, and it gave its name to his church. It was usually raised on a dais so that the bishop looked down at the congregation across the holy table. This arrangement can be seen in Norwich cathedral, where the ancient stone chair was probably brought from Elmham via Thetford, as the centre of the diocese changed. In the Middle Ages, when bishops' duties frequently took them away from their cathedrals, the chairs were used only for the ceremony of enthronement. They were then moved to the south side of the chancel, like that of Bishop Hatfield (1345–81) at Durham.

Each cathedral had its own individual history and eight of them (plus Bath) were monastic and eight (plus Wells) were secular.[1] The former were directed by a prior and chapter (i.e. the senior monks), the whole community obeying a code of regulations – the Rule[2] – and living within the walls of the monastery. The latter were staffed by clergy who, like the monks, took part in the daily services; however, unlike the monks, they lived in the world at large and were each supported by their own share of the revenues – an estate, church or manor – known as a prebend (from the Latin *praebenda*, an allowance). They themselves were called prebends or canons, the chief one being the dean. A prebend often took the income but put in a vicar-choral to live on the spot and do the actual duties. Both types of governing bodies became powerful enough to resist the claims of their bishops. By the fifteenth century, after many struggles about authority, the bishops conceded defeat, although it was agreed that they had the nominal right to 'visit' the secular foundations and of being recognised as titular abbot of the monastic ones.[3]

---

[1] The cathedrals of the first eight dioceses listed in the footnote on page 106 were monastic and those of the next eight were secular. Bath and Wells were used alternately as the seat of the bishop of Bath and Wells.

[2] The Benedictine Rule was adopted by all except Carlisle, which followed the Rule of St. Augustine.

[3] To this day the bishop of Durham's stall is on the south (or abbot's) side of the chancel in Durham cathedral, and the dean's is on the north (or prior's) side, and this arrangement may apply to other formerly monastic cathedrals.

2. CONSECRATION, THE INSIGNIA AND ENTHRONEMENT

On appointment a bishop was consecrated by his archbishop, generally in the metropolitan's own cathedral, through prayer and the laying-on of hands. In this way it was believed that the true faith was transmitted in unbroken descent from the apostles.

After they had been consecrated archbishops and bishops thought of themselves as the fathers of the people in their dioceses and the word 'father' became part of their formal designation. From early days they were always referred to or addressed respectfully by suitable religious phrases. Bede mentions 'the venerable Archbishop Paulinus', 'the most holy Bosa' and 'the most reverend Bishop Cedd'. The latter phrase is the commonest and was also used by Pope Gregory in a letter to Archbishop Etherius of Arles: 'To his most reverend and holy brother'. Eventually it was reserved for archbishops only, bishops being distinguished as 'right reverend'. By the beginning of the sixteenth century the full titles of archbishops and bishops, respectively, were 'the most reverend father in God' and 'the right reverend father in God'.

During the consecration ceremony the bishops were invested with their insignia. The pastoral staff was a symbol of office in the same way that a king's sceptre was. Its importance is shown by the story of Rannulf Flambard, bishop of Durham, who was imprisoned in the Tower of London in 1100 by Henry I. A daring fellow, he escaped by climbing down a rope from his window, at the same time remembering to carry his pastoral staff. It was necessary to take it with him as it was both an emblem and a proof of his episcopal authority.

Those staffs which had rounded ends reminded bishops of their role as shepherds, so that such crooks became customary although not essential. Thomas Becket's staff, shown to Erasmus at Canterbury in 1512, was short, but in later years shoulder height or the height of the holder became normal. A bishop held his staff in his left hand in order to leave his right free to raise for the blessing. In procession the staff was usually carried by a bearer known as the crociarius (i.e. the bearer of the crook) and this Latin term was at length transferred to the staff, so that by the sixteenth century it was often known as a crosier. Pastoral staffs belonging to two medieval bishops of Winchester are kept by the Oxford colleges of their own foundation, that of William of Wykeham (d.1404) at New College and that of Richard Fox (d.1528) at Corpus Christi. Representations of others can be seen on the tombs of some bishops.

The episcopal ring was looked on as emblematic of the bishop's marriage to the Church. It was made of gold and set with a large unfacetted stone, perhaps a sapphire, amethyst or ruby. The bishop wore it over his glove so that it could be seen when the hand was lifted to give the blessing.

Originally a papal head-dress, the mitre was assumed by all bishops and it became part of the investiture ceremonies. By the late twelfth century it was triangular in shape, with the double points worn front and back. A contemporary example of this is shown on an episcopal figure painted on a wall of the Galilee chapel in Durham cathedral. The height of mitres increased during the later Middle Ages, and the material changed from the simplicity of white linen to silk or cloth of gold adorned with jewels. The remains of William of Wykeham's can be seen at New College.

Archbishops possessed two additional items of insignia which were not given until their enthronement. One was a staff with a cross (sometimes a crucifix) at the top. The right to have this carried before them was granted by the pope about the beginning of the twelfth century, following his own custom. When Thomas Becket was attacked by the four knights in his cathedral, his cross-bearer, Edward Grimm, used the cross to try to fend off the blows and it was broken as a result.

The most important part of an archbishop's insignia was the pallium, a narrow scarf with tails, which encircled the shoulders so that its shape appeared like the letter Y, both front and back. Pope Gregory the Great (590–604) sent one to Augustine in 601, after his consecration as archbishop of Canterbury, following the success of his mission to England. Then, for the first time, the pallium became an essential mark of rank and was linked with the right to exercise metropolitan government of a province. Henceforth it was a symbol of delegated papal authority and a written acknowledgement of the supremacy of the Roman see was required from recipients as well as a burdensome 'voluntary' payment. As papal power increased so did the importance of the pallium – an archbishop could not be enthroned or perform any of his archiepiscopal functions or even use his title until it was obtained. In 1093, Anselm, clad in his vestments, but barefoot, met the messenger bringing the pallium at the gates of Canterbury. It was then borne in solemn procession to the cathedral where the enthroning ceremony began. The archiepiscopal status of the sees of Canterbury and York was shown by placing a heraldic form of the pallium on their armorial bearings (still remaining on those of the former).

At death an archbishop was buried with his pallium about his shoulders, so that, after his consecration, each new archbishop had to request another for himself. The lack of a pallium was considered a serious deficiency in Stigand, archbishop of Canterbury from 1052–70 (ignoring the one he got from a pope who was later said to be a false intruder). This was the reason that caused Pope Gregory VII to support the Norman invasion of England in 1066, although Stigand was not deposed till four years later. From that time archbishops went unquestioningly to Rome for their pallia or sent their deputies for them. Even Henry VIII considered it to be necessary for Cranmer in 1533 and he put financial pressure on the pope so that he provided one. Twelve years later, after the break with Rome, the pallium was still considered to be an essential part of an archbishop's clothing and Cranmer himself gave one to Robert Holgate, the new archbishop of York. His own successor at Canterbury, Cardinal Pole, received his pallium from the pope in 1556, being the last English archbishop to wear one. (He died in 1558).

As soon after consecration as possible a bishop went to his own cathedral for the ceremony of his enthronement in the episcopal chair. This act signified his formal assumption of power to govern the diocese.

3. CHOOSING A BISHOP

In the early days of the Conversion the Church's mission was dependent on the Anglo-Saxon kings and it was they who appointed the bishops. When cathedrals were established the monks or canons there had the theoretical right to elect their bishops, but, in practice, the king continued to make the choice. On appointment, bishops received their rings and pastoral staffs from the king and also, as land-holders, swore fealty to him. The system was satisfactory when well-meaning kings appointed good bishops, but it could be abused by putting in unworthy men or by leaving a see vacant so that the king received the rents and dues. In 1075 Pope Gregory VII forbade investiture by kings, although William I ignored this command. The matter was more or less settled by compromise in the reign of Henry I in 1106. Thereafter the monks or canons of a cathedral elected their bishop, who then did homage as a baron to the king for his lands, 'the temporalities'. Consecration followed, performed by the archbishop of the province, who invested the new bishop with the ring and staff, the symbols of 'the spiritualities'. In

1214 King John said that the royal *congé d'élire* (permission to elect) was to be obtained before proceeding to election, which was afterwards to be confirmed by the king. This settlement remained in force during the reigns of succeeding medieval kings, although disputes continued to occur from time to time.

Left to themselves monks or canons were likely to choose a scholar of repute or the most distinguished member of their own body. Kings saw bishops as feudal lords who owed duties to the crown and who might serve as advisers on national and foreign affairs. For these reasons they put forward their own nominees and cathedral chapters usually acquiesced in electing them. The kings tended to bestow bishoprics on their relatives, members of noble houses and their own civil servants who were thus supplied with a handsome income. Such men generally viewed their new position as a lucrative political one giving them the financial means to live in an opulent manner. Being more interested in diplomacy and the business of the king's court, the spiritual side of their duties became, for many, of secondary importance and they were inclined to ignore the calls of the diocese.

Any capable man, whatever his social status, might rise to episcopal rank. Some saw in this an opportunity to advance themselves which was denied elsewhere. It was necessary to be in holy orders although some men did not enter these until a bishopric was in the offing. The career of William of Wykeham (1324–1404) furnishes a good example of an ambitious man using the Church to reach one of the highest and wealthiest ecclesiastical dignities. Up to the age of thirty-eight he had been mainly a supervisor of Edward III's building works. His reward was a large number of rich benefices, given between 1356 and 1364, although he was not even an acolyte till the end of 1361 and a priest only from July 1362. His aspirations were achieved when he became bishop of Winchester in 1366 and also chancellor of England (the leading minister of the king) some months later. These two posts gave him an annual income of about £250,000. It was only after losing the chancellorship in 1371, when blamed for the failures of the French wars, that he began to devote time to his diocese and the founding of his school at Winchester and New College at Oxford.

While many bishops were of the same self-seeking nature as Wykeham, there were also some worthy men who were determined to raise the spiritual level of their dioceses. Perhaps the most illustrious of these was Robert Grosseteste, bishop of Lincoln from 1235 to 1253. A scholar of international reputation, he travelled throughout his large diocese rectifying wrongs and instituting reforms. A hard-working and outspoken man, he was yet a very human figure – he once ordered a melancholy friar to drink a cup of the best wine as a penance.

4. THE ARCHBISHOP OF CANTERBURY'S RIGHT TO CROWN THE SOVEREIGN

The happy partnership of kings and bishops during the Conversion led the Church to opine that monarchy was ordained by God. Because of this a king's crowning became its concern and so it added a sense of sacred mystery to the coronation ceremony. In 973 Dunstan, archbishop of Canterbury, consecrated and anointed King Edgar (one of the earliest kings of the whole country) like a bishop, as well as crowning him, and this set the pattern for the future. (The first known anointing was of Offa of Mercia's son, Ecgfrith, in 787, following the example of Charlemagne in 781). The Church placed the emphasis on the priestly element of anointing, as setting the king apart as the Lord's Anointed. It was to this idea of kingship by divine right that Shakespeare's Richard II appealed when threatened with deposition:

> Not all the water in the rough, rude sea
> Can wash the balm from an anointed king.
>
> (*Richard II*, III, ii)

The privilege of crowning the king was assumed as a right by all archbishops of Canterbury after Dunstan. Necessity obliged archbishops of York to crown William I (and probably Harold II) in 1066, and the son of Henry II during his father's lifetime in 1170. The latter deed caused the returned Becket to excommunicate his fellow archbishop and this led to Becket's murder and eventual canonisation. The most that York could claim after that was simply to be present at a coronation. If for any reason Canterbury could not perform the ceremony it was to be done by his chief suffragan bishop and this happened at the coronation of Henry III in 1216, when the king was crowned by the bishop of Winchester.

Certain bishops were interested in playing their parts during the rite. At the coronation of Edgar the king had been brought into the church by two unnamed bishops, and this episcopal escort had probably been continued at later crowning ceremonies. Supporting Richard I throughout his coronation in 1189 were the bishops of Durham and Bath (united with Wells in 1219), and their successors maintained this presence as their traditional right ever after.

5. THE ARCHBISHOP OF CANTERBURY'S RIGHT TO MARRY THE SOVEREIGN

The king's marriage also became a matter of concern to the Church. The first marriage ceremony of a sovereign after the Conquest, that of Henry I in 1100, was performed by Anselm, archbishop of Canterbury, and his successor upheld this privilege as a right of office at the same king's second marriage in 1121. In the event he was ill and chose his suffragan, the bishop of Winchester, to marry the royal pair. These were occasions when the chief parties were doing honour to each other. Unusual circumstances due to which the ceremony was performed by someone else – Richard I's wedding to Berengaria of Navarre, in Cyprus, in 1191, en route to the Holy Land, for instance – did not invalidate the marriage.

6. THE LORDS SPIRITUAL

When parliament began to develop in the thirteenth century the bishops were liable to be summoned to its meetings, should the king desire their presence. If the twenty-one bishops were all there, together with about seventy abbots, the lords spiritual outnumbered the barons. No bishop or abbot or, for that matter, a baron, had a right to a summons and the king invited those whom he wished. They were not called as representatives of the Church but, like the barons, because they held land by military tenure-in-chief of the crown; that is, their lands owed military service and they were therefore barons as well as prelates. In practice most of the bishops were called and did attend but the majority of the abbots found reasons for not attending.

The meeting place of parliament was normally the hall of the king's palace at Westminster but it could equally as well be held at other places – York, Lincoln or wherever the king happened to be. While the chancellor and other members of the council were accommodated on wool-sacks, the barons, bishops and abbots sat on benches. The bishops' bench ran down from the right of the throne and the bishops sat there in their order of precedence with the abbots behind them. The sight of so many bishops in one place caused people to refer to them collectively as 'the bench of bishops', and to be 'raised to the episcopal bench' meant promotion to a bishopric.

7. DIOCESAN DUTIES

To the medieval bishop the idea of being a shepherd of the souls in his care was no more than a pleasant theory. In practice he saw himself as a stern corrector of the faults of both clergy and people. His diocesan duties were to go on visitations (tours of inspection), hold law courts for spiritual offenders, consecrate churches, institute rectors to benefices and confirm the faithful. By the fifteenth century many bishops, especially those in the king's governmental and administrative service, managed to avoid most of these responsibilities for years; at the same time there were some who preferred to turn their backs on the London scene and to conduct diocesan affairs with energy.

After his enthronement a bishop was supposed to make a primary visitation of his diocese, and thenceforth a triennial one, but this rule was not strictly kept. A visitation, when it did happen, was more of a grand progress through certain central places to which clergy and churchwardens were summoned from the surrounding areas. On his journey the bishop, wearing the secular clothing of a great lord, and accompanied by a large retinue, would reside at his many manor-houses, or else he expected hospitality to be offered by abbeys, local notabilities, wealthy tenants and rectors. He did not often stay at his palace in the cathedral city, as he and the cathedral authorities were not generally happy to be in such close proximity. Making stops for enquiries and the performance of duties took a lot of time and the tour might be spread over several years. A visitation was not welcomed by either clergy or people, for they did not wish to have critical eyes cast upon their affairs or to suffer the expense of entertaining the important company. Those who could muster an excuse (perhaps the poverty of the parish or abbey due to agricultural disasters) tried to buy off the visitor by offering a fee instead and this was often accepted.

As absentee bishops could not fulfil their diocesan obligations in person they appointed deputies to take them over. From the thirteenth century a vicar-general was chosen, usually a member of the cathedral chapter, for the work which did not require episcopal orders. He could do all the routine work: summon and hold diocesan synods, oversee elections of heads of religious houses, arrange for ordinations to be celebrated by assistant bishops, institute incumbents into their benefices and receive their oaths of obedience, issue dispensations for non-residence, collect the incomes of vacant benefices for his master, free the bishop's prisoners and collect Peter's Pence.

8. THE CONSISTORY COURT AND ITS PERSONNEL

As part of his office every bishop was a judge ordinary, usually called 'the ordinary', with jurisdiction concerning ecclesiastical matters within his diocese. He generally delegated his powers to a lawyer called the official-principal, more often known as the official. This representative presided over the consistory court, which was held in the capital of the diocese, often in the cathedral building itself. There he heard cases respecting such things as non-attendance at church, Sunday trading, wills, tithes, brawling, attacks on clergy and the drunkenness of clerics.

Those defendants who were judged guilty had to pay the costs and were given punishments: a public whipping; the wearing of a placard proclaiming their fault; or walking in the Sunday church procession, carrying a candle in one hand and a shoulder of lamb in the other (for selling meat on Sundays). Some chose to commute their penances into money payments; such sums were supposed to be used for charitable purposes but it was suspected that the court officials pocketed them. To appear in court, often many miles from home, might be inconvenient and some defendants failed to turn up. The court, however, possessed powers to enforce attendance – a fine or even excommunication and, in the end, the arrest of the offender by the secular authorities.

There were other servants of the court – proctors (equivalent to barristers, who could be hired by both plaintiffs and defendants), registrars, scribes and apparitors (who were better known as summoners). The latter summoned defendants to appear in court, by letter if they were literate or else by word of mouth. As they went about their business in towns and villages they became well-acquainted with local gossip. They were thus in a position to report to the judges on the moral lapses of both clergy and lay people, although their silence could be bought. Their inquisitorial activities brought the whole legal process of the consistory courts into disrepute. The bishop's official and the rest of the court personnel derived much of their income from the fees that they charged their clients. The more cases they handled the better it was for them, so they were not averse to the meddling ways of the summoner.

9. THE BISHOP'S COURT

The most serious offences were dealt with by the bishop himself (or, in his absence, by the vicar-general) in his own court, held at whichever of his manors he happened to be staying at. There he decided cases of murder, rape and burglary by the clergy, fraudulent behaviour by executors, heresy, simony and assaults on the clergy or the bishop's officers. Besides the sort of punishments meted out in the consistory court, the bishop's court might send a guilty person on a long pilgrimage, suspend clerics temporarily from their livings and even (although rarely) deprive them altogether. The final measure could be a term of imprisonment, for all bishops were required to have one or two prisons in their dioceses, according to the statutes of the Council of Lambeth (1261).

10. ARCHDEACONS AND THEIR CHAPTERS

Every bishop had one or more archdeacons as his chief administrative officers. These were known as 'the bishop's eyes' because they saw the state of the diocese and brought it to their master's attention, where necessary. They themselves were empowered to deal with matters which did not require the direct intervention of the bishop and so were possessed of authority in their own areas almost as great as that of the bishop himself.

Large bishoprics were divided into archdeaconries, which were based on county divisions and given local titles. In a small diocese, such as Rochester, one was enough but Hereford and others had two and Lincoln had eight. The cathedral city gave its name to the chief archdeacon and he took precedence over the others. As archdeacons' duties were administrative and nothing to do with the ministry of the sacraments it was not necessary for them to proceed to priests' orders; most of them did so as it could prove to be a step towards a bishopric.

Archdeacons were responsible for the inspection of church buildings and also for enquiring into the moral behaviour of both clergy and people. As, in the performance of these duties, they claimed free accommodation for themselves and their retinues, an archidiaconal visit was dreaded by all. Where possible, some parishes tried to buy off the inquisitor by paying him not to come.

Archdeacons (or their officials) exercised their supervisory powers by holding visitation inquiries at courts known as chapters. To these were brought the vicars accused of having hearth-mates or slighter connections; the couples who were said to be married within the prohibited degrees; peasants who had worked on Sunday and others who could be called on as witnesses. All were closely cross-questioned about their own and others' private affairs. Out of these human faults and miseries came money for the archdeacon. Those who could afford it paid to evade citation in the first place. Those who were pronounced guilty were either fined or sentenced to public floggings round their market place or parish church. The threat of disgrace and pain was enough to make some people pay to avert it – like the husband of an innocent Scarborough woman accused of adultery in 1158, who made a payment so that his wife should be gently treated. If a defendant escaped these penalties he might be caught by unlawful exactions, like the one in thirteenth-century Winchester commonly called the 'archdeacon's pig'.[1] All of this money brought in good returns for archdeacons, and Henry II declared that they had larger incomes than he had himself.

The minute inquiries into people's most private affairs and the acquisitive behaviour resulted in the general unpopularity of all archdeacons and caused men to ask whether they could be saved. Indeed, a correspondent of John of Salisbury stated that salvation was wholly barred to them because they thrived on the sins of others, on bribes and on false accusations. William Langland referred to archdeacons who were willing to ignore sins such as adultery, divorce and usury, if in return they were 'saddled with silver'. The inescapable power of these diocesan officers was so felt and feared that a twelfth-century preacher commented in surprise, and doubtless relief, that even popes and archdeacons died. One such, William Doune, archdeacon of Leicester (d.1361), was moved to refer in his will to the rapacity of himself and others like him, who dealt 'busily, nay, harshly with those who are subject to them; and of these I have been and am one.'

An archdeaconry was a large area to supervise, so it was sub-divided into smaller parts called rural deaneries which were composed of several parishes. These smaller, more manageable administrative units were well-established in England by the end of the twelfth century. One of the

---

[1] This charge must have taken its name from the 'pig' which, in this context, would have been a pot, jar or other container in which, presumably, the archdeacon concerned kept his spoils.

resident clergy was appointed rural dean by the bishop with the duty of supervising his group of parishes. He was always on the spot and thus well-placed to hear of the sins of his fellows and their flocks and worked closely with the archdeacon or his official, often presiding at the chapter.

The man who had the task of bearing the summons to appear in court to the person cited was the archdeacon's apparitor or summoner. On his travels he had the right to be lodged one day and night at the homes of vicars or rectors. When the court was in session he carried a wand or staff and acted as beadle or marshal, being in charge of witnesses and the movements of people about the room. These duties did not require a specially-trained person, but an ability to read and write was useful and sometimes the apparitors were clerics. The profits of the court were shared, probably on a percentage basis, the archdeacon or his official taking the larger amount, and the rural dean, the summoner and possibly other hangers-on a lesser amount. Some summoners may have done their work conscientiously but the majority of them used their opportunities to prey upon the uneducated country-folk, ferreting out personal follies, frightening their victims, offering to ignore an offence in return for a bribe or making false accusations in the hope of receiving money to keep quiet. They acquired an infamous reputation and were castigated in the literature of the day; as the Friar in the Prologue to Chaucer's *The Friar's Tale* stated, 'of a summoner may no good be said'. The Friar went on to tell of one who had his own spies ready to report to him those faults of others that were likely to bring him profit. As a result of this kind of thing feelings sometimes ran high and more than one summoner was ambushed and attacked, a consequence due entirely to their own abuse of their powers. To simple illiterate folk the summoner seemed to represent the stern authority of the universal Church reaching out to discipline the humblest of straying sinners.

11. SUFFRAGAN BISHOPS

Certain of an absentee bishop's duties could only be performed by a holder of episcopal orders: consecration of churches and graveyards, and of holy oil and chrism on Maundy Thursday, as well as confirmation and ordination. For these acts suffragan bishops were chosen. These were first appointed in the thirteenth century and proved to be so useful that there was a steady succession of them in most dioceses. They were often learned members of a friars' house and were probably graduates in theology. Having chosen his candidate the diocesan bishop applied to the pope to nominate him to a titular see. The names of suffragan sees were taken from towns in eastern Mediterranean lands, once within the bounds of Christendom but later in infidel hands – Ascalon, Laodicea, Philopolis, Pharensis, for example; or Irish sees which were difficult of access – Annaghdown, Kildare, Dromore and Achonry, among others. The suffragan was consecrated and given episcopal insignia; referred to (like his diocesan) as 'reverend father in Christ, by divine permission, bishop of (for instance) Edessa'; and addressed as 'lord'. He was thus shown to be a person of some importance. Even so, he was always known to be a paid deputy, whose appointment had to be renewed from year to year. He received a salary from his diocesan bishop who augmented this by the granting of benefices.

The suffragan had much to do and travelled widely about the diocese performing the bishop's sacerdotal functions. He had no other powers and was subordinate to the vicar-general. He was merely the diocesan bishop's humble servant, a fact made plain in an entry in the register of Thomas Langley, bishop of Durham. In 1437 the newly-elected abbot of Alnwick abbey was unable to travel the sixty miles south to Bishop Auckland to receive the bishop's blessing, because of the expense and the danger of Scottish raids. The canons asked if instead the suffragan could be sent north to bestow the episcopal benediction. This request was granted and the bishop of Dromore was sent off on the long and possibly dangerous journey. A later suffragan of Durham, in office from 1458 till his death in 1484, was William, prior of Brinkburn, in Northumberland, appointed to the titular Irish see of Clonmacnoise. He was buried in his priory church and his grave-slab, calling him 'bishop of Clunensis', shows an incised mitre and pastoral staff.

The organisation of the Church from province to parish enabled the hierarchy to keep in touch with the least of its children, although not in the same way that Christ had suggested. To the children themselves their father-in-God was a largely unknown and distant figure and his rule by deputies seemed to them more judicial than paternal. The only people to benefit from the system were the office-holders, of one sort and another, who made their living out of it at the expense of the lowliest whose need was the greatest.

SELECT BOOK LIST

BARLOW, F. *The English Church, 1000–1066* (1963).
DEANESLY, M. *Op. cit.*
GIBBS, M. and LANG, J. *Bishops and Reform, 1215–1272* (1934).
HASELMAYER, L. A. 'The Apparitor and Chaucer's Summoner', in *Speculum*, Vol. xii (1937).
HILL, G. *The English Dioceses* (1900).
LEVISON, W. *England and the Continent in the Eighth Century* (1946).
MACKENZIE, K. D. *The Case for Episcopacy* (1929).
MOORMAN, J. R. H. *Op. cit.*
NORRIS, H. *Church Vestments*. Their origin and development (1949).
POLLARD, A. F. *The Evolution of Parliament* (1920).
ROCK, D. *Op. cit.* Vol. II.
RODES, Robert E. Jr. *Ecclesiastical Administration in Medieval England* (1977).
SAYLES, G. O. *The Medieval Foundations of England* (1948; revised and reprinted, 1961).
SCAMMELL, J. 'The rural chapter in England from the eleventh to the fourteenth century', in *The English Historical Review*, No. CCCXXXVIII (January 1971).
SCHRAMM, P. E. *A History of the English Coronation*, trans. by L. G. W. Legg (1937).
STOREY, R. L. *Diocesan Administration in the Fifteenth Century* (St. Anthony's Hall Publications, No. 16, 1959).
STOREY, R. L. *Thomas Langley and the Bishopric of Durham, 1406–1437* (1961).
TELFER, W. *The Office of a Bishop* (1962).
THOMPSON, A. Hamilton. *The Cathedral Churches of England* (1925).
THOMPSON, A. Hamilton. *Op. cit.*
WOODCOCK, B. L. *Medieval Ecclesiastical Courts in the Diocese of Canterbury* (1952).

MEMBERS OF THE RELIGIOUS ORDERS

1. MONKS, CANONS AND NUNS

a. *The monasteries*

The first monasteries were religious institutions where groups of people could serve God in seclusion. Although it was necessary for entrants to take vows of poverty, chastity and obedience (i.e. to the Rule, a detailed code of conduct which had been drawn up by St. Benedict in the sixth century) many men and women were attracted to the life. There were already monasteries of the Benedictine order in late Anglo-Saxon England and more were established after the Conquest.

Other monastic orders were then introduced, the most important being the Cluniac, Cistercian and Carthusian. There were also orders of regular canons (i.e. priests living according to a monastic Rule) – the Augustinian (or Austin) and Premonstratensian. All of these, except the Carthusian, had houses for nuns as well as monks or canons. In addition there was the only native English order, the Gilbertine, which was founded at Sempringham, Lincolnshire, by a secular priest, Gilbert, for nuns and for the regular canons who served the community as priests. Each order in England made fresh foundations up to the beginning of the fourteenth century when there was a total of about eight hundred houses. Few were founded after that. Besides these there were more than a hundred daughter houses of Norman and French monasteries and these 'alien priories' were subsidiaries of their parent monasteries.[1]

There was a great difference between the wealthy monasteries of local

---

[1] These were all closed in the French wars of the fourteenth and fifteenth centuries, their revenues being used mainly for new religous foundations.

or national importance with close on a hundred brethren and the smaller houses with only half a dozen. St. Mary's abbey, York (annual income over £400,000 in 1535), was obviously superior to the nun's priory at Nunburnholme (annual income about £1,600 in the same year) a few miles away. In wealth and influence the two may be compared with a modern London department store and a village shop, respectively.[1] Large or small, they were scattered about all over the country, in towns or on remote moorland, in secluded villages or on busy highways. They became almost as much a part of the English scene as the parish churches and, like them, many have left their traces on place-names. Monk Bretton in Yorkshire was home to a monastery, as Nuneaton in Warwickshire was to a nunnery. There was a priory for Carthusian monks at Hinton in Somerset and the word 'Charterhouse' was added to the village name (derived from La Grande Chartreuse, the mother house in France). The white robes of the Cistercian nun owners gave the name of White Ladies Aston to a Worcester manor. Similarly, Brewood Black Ladies, Staffordshire, was named from the priory of black-clad Benedictine nuns there. Canons Ashby, Northamptonshire, was the seat of a priory of regular Augustinian canons. The village of Crowmarsh Battle, Oxfordshire, received its suffix from Battle abbey in Sussex, which owned it. The agricultural centres worked by Cistercian lay-brothers were called granges (a word sometimes adopted by the Benedictines also) and several present-day farms have that name attached to them.

St. Benedict said that a company of monks was a family and that the head of that family was the father or abbot. By transference, a monastery came to be referred to as an abbey. The abbot's deputy was the prior. Where the monastery church was also the cathedral of the diocese the bishop was the nominal abbot, but the actual governing was done by the prior. In this case the monastery was called a cathedral priory. If a daughter house was founded on some part of the monastic property it was ruled by a prior chosen by the mother house and was known as a priory. The heads of the Cistercian and Premonstratension houses were also called abbots while the Cluniac, Augustinian and Carthusian heads were called priors. The same nomenclature obtained for the houses for nuns of each order. Any monastery of monks or nuns might be referred to as a convent[2] (from the Latin *conventus*, 'to come together').

[1] This comparison is drawn by A. G. Dickens in *The English Reformation*, 52.
[2] The restricted use of this word to a nunnery dates only from the end of the eighteenth century.

b. *The monks*

For centuries followers of the Rule of St. Benedict lived in self-supporting communities dividing their quiet day between worship, study and manual work. All their efforts were bent on the ordered life within the enclosure, with no thought given to the world outside from which they had withdrawn. They had all the necessities of life but no luxuries – a vegetarian diet, the simple clothing of peasants, no personal items of property or separate rooms – , the whole existence being bounded by the monastery walls with few opportunities to travel outside them.

Although Benedict was anxious that there should be no class distinction recruits came mainly from those families rich enough to be able to spare a member to an unworldly life-style. In medieval England the greater proportion of entrants came from the families of the lesser land-owners and those of tenant-farmers and merchants. The Augustinian order gave precedence to those from the upper-classes.

Novices gained their places by means of endowments made by their families – whether gifts of money, houses, manors or appropriated churches. Most of these middle-class young men expected a standard of living commensurate with that to which they had been accustomed and only a few entered the monastery because of a genuine religious vocation. Others saw in it an opportunity for study, whether of theology or history, or for developing their artistic gifts. Those with business inclinations could work as accountants or treasurers, those with good organising abilities hoped to become heads of departments and those with an interest in the land might control the monastic estates. The ambitious might see it as a step to life at court or foreign travel (as the king's envoy) or even episcopal preferment. In short, the monastery was a place to satisfy career aspirations and the early strivings after spiritual perfection ceased to be attempted by the majority of the monastic community; it became, in fact, more of a gentleman's club.

With all these secular pursuits, it was only natural that some monks were increasingly unhappy and it was this dissatisfaction that produced new orders. Most of these failed to live up to their primary ideals and only the Carthusians and the Bridgettines (a fourteenth-century Swedish order for monks and nuns, with one abbey at Syon, Middlesex) followed their high calling and kept their ascetic way of living to the end.

There were about 10,000 monks and regular canons and about 3,000 nuns in English and Welsh religious houses in 1348 when the population as a whole was approximately 3,700,000. Following the Black Death and further outbreaks of the plague in the later fourteenth century the numbers were reduced by forty or fifty per cent. They only slowly improved to about 6,000 for the men and nearly 2,000 for the nuns by 1534.[1]

c. *Life in the medieval monastery*

In a Benedictine house the monks' day began and ended some five hours before that of the present working day. The most important part of this, according to Benedict's Rule, was the reciting of prayers and psalms at several services throughout the day, known collectively as the divine office; altogether about four hours were devoted to this. In winter the monks rose about two o'clock and went from their dormitory into the church for the first prayers. During the rest of the day there was a time for reading, a meeting in the chapter house, a period for work – manual, intellectual or artistic –, mass, dinner at two o'clock, study in the afternoon and then a supper drink – all punctuated by the sequence of 'offices', the last of which was compline. Bed-time was at about six o'clock so that they had eight unbroken hours for sleep. This time-table was slightly different in the summer and was varied by the different orders.

Those monks who were priests, and by the thirteenth century this applied to most of them, said private masses once or twice a week at the different side-altars in the church. These were for the souls of benefactors who had paid for the privilege and they were fitted in during the mornings. In some places this was looked on as an onerous task and chaplains were employed to relieve the monks of the duty.

The monks ate well – fish, eggs, poultry, fruit, nuts and simnel cake, with wine and beer. In addition they had pittances, which were special tasty dishes supplied as extras on certain days of the week and important church festivals. In the larger monasteries these became so numerous that a special obedientiary, the pittancer, who had his own funds, was appointed to be in charge of their provision. They got round the old rule about not eating meat by considering that that referred to the refectory only and finding reasons to dine elsewhere – at Durham they used the 'loft', a smaller room at the west end of the refectory.

The simple peasant garb of St. Benedict's time was replaced, in a colder climate, by warm outfits which were renewed at intervals. If

---

[1] The numbers of religious persons are taken from Knowles and Hadcock, *Medieval Religious Houses, England and Wales*. The population estimates are taken from Russel, J. C., *British Medieval Population (1948)*; these are for England only, but the Welsh figures, if known, would probably not make any appreciable difference.

clothes were in good condition when the time came for the issue of new ones a cash payment was often made instead. With this (plus the pocket money that some monasteries supplied) individual monks bought items made of fur (cat, squirrel, miniver) and silk and even colourful secular garments. This clothes money was also used for smaller purchases which were kept in bed-side lockers or in the carrells which were erected in the cloisters for scholars. The possession of all this personal property was against the Rule and visiting bishops tried to put a stop to it, but in vain.

The manual labour which was an integral part of the early monks' day had been given up by the thirteenth century. From its inception the Cistercian order had lay-brothers to do this, and the Benedictines and others eventually employed servants. Among these might be found a butler, cook, carpenter, stableman, boatman, bath-attendant, a plumber and his mate and even a washerwoman (although women servants were not allowed by the statutes). There were often twice as many servants as monks: the 62 monks at Norwich in the thirteenth century had 146 paid employees. Abbots saw to it that the monks were given other occupations – mainly reading, making new copies of manuscripts and illuminating fine books. Young monks with an aptitude for learning were sent to Oxford or Cambridge so that when they returned they would be able to give lectures in theology to the novices.

The secluded existence of Benedict's monks gave way to many excursions into, and contact with, the outside world. There was much coming and going through the abbey gate and mixing with the townspeople or village-folk beyond; some monks went hunting or hawking; all had their turn to have a holiday at one of the monastery's manors; and several rode out to supervise estates. In the large monasteries it was possible that, at certain times of the year, as many as a third or even a half of the monks might be away.

From time to time strolling players, wandering minstrels, buffoons, jesters and dancers came to the monasteries. They were received with pleasure, both for the interest of their performances and for the opportunity it gave to have news of other places and people visited by the entertainers.

Since the monastery walls no longer prevented outsiders from coming in or monks from venturing out, and since women could enter as servants, guests or corrodians, it is not surprising that the vow of chastity was sometimes broken. There is evidence of immorality in some communities concerning both abbots and priors as well as monks and nuns.

d. *Obedientiaries*

As the life of a monastery became more complex and as its possessions and income grew, the organisation was divided into departments each with a monk, known as an obedientiary, as its chief. Such men had their own incomes and estates, their own households and servants. About a quarter of the total number of monks were obedientiaries so that any capable man could expect to receive such promotion in time. Among them were the sacristan, who looked after everything needed for church services; the bursar (or treasurer); the cellarer, who was in charge of catering; the chamberlain, who saw to clothes and bedding; the forester; the librarian and the terrar (or land agent). These were business men handling huge sums of money. At Durham, a wealthy and important cathedral priory, the bursar alone had an annual turn-over of nearly £750,000 at the end of the thirteenth century. The obedientiaries had full-time jobs looking after their departments and this fact was used as an excuse to avoid the full round of services in church so that they went only occasionally, probably arriving late and leaving early.

Founders and other benefactors gave land to monasteries mainly because of their fears of purgatory and hopes of prayers. The great estates and the appropriated churches which the monasteries accumulated in this way were at once a source of wealth and a heavy responsibility. Terrars or their deputies had to be on the spot to supervise harvests, collect rents, see that tithes were gathered in and maintain property. Some land-agents were not capable of this sort of work, and in this case the land tended to become a drain on the monastic resources. In an effort to settle debts some estates were 'farmed' (see page 14), others were sold, the appropriation of more churches was sought or a corrody was awarded. The latter meant that board and lodging at the monastery was granted to an elderly, wealthy layman (and sometimes his family) who paid a lump sum for the privilege; this was only of advantage to the monastery if he did not live very long – otherwise he also became a burden. The best way to get out of financial difficulties was generally the last to be thought of – the exercise of rigorous economies in food, drink and clothing and the curbing of lavish hospitality.

e. *Abbots and priors (heads of houses)*

In the interim period between the death or retirement of one abbot and the appointment of the next, medieval kings claimed the revenues of the abbey. To avoid such a serious reduction of the abbey's income it was thought expedient to divide the lands and possessions between the abbot and the community. This encouraged the abbot to have quite separate quarters with his own household. As well as living accommodation there was also a private chapel where his chaplains could say mass, thus obviating the need for him to go to the monastery church. He also had his own manors which provided him with food and fine houses to stay at for holidays and on his journeyings.

Abbots and priors were supposed to be freely elected from among their own number by the monks themselves. As the appointment of these wealthy landholders mattered to the king he sometimes made his own choice known to the monks, and they generally agreed with this. These elevated Church dignitaries were expected to attend on the king from time to time as advisers and were used by him as ambassadors and diplomats. Like bishops, they could be summoned to parliament as tenants-in-chief although they preferred not to go. They were so successful in securing exemption that, in 1513, the judges declared that their presence was not essential.

There were some holy abbots, like Ailred of Rievaulx (1147–67), and some practical, hard-working ones, like Samson of Bury (1182–1211), doing their best to run well-ordered houses. By the fourteenth century most were popularly held to be experienced men of the world, having little to do with leading a spiritual life and spending the minimum of time in their monasteries. Chaucer's Monk, riding his fine horse in a mixed company, fastened his hood with a gold pin in the shape of a love-knot and trimmed his sleeves with squirrel fur. He liked hunting and good food, but not studying in the monastery. With all these mundane ways he struck the pilgrims as an obvious candidate for an abbacy.

As wealthy landowners, the abbots were the equivalent of lay barons and kept great state both at their abbey houses and their manors. Even nobles were glad to send their sons to be given a social and educational training in their households. To the rest of the people they seemed to be no different from any other feudal lord. Their reputation is best mirrored in the anonymous fifteenth-century poem, *A Lytell Geste of Robyn Hode*,[1] in which the abbot of St. Mary's abbey, York, is pictured as a rich, grasping landlord, caring only about gaining more possessions and turning the predicament of Sir Richard at the Lee to his own advantage. Many readers and listeners would feel that he was typical of his kind.

Moving about the country and attending at the king's court, as many

---

[1] Later printed by Wynken de Worde between 1492 and 1534.

of them did, some heads of monasteries rose to even greater heights, for they might be chosen to be bishops or even archbishops. Lanfranc, the first Norman archbishop of Canterbury, was called from the Benedictine abbey of Caen in Normandy, and in 1186, Hugh, prior of the Carthusian house at Witham, became bishop of Lincoln. In the later medieval period such promotions were generally to the less important sees, like Hereford, although Henry Dean (d.1503), the Augustinian prior of Llanthony, Gloucestershire, became bishop of Bangor, then bishop of Salisbury and finally archbishop of Canterbury.

Abbots and priors were usually buried in splendid tombs which they themselves had planned and paid for: Thomas de la Mare (abbot of St. Albans from 1349 to 1396) is depicted on a splendid brass in his abbey; the effigy of Walter Newbury (abbot from 1428 to 1473) lies on his tomb-chest at Bristol; and the likeness of Richard Beauforest, prior of Dorchester, Oxfordshire, is engraved on a brass (dated c.1510) in his former priory church. All of these hold pastoral staffs and the first two wear mitres, a distinction granted by the popes to the heads of those wealthy abbeys and priories which were willing to pay for it.

f. *Nunneries*

Nunneries were, on the whole, smaller and less important versions of the monasteries. This was probably because most founders and benefactors preferred to give their money and land to the monks' foundations. In return for their endowments they wanted masses said for their souls and this the nuns, being women, could not do, as they were not admitted to holy orders.

The inmates of nunneries were from the upper classes, the country gentry and wealthy merchant families. Many were sent there as a way of providing for them if a handsome marriage portion was not available to obtain a husband of their own rank. To people of their superior status only the nunnery was considered as a suitable alternative to marriage. Not for them the useful tasks taken on by the unmarried daughters of villeins and tradesmen, who could turn their hands to spinning, brewing and generally helping with the work of their parents. Working-class girls could not become nuns because the nunneries only accepted those who brought dowries (smaller than marriage dowries) with them, although this was against canon law.

Men of higher social standing, including the clergy, used the nunneries as permanent homes for unwanted dependants such as mentally and physically handicapped girls, illegitimate offspring

(Cardinal Wolsey's daughter was at Shaftesbury Benedictine abbey, Dorset) and even erring wives and former mistresses. Among these unfortunates were those child-heiresses whose guardians removed them to a nunnery while they themselves took their heritage. They were often placed as very young children and quickly professed as nuns, although the official minimum age for this was sixteen. After that they were unable to have a claim on their father's estate. A few petitioned the bishop for their freedom (vows could be cancelled if influential friends could prove that they had been made under duress) and one at least actually escaped. Margaret of Prestwich was sent to the small Benedictine priory at Seton, Cumberland, at the age of eight. After some years she was carried to the church and professed, loudly protesting the while. Although treated as a prisoner she seized an opportunity to gain her freedom. She married Robert of Holland, after the banns had been called, and then appealed to the pope. Richard of Stretton, bishop of Coventry and Lichfield (1360–86), inquired into the matter and found that her story was true, so she was formally released from the religious life.

Among the nuns, then, there may have been a few who went voluntarily because they felt drawn to a religious vocation; others saw it as an acceptable career when marriage within their social class was not possible; many had no choice but to go, and to them the nunnery was a prison and the ring they were given, on taking their vows as a bride of God, was a manacle; there were also some wealthy widows who decided to take the veil in retirement. As so many of them had so little spiritual inclination they fell a prey to the same temptations as the monks – breaking the food rules, dressing in secular garments, having private possessions, going on excursions outside the nunnery, enjoying entertainments within its walls and in certain cases breaking their vows of chastity. Contact with and news of the world beyond contrasted unhappily for some with the repetitive routine of their lives and many must have fretted in misery and longed for an untrammelled existence with family and friends. One nun, Agnes Butler, of St. Michael's Benedictine priory, Stamford, hated it so much that, in 1440, she ran away with a travelling harper, preferring the uncertain life of the road, with the risk of an awesome punishment awaiting at the end, to the cloistered calm and the reward of heaven.

According to St. Benedict's Rule, the movement of nuns outside the nunnery was to be restricted but was not entirely forbidden. Popes and bishops thought that temptation lay that way, and during the Middle Ages they tried repeatedly to order stricter, if not total, enclosure of the nuns. The nuns themselves wanted as much contact with other folk as monks had, so they saw friends in town and village, sat in taverns, went away for holidays and visited their homes where they joined in family games and dancing. The bishops met such determined opposition to enclosure – the nuns of Markyate, Hertfordshire, threw the statute about it left by Bishop Dalderby of Lincoln, in 1300, at his retreating back – that most of them were satisfied with some sort of compromise and hoped, although usually in vain, that it would be observed. The world came into the cloister, also, for there were many friends and relations, workmen, travellers in the guest houses, corrodians, long-term boarders and short-stay lodgers,[1] all introducing a disturbing whiff of secular air, not to mention passing monks, friars and scholars.

The high-born girls who arrived in the nunneries had little to offer other than their dowries. They were supposed to know or to learn Latin but rarely did; they sang the Latin words of the services without understanding their meaning and the Rule of St. Benedict was translated into English for them. Some reading (in English) was done, but no copying of manuscripts nor writing of original work – no nunnery produced a chronicle, for instance – for women were not expected to be so clever. When not in church they spent some of their time in making vestments and embroidering altar cloths. Skill with herbs and in home medicine, such as any lady of their class would know, was probably among the accomplishments of the nuns. Some would be able to bleed each other (a common preventive or treatment for many illnesses) – the prioress of Kirklees in Yorkshire bled Robin Hood when he went to her for help. Some nunneries took in a few girls and very young boys from aristocratic and gentry families as pupil boarders. This was done purely for the benefit of the fees received, and the education given was limited by the low standards attained by the nuns themselves.

The round of services in church was the same as that for monks, but it was necessary to have one or more resident chaplains to say mass and hear confessions. The business affairs of the house were conducted by the more capable nuns who were promoted to be obedientiaries. Since they lacked training and experience they were generally not very competent and, if they employed unsatisfactory or dishonest lay servants, they found themselves in financial difficulties. For these reasons and others beyond their control – natural disasters, corrodians

---

[1]The bishop of Norwich arranged for Margery Paston to stay at Blackborough priory, Norfolk, before her marriage, because her mother would not have her back at home. Richard Calle also lodged there. (See Chapter 2, Section 5b).

forced on them by patrons, and so on – nunneries were perpetually complaining of poverty. Even the abbey of Shaftesbury, with such extensive endowments that it was popularly said, 'If the Abbot of Glastonbury could marry the Abbess of Shaftesbury, their heir would hold more land than the King of England', was often in trouble. By appeals to king, bishop and public the nunneries managed to survive, but the nuns of the smaller, ill-endowed ones were sometimes known to beg in the streets.

The nuns chose their abbess or prioress from among themselves (having first obtained the *congé d'élire* from their patron) and subject to the confirmation of the bishop. Pressure was sometimes brought to bear on them by great outsiders on behalf of a relative and it often seem expedient to choose the nun of highest family who would be able to use her influence for the financial advantage of the house. It would be almost impossible to overlook a former queen, a princess or the daughter of a powerful earl, and all of these were abbesses of Barking in Essex, not too far from London. Aspirants to the position needed only to be of legitimate birth and over twenty-one years old (thirty for Cistercians), but anyone lacking these qualifications could apply for an episcopal dispensation (Margaret Botetourt became abbess of Polesworth, Warwickshire, in 1362, before she was twenty).

At their consecration abbesses and prioresses received a pastoral staff, as did abbots, and also a ring. They had the same autocratic powers as abbots over the ruling of their houses and property, but were never called to parliament. They were the social equals of the local gentry and when they rode forth, whether on business or to a private function (the prioress of Carrow, Norwich, attended the funeral dirge of John Paston at St. Peter Hungate church in 1466), it was with a dignified retinue. Even on pilgrimage Chaucer's Prioress was accompanied by a nun and three priests. Their journeys brought them too closely in contact with the world so that the breath of scandal sometimes touched their names. The typical abbess or prioress was a well-meaning autocrat who liked to wear furs and silks, gold and jewels, and to travel outside the nunnery. She was like Chaucer's Madame Eglentyne, who stayed with the assorted and mostly male pilgrims at the inns on the way to Canterbury, talked over drinks with the experienced Wife of Bath, showed her forehead which ought to have been covered by a seemly veil, enjoyed some questionable stories and expected to be treated as a cut above the others. She may have been a good ruler of her house but she was happy to leave it for a change of scenery and companions. There were few like the saintly Euphemia, abbess of Wherwell, Hampshire (1226 to 1257), who 'provided for the worship of God and the welfare of her sisters.'

Heads of nunneries were buried with honour in their convent churches and their graves were often marked with a brass. Few of these have survived, but that of Elizabeth Herwy, abbess of Elstow, Bedfordshire (d. 1527), showing her holding her pastoral staff, can be seen in Elstow parish church (her former nunnery).

g. *Visitations*

Monasteries were under the jurisdiction of bishops and they were subjected to the visitations of their overlords. Records show the probings into every aspect of the occupants' behaviour, whether connected with their morals, private property, secular clothing, pocket money, travelling too much outside the cloister and having overmuch contact with the laity. The heads of the houses and their monks and nuns must have viewed these close scrutinies of their affairs with apprehension, for changes were ordained and punishments meted out – penances, curtailment of movement, transference to another house, even deposition. Afterwards some attempts were made at improvement, but when the bishop rode away they knew that he would not be back for some years, if ever, and gradually they fell back into their old, comfortable, relaxed routine.

The Cluniac, Cistercian and Premonstratension orders, as well as certain of the greater Benedictine houses, obtained exemption from these inspections, acknowledging only the authority of the pope. They did not escape visitations altogether, as each order had its own system of inspection and correction of faults.

h. *Social impact*

Lay people were affected in different ways by the monasteries. The king knew that he and his family were prayed for in each one every day, whether or not he or his forebears were founders; this was very sustaining as the monks were deemed to be the greatest of intercessors. Edward I had felt this; he wrote to the monks of Durham that he had 'often experienced the patronage and help of St. Cuthbert in various troubles and dangers, through your prayers'.

Similarly, any patron would expect to have the prayers of his own house. Occasionally he would call at the monastery with his retinue and perhaps his wife and family, dine at the abbot's table and stay a night or two. At death he had the honour of being buried in the monks' church. A less-exalted donor might make a gift of land in order to have an annual obit. Even a thrifty peasant could give half an acre in order to be named in the monks' prayers.

St. Benedict's Rule said that a guest should be received 'as if he were Christ', so hospitality to all comers was seen as a necessary duty. Royalty, patrons and the great magnates would be greeted by the abbot and accommodated in his house. For the rest there would probably be one or two guest-houses, perhaps a superior type for the better off and another for the poor. The former were given greater care and attention, for it was hoped that they might become benefactors.

The obedientiary in charge of arrangements for guests was the hostillar. If he had a cheerful personality people felt welcomed and looked after. It followed that 'the reputation of the monastery increased', as would also the gifts made to it. The monastic guest-houses of Westminster and Canterbury, as well as of those on important main roads, like Reading and St. Albans, must have been permanently busy, although visitors would have been rarer at the smaller houses in out-of-the-way spots. Whenever monasteries fell on hard times and appealed for financial help one of the reasons given was the need to provide hospitality. Among the travellers were pilgrims on their way to the shrine of a saint. Some monasteries possessed their own shrine and so were journey's end themselves.

Another duty of the monasteries was to care for the poor and this was done in a variety of ways under the direction of the almoner and his staff. The broken-meats (or left-overs) from each meal were supposed to go to the poor who waited for them at the known time, but this food sometimes went to friends of the monks or even to the dogs. Food, as well as items of clothing and fuel, was distributed at the gate of the abbey or delivered to the houses of the poor and sick. Sometimes half a dozen poor men actually lived in the almonry building, perhaps going to the church at certain times to pray for the souls of the benefactors. Kings, bishops and abbots left money for a dole of food to be made to the poor on their anniversaries and this might be given out at the gateway or at a room within the monastery – thirty were fed in the parlour at Evesham on Prior Thomas's anniversary.

Being landowners brought the monks into close contact with their tenants and it was as the lords of the towns outside their walls, the owners of manors and the appropriators of churches that they were seen to be less than holy. The monastic overseers could be hard taskmasters, insisting on their rights and heedless of the impoverishment of their tenants. There was nothing the tillers of the soil could do to improve their conditions and they watched in desperation as much of their produce went to feed their monkish masters. The men of the townships at the gates of the great monasteries also felt wronged; they wished to have charters granting them self-government, like some towns on the king's manors, but most monasteries refused to give this right, for it would have raised up powerful opponents on their own doorsteps.

Resentment smouldered for centuries and erupted into violence from time to time. Then, people who were treated as chattels and who saw the monasteries as oppressors were goaded into doing desperate deeds: refusing to pay tallage – an irregular tax made at the whim of the lord – to the prior of Dunstable in 1229, and declaring, when excommunicated, that they would rather go to hell than be beaten; failing to pay tolls at the annual fair at Norwich in 1272, which led to a pitched battle between the townsmen and the monks (plus their hired armed men), during which most of the cloister buildings and part of the cathedral church were burned; assaulting the abbot of Combermere, Cheshire, in 1309, killing one of his monks, burning his grange and stealing his goods; plundering the abbey of Bury St. Edmunds, in 1327, and burning many of the outbuildings; and, in the same year, demanding a charter for the people of St. Albans, besieging the abbey when it was refused.

All this had its climax in the Peasants' Revolt of 1381, when certain monasteries of southern and eastern England, together with other landlords, reaped what they had sown in their operation of an unjust and divisive agricultural and local governmental system. The townsfolk of Bury St. Edmunds 'tried' the prior and cut off his head. The people of St. Albans compelled the abbot to give them a charter, although afterwards, when the rebellion had failed, the ring-leaders were hanged. These town uprisings were supported by many villages in the ownership of the two abbeys.

The harsh crushing of the uprising did not quell the desire of the labouring classes for freedom. In 1394 seven 'poor tenants' of Winkfield appealed to the king, whose inquiry proved that they were the king's own tenants. Nevertheless, the abbot of Abingdon maintained that they were his serfs and imprisoned their three leaders. The prophecy in *Piers Plowman* may have been made following this event:

> But there shall come a king, and confess you Religious,
> And beat you, as the Bible telleth, for breaking of your Rule, ...
> And then shall the abbot of Abingdon, and all his issue for ever
> Have a knock of a king, and incurable the wound.[1]

Plowman. B Text, x 317 ff, quoted by G. G. Coulton, *The Medieval Village*, 149.

By the time that this was fulfilled most monasteries had travelled a long way from the spirit of St. Benedict's Rule, and there was too much evidence of worldly, even deplorable behaviour, for them to keep the national respect.

2. FRIARS

a. *The first friars*

The early ideal of the monastic life envisaged a retreat from the world in order to attain personal salvation. It did not entail any responsibility for the world thus left. In the first decade of the thirteenth century a new concept of holy living by service in the world was taught by Francis of Assisi (1182–1226). He did not intend to found an order, but others, fired by his example, joined him and so the order of the Friars Minor (the 'lesser brethren') came into being. A simple Rule was prescribed and the members tried to live as Christ had lived, working among others, and, poor themselves, serving the poor.

Women, too, joined the order under the direction of Clare, who, like Francis, belonged to one of the élite Assisi families. Because it was not considered seemly for them to wander about, they lived a very austere, enclosed life in their abbeys. In England they were called the Minoresses.[1]

Living at the same time as Francis, a Spanish Augustinian canon, Dominic (1170–1221), trained a company of priests, who were not dedicated to poverty, to preach against heresy. This met with the approval of the pope who formally recognised Dominic's Order of Preachers in 1216. The new canons (soon called friars) travelled all over Europe with their message. Groups of Dominican nuns were also formed and they lived in a similar way to the Minoresses.

b. *The introduction of the Dominicans and Franciscans into England*

Both orders sent missions to England: the Dominicans arrived in 1221 and went to Oxford to study and preach there; the Franciscans landed in 1224 and also went to Oxford hoping to attract eager young men to join them. By that time the ragged garb of the Franciscans had become a standard grey habit which gave them the popular name of the 'grey friars', to distinguish them from the Dominicans who wore a black cloak

---

[1] Now known as the Poor Clares.

and hood over a white tunic – they were the 'black friars'. These two different orders assimilated much of each other's ways: the Dominicans embraced poverty so that they would not be a target of heretical criticism of the wealth of the Church and also because of the example and greater popularity of the Franciscans; the latter, through the influence of Robert Grosseteste, chancellor of Oxford, and the intake of learned recruits, included serious study on their time-table and many of them were eventually among the foremost scholars in the country.

In their missionary work the friars always went to towns because prospective listeners were congregated there, some of whom were able to contribute to their support. They were aided by certain bishops who desired to revive a new spirit in the Church. Such men helped to establish friars of both orders in the major towns of their dioceses. By 1250 there were 25 Dominican friaries (each ruled by a prior) and over 40 Franciscan houses (under guardians or wardens) holding about 1,000 friars.

The sight of the newcomers, living in the poorest parts of town, eating leftovers and tramping barefoot through the snow on their missionary work impressed everyone. Here were men not afraid to practise what they preached, who wanted only to serve Christ and others in poverty and who were not moved by ambition to attain rich benefices or plum bishoprics. It was an example people of the Middle Ages had not seen before and it stirred them to offer help – food and clothing or the provision of a house as headquarters. About the Franciscans, Matthew Paris wrote, 'Wherever men are most wretched, stricken down by the most loathsome diseases, starved by famine, or trodden down by the great, there went the Grey Friars of St. Francis.' Such a way of life might be compared today with that of the Salvation Army.

The early friars kept alive by begging enough for the day or by their own labour. Generous lay-folk also brought them gifts and, as a result, there was some dissension in the orders (especially the Franciscan) about the morality of owning property. A compromise was reached with a legal fiction in 1247, when Pope Innocent IV said that the friars could have material objects for their use but that actually they would belong to the popes. This was acceptable to all except the most fervent Franciscans, who were known as the 'Spirituals'. Their movement was mainly continental and did not have much influence in England.

The first houses that the friars built for themselves were small and simple, often made of wood or wattle. All they needed was an oratory, a lecture room and the simplest of living quarters. When in residence the friars sang the daily office but were allowed to do this quickly, for religious study took priority. Each friary had its own school, under the direction of a doctor of theology, and the most promising students went on to work for their degrees at a university. The emphasis on scholarship limited the type of recruit to the educated classes – young men of well-off town families and the gentry – so that peasants, who had been welcomed by Francis and Dominic, were no longer encouraged.

From their centres the friars went forth to preach in the parish churches or churchyards, in the market places or on the village greens. To listen to a friar was to receive spiritual uplift but also entertainment. Their training gave them an insight into the best way of gaining the attention of an unlettered audience. They had a fund of good stories gathered from experience or culled from books specially written for the purpose. A friar sent his hearers away with cheerful hearts, not the frightening thoughts of doom with which the parish priests threatened them.

Another point in their favour was that they came with the pope's permission to hear confessions. Many people preferred to confess to a friar rather than to their local clergy, for he listened sympathetically, did not make a mountain out of a molehill, generally awarded a light penance and then passed on his way so that a parishioner was relieved of the permanent presence of one who knew the worst things about him.

c.   *Dominican and Franciscan nuns*

The Dominican nuns in their abbey at Dartford, Kent, and the Minoresses in their three abbeys at London, Denney in Cambridgeshire and Bruisyard in Suffolk, lived in much the same way as nuns of the older orders. 'Lady Poverty' was forgotten and replaced by ladies from royal and noble houses and prosperous town families, who all brought dowries with them. The nuns were allowed to possess a good deal of property – land, houses, and appropriated churches – to provide them with an income. A friar or lay steward supervised this. To assist their finances the nuns also took in corrodians, and the London house, commonly known as the Minories, even had paying guests – Sir Thomas Palmer, a knight on business from Calais, used it as a hotel in 1537.

The sequestered life led by Clare's women and girls was disregarded. Friends and relatives were allowed to pay visits and to bring personal gifts. The rules about enclosure were not over-strictly enforced. On three occasions in 1355 and 1356 all the London Minoresses went out to dine at the home of their patron, Elizabeth de Burgh, who was a connection of the royal family. When this important lady died in 1360 she chose to be buried in the church of these nuns, like many others who were rich enough to pay for the privilege.[1]

Echoes of the outside world must have made some nuns pine for a life that was different. One of them, Mary Felton, managed to make her escape from the London house in 1385. Although there was an order for her arrest as 'an apostate and vagabond sister', she married John Cursoun and her plea that she had not taken her vows was upheld by the bishop of London's court. Probably she had been sent to the nunnery in early youth without having any sense of vocation. Others like her would have welcomed the closure of the nunneries in 1539, as did 'half a dozen' out of the thirty-five nuns at Denney. The abbess, Elizabeth Throckmorton, however, retired to her family home at Coughton, in Warwickshire, with two or three of the nuns, and continued to follow the strict rules of the convent until her death in 1547. These two conflicting attitudes must always have been present in the nunneries of the friars' orders.

d. *Carmelite, Augustinian and Crutched friars*

In the mid-thirteenth century some other orders of friars sent groups to England. The most important of these were the Carmelites (named from Mount Carmel, where their first members lived as hermits) and the Friars Hermits of St. Augustine (Austin Friars). They developed in much the same way as the two older orders, sending their men to the universities and becoming preachers. With the Franciscans and Dominicans they became the 'four orders' mentioned in *Piers Plowman*. By the beginning of the sixteenth century there were 37 Carmelite and 35 Austin friaries in England and Wales. There were also one or two lesser orders, but, of them, only the Friars of the Holy Cross (or Crutched Friars) stayed in being, with 2 houses, until the sixteenth century.

e. *Confraternities*

Such was the godly reputation of the friars that many men and women joined them as associate members, paying a considerable subscription to do so. Their names were then entered in the records of the chosen house

---

[1] In December, 1964, during excavations on the site of this former Franciscan nunnery, the coffined remains of Anne, the child-wife of Richard, Duke of York, were found. She died in 1481 at the age of eight and her body was buried in the Minories church after being transferred there from Westminster abbey. It was re-interred in the abbey in June 1965.

so that after death their souls would be prayed for there. They also had the right to be buried clothed in a friar's habit (thought to be a guarantee of entry into heaven); the effigy of a layman wearing Franciscan dress, dated about 1300, can be seen at Conington, Huntingdonshire. They could even be buried in the church or churchyard of their friary, and hundreds of people availed themselves of this opportunity. *Piers Plowman* gives an example of someone buying her way into a friars' community when the sinful Lady Mede says (in modern paraphrase): 'And I shall roof your church, and have your cloister built, your walls whitewashed and your windows glazed, have paintings and statues done, and pay for the work, so that everyone will say I'm a lay-sister of your house.'

f. *Opposition of parish priests and monasteries*

It soon became evident to the parish priests that the friars posed a financial threat to them, for offerings given after confession and some burial fees deprived them of part of their income. This problem was settled by the pope in 1300 (restated in 1311). Thereafter the friars could preach freely in public places but only by invitation in parish churches; to hear confessions they had to have a bishop's licence; and a quarter of the dues, as well as of the legacies, of those buried in friary churches and churchyards had to be handed over to the parish priest.

The monasteries, too, began to resent the presence of the friars, for they lost some scholarly recruits to them, besides gifts and bequests. Their hostility was expressed by the abbot of Peterborough in the middle of the fourteenth century; referring to the year 1224, he wrote, 'In that year, O misery! O more than misery! O cruel scourge! The Friars Minor came to England.'

g. *Support of royalty*

From the beginning the friars were welcomed by royalty, who supported them with gifts of money, buildings and clothes. Henry III made annual grants from the Exchequer to the Franciscans of Oxford, Cambridge and Berwick and Edward I gave the price of a day's food to every friar living in any town through which he passed. As patrons, members of the royal family treated the friaries as guest houses while on their journeys, making suitable payment for their stay. The young Edward III and his mother lodged at the Franciscan house in York for six weeks duing 1327. While she was there the queen gave a feast in the friars' dormitory, where at least sixty ladies sat at table with her. Mendicants were chosen as confessors to the royal family and were employed on confidential errands or for high-level negotiations, whether at home or abroad. Such men were generally rewarded with a minor bishopric.

h. *Friars during the Peasants' Revolt*

As the majority of the friars travelled about the country in the second half of the fourteenth century they must have become aware of social unrest among the oppressed lower classes, with whom they doubtless expressed sympathy. Langland says that they preached communism: 'all things under Heaven ought to be in common.' This attitude would add to their popularity among the under-privileged and their houses did not suffer in the Peasants' Revolt as did some of those of the monks. Indeed, according to Thomas Walsingham, the monastic chronicler of St. Albans, one of the peasants' leaders, Jack Straw, said that he would like to get rid of the monks and the secular clergy but would keep the friars for celebrating the sacraments.

i. *Development of buildings*

Friaries were never built on the same massive scale as the greater monasteries but were always more compact and planned for practical use. It was thought expedient to build spacious churches in the leading towns, if land was available, to provide plenty of room for those who wished to be buried there and for the large congregations which gathered to hear the friars' sermons. These last took place in the nave, separated from the choir by a passage, 'the walking place', which led to the living-rooms. Over this was erected a slender bell-tower, like the fine one that remains at King's Lynn. Not many friars' churches are left, but a good fifteenth-century example can be seen at the former Dominican friary in Norwich (now St. Andrew's Hall). Sometimes sermons were preached in the open air from a pulpit outside the friary; one can be seen at Hereford, where it stands to the west of the place formerly occupied by a Dominican priory church.

Little remains of friaries because, when they were all closed, their mid-town sites tended to be snapped up by the townsfolk for domestic or civic purposes. The best preserved cloister buildings (after restoration) are probably those of the Blackfriars in Newcastle, although the south and west walks of the Carmelite friary at Aylesford, Kent, survive, with their residential quarters behind them.

In many cases, while friaries may have completely disappeared leaving no trace, street-names still tell of their former presence – Friargate in

Derby, Friary Street in Guildford, Friars Road in Ipswich and Friary Lane in Salisbury. In Hull there are both Blackfriargate and Whitefriargate, from the Dominican and Carmelite houses there; in Gloucester there is Greyfriars, from its Franciscan house; and in London there are streets called Austin Friars, and Crutched Friars. Also in the capital the Minoresses gave their name to The Minories, the street just north of the Tower in which their house was situated.

j. *Criticism of the friars*

The very success of the friars was their undoing, for the money and goods that they were given, the worldly lives in which they were invited to share, the holding of senior teaching posts at the universities and the promotions to the hierarchy (Robert Kilwardby, a Dominican, and John Pecham, a Franciscan, were archbishops of Canterbury in the late thirteenth century) were a far cry from the humble ideals of St. Francis. They still maintained themselves by asking for alms, but the different orders began to dispute with each other about their own areas for doing this. They were very persistent beggars, like Chaucer's Friar, who 'would have a farthing (i.e. 50 pence) ere he went.' St. Bonaventure (c.1217–74), himself an Italian Franciscan theologian, said that people were as afraid to meet a friar as a highway robber, for both would take money from them.

Everyone honoured the memory of St. Francis, and the behaviour of his later followers was measured against his. 'I have seen Charity also', wrote Langland,

> And in a friar's frock he was found once
> But it is far ago in Saint Francis' time.

Gradually, the high estimation in which they were first held gave place to suspicion and dislike. This is witnessed by the fourteenth-century writings of Langland, Chaucer, Wyclif and lesser authors, in none of whose pages can a good friar be found. Their best-quality clothes, their fine buildings and their seeking out of rich men's houses for free meals were criticised. Their ready granting of absolution in expectation of a fee – £12 would absolve a penitent from patricide and incest – was attacked. Facile promises that a soul would go to heaven if the glazing of a new window in the friary was paid for, with the donor's name 'engraved in the glass', were censured. Friar Flatterer, or 'Slinker-into-houses', might be the nickname of all those who visited homes ostensibly in order to counsel and to beg, but also to flatter and to seduce; as the Wife of Bath said in her story, women could 'go safely up and down' and only a friar would do them dishonour. In fact, their behaviour was so far removed from the example of Christ that Langland says of the Nativity (in modern paraphrase), 'I bet you five shillings[1] there wasn't a friar found there.'

This sort of conduct must have come as a shock to those men who felt a religious call to join the friars and disillusionment followed. A contemporary of Chaucer's wrote of such a one:

> I was a friar full many a day
> Therefore the truth I wate [know],
> But when I saw that their living
> Accorded not to their preaching,
> Off I cast my friar's clothing,
> And quickly went my gate [way].

Probably few were so honest.

Criticism of the friars came from all levels of the community and this sometimes erupted into physical ill-treatment – being driven away with stones, having their habits torn off or their houses sacked. This reached such a pitch that in 1385 there was a royal proclamation for their protection. At the same time, the ancient respect for their (now largely theoretical) lives of poverty and service, together with a life-time's belief in their powers of assisting folk into heaven, kept the support of many and bequests continued to be made to them.

A friar in his cowl and gown with knotted cord can be seen engraved on a brass (c.1440) in Denham church, Buckinghamshire.

k. *The Observant friars*

There were, doubtless, always men in the Franciscan order, like the early 'Spirituals', who wanted to return to the original poverty of Francis. Towards the end of the fourteenth century a group of Italian friars started a movement for the strict observance of the Rule. They were called Observants, although it was not until 1517 that an independent order was formed. Edward IV introduced a small group of Observants from the Netherlands into England in 1482. Their house at Greenwich was treated as a royal chapel and Tudor christenings took place there. A few other houses were either transferred to or founded for them but the foreign influence continued and few Englishmen joined them.

---

[1] i.e. 25 pence, now equivalent to £50.

1. *Numbers of friaries and their occupants*

Altogether there were 187 friaries in medieval England, and in the heyday of their popularity these were occupied by 5,000 friars. After the Black Death the numbers fell to about 2,000, then climbed to 3,000 by 1500. They then declined again to 2,300 in 1534. In the latter year there were about 70 Dominican and Franciscan nuns in their 4 houses.

3. KNIGHTS OF THE MILITARY ORDERS

a. *The Knights Hospitallers and the Knights Templar*

Some men wanted to devote a lifetime's service to the defence of the Holy Land and at the beginning of the twelfth century they formed military orders which were dedicated not only to fighting for the cause but also to living in a partly-monastic way. The Knights of the Order of St. John of Jerusalem (called the Hospitallers from their care of sick pilgrims in a hospital near the Holy Sepulchre in Jerusalem) kept a Rule based on that of the Augustinians. Their uniform was a black mantle with a white eight-pointed cross[1] sewn on the front. The members of the Order of the Poor Knights of the Temple of Solomon, usually known as the Knights Templar, followed a Rule drawn up by the Cistercian abbot, Bernard of Clairvaux. They wore white cloaks, each with a red cross sewn on it. Neither group adopted the tonsure and they were usually bearded.

Both orders were international and were organised in much the same way, with a Grand Master at the head. They manned their own castles and constituted a permanent force to keep the pagan enemy at bay. The knights had a reputation for outstanding bravery, always being in the forefront of the battle and never surrendering. Royalty relied heavily on their experience and ability when they arrived to lead a crusade. So highly did Richard I learn to value the Templars during his campaign of 1191–2 that, when he sailed for England with an escort of them, he himself and his entourage wore their uniform as a disguise. Such a party, riding home across Europe from the Mediterranean would be watched with respect and cause no surprise to any onlookers. It was unfortunate for Richard that shipwreck caused the scheme to miscarry.

In order to gain the prayers of the military monks wealthy people made gifts of land to them, the rents of which were for the support of the orders

---

[1] The cross of St. John, first pictured on a wax seal, dated 1207–28. After 1530 it was known as the Maltese cross.

and the promotion of their campaigns. Nearly 700 Templar estates were spread throughout Europe and there was probably a similar number belonging to the Hospitallers. Each country, or province, was ruled by a Grand Master (for the Templars) and a Grand Commander or Prior, (for the Hospitallers[1]). Houses were founded, known as preceptories by the Templars and commanderies by the Hospitallers, each with a preceptor in charge. These were small houses with chapels, run by two or three members of staff. They were centres for recruiting, the overseeing of the estates and the collection of rents, and also for assisting pilgrims and travellers. At the beginning of the fourteenth century there were about 50 Templar and 40 Hospitaller houses in England. The former Templar manor house at Strood, Kent, still exists (and is open to the public). Sometimes chapels were specially built and some of these had round naves and rectangular chancels, being based on the plan of the Church of the Holy Sepulchre in Jerusalem. One of them, belonging to the Hospitaller commandery of Little Maplestead in Essex, is now in use as a parish church.

A number of former Templar houses and estates can be detected in place-names, as at Temple, in both Cornwall and Hampshire, and in the prefixes to village names, such as Temple Bruer in Lincolnshire and Temple Combe in Somerset. A Hospitaller commandery is remembered in the name of Kemeys Commander in Monmouthshire. To an estate in Herefordshire, in their possession by 1168, the Templars gave the name of Baldock, the French form of Baghdad, presumably from some association with the original city during their service in the east.

Both orders had their English headquarters in London and these were the only places that had extensive buildings. That of the Hospitallers, the priory of St. John at Clerkenwell, was founded about 1144. The southern gateway, built in 1504, spans St. John's Lane.[2] The Templars' headquarters lay south of the Strand beside a road-barrier known, from its proximity to the Temple, as Temple Bar. Only the church remains, the finest of the five round churches in England, although it is much

---

[1] After its dissolution, this order was briefly revived by Queen Mary, with Sir Thomas Tresham as its Grand Commander. The alabaster effigy of the latter (d. 1559), bearded and in the robes of the order, can be seen on his tomb-chest at his own parish church of Rushton, Northamptonshire.

[2] This gatehouse is now the headquarters of the order, which was revived in 1831. It was constituted an order of chivalry with the sovereign at its head in 1888. The St. John Ambulance Brigade was founded at this time; its members wear black uniforms with the white eight-pointed cross of the Hospitallers as their badge.

restored after the enemy action of 1941. In the pavement of the nave are eight grave slabs with marble effigies of knights in full armour. These were not Templar knights but wealthy men who joined the order as associate members for the same reasons as people joined the fraternities of the friars. Even a king, Henry III, had wished to be buried there, but when the time came he was entombed in Westminster abbey.

As the main forces were always serving abroad the numbers of men in England and Wales were not large compared with those of the other religious orders, there being between 100 and 200 members – knights, sergeants and chaplains – in each of the orders. Except for those in the London houses these were all working in small groups in the different preceptories and commanderies. Some of them may have been new recruits, some soldiers on leave and others were likely to have been older men retired from an active military life.

The income from the estates, as well as from charitable bequests, came into the London houses and the Templars are known to have had a gross revenue of nearly £1 million in 1308, the equivalent of that from perhaps twenty-five medium-sized monasteries.[1] This money was for the defence of the Holy Land and the funding of future knightly ventures there. When it was necessary to move it to the east it was taken from one Templar or Hospitaller estate to another under an armed guard. The possession of so much money in London and other capital cities led to the Templars becoming bankers, and the kings of Europe depended on them as their financial advisers and for loans. They were so reliable that rulers and great lords were happy to deposit their valuables with them.

The international connections of both orders made them knowledgeable and trustworthy negotiators and they were sometimes called on as guarantors of treaties and transactions – the Grand Master of the Templars was one of the witnesses of Magna Carta. In England the Grand Masters ranked with the great abbots and could be called to parliament; and some brethren were given posts of responsibility in the royal household.

The great wealth acquired by these soldier-monks, their superior positions among the mighty and their unique military and political knowledge of the Holy Land changed the humble attitude current in the early twelfth century to one of arrogance. This outlook even extended to each other, so that Templars and Hospitallers behaved at times as rivals and, on one occasion in 1254, actually fought on opposite sides. For all

---

[1] This comparison is made by D. Knowles, *Medieval Religious Houses*, 27.

that, they stood shoulder to shoulder at the bitter siege of Acre in 1291 when they were finally driven from the Holy Land and only a remnant escaped to Cyprus.

Both the Hospitallers and the Templars were then in something of a quandary for they had lost the purpose of their existence while still possessing the funds from their European lands which were intended to secure the holy places from the infidel. The Hospitallers were shrewd enough to find another associated cause – the pursuit of the Turks at sea. In Cyprus they built a navy and then captured the Greek island of Rhodes, which henceforth became their headquarters. The Templars remained true to their primary objective and in 1306 the Grand Master was summoned to Poitiers to discuss the organisation of a new crusade with the pope.

b. *The suppression of the Templars*

At this time Philip IV, King of France, known as 'the Fair', was in financial straits and he cast covetous eyes on the wealth of the Templars. He laid his plans well and, in October 1307, all the Templars in France, including the Grand Master, then in Paris, were arrested on trumped-up charges and their goods were seized. About 600 men were involved of whom between 50 and 100 were knights. All were charged with denying Christ, spitting on a crucifix, worshipping an idol and encouraging homosexuality. Such accusations were nothing new, for both Church and State had used them previously to discredit the heretical sects of the Cathars and Waldensians. The Templars were chained in solitary confinement, kept on bread and water and tortured until they 'confessed', although some died in the process.

Philip wrote to other European kings, including his son-in-law, Edward II of England, informing them of the Templars' guilt and suggesting that they, too, arrest the members of the order in their dominions. No other ruler did so at that time. They probably believed, with a correspondent of James II of Aragon, that 'the pope and the king did this in order to have their money'. The twenty-three year old Edward II, who had ascended the throne only three months before, wrote to the other kings advising them to leave the Templars alone until such time as they were legally convicted.

The pope, Clement V, himself wrote a letter to the kings stating that the Templars should be arrested in the name of the papacy. Edward II gave orders for the detaining of the English Templars, but many of them were left under house arrest in their preceptories and those who were imprisoned had comfortable conditions.

Formal inquiries did not begin until the end of 1309 when the pope sent two members of the Inquisition – the organisation for dealing with the suppression of heresy. The inquisitors who came were the only two ever to enter the British Isles. They were given facilities for lengthy interrogations in London, Lincoln and York, and examined 144 Templars, of whom 6 were knights, 8 were chaplains and the rest sergeants. When they met with denials they pressed for the power to use torture. They were supported by the bishops of the province of Canterbury, who petitioned the king for this. Edward agreed but put obstacles in the way. A year later the pope wrote to him: 'We hear that you forbid torture as contrary to the laws of your land, but no State law can override Canon Law, Our Law; therefore I command you at once to submit those men to torture.' He then offered Edward remission of his sins if he would do this. Edward gave in and in June 1311 the machinery of torture was ready for action. Then its use, or the threat of its use, produced the desired confessions. In July the brethren publicly abjured their heresy outside the south doors of either St. Paul's in London or the minster in York. They were then formally reconciled to the Church, after which they went in to take part in high mass. Many of those in London were too weak to go to St. Paul's and they were reconciled at St. Mary's chapel near the Tower. Afterwards they were all separated and sent to different monasteries for life, under threat that if they withdrew their confessions they would be burned.

Two Templars were left in London. In spite of torture William de la More, the Grand Master of England, continued with his denials and was sent to the Tower until the pope's judgement was known. He died there in December 1312 and was henceforth known to the Hospitallers as 'the martyr'. Visiting London at the time of the arrests was a French preceptor, Imbert Blanke. He, too, stoutly maintained his innocence and that of his order. Because of his resolution he was kept in prison under the most vile conditions, possibly being subjected to torture. By February, 1314, he may have been released to live in a monastery, for at that time Edward II ordered the Hospitallers to pay him an allowance of £20 a day.

Much the same sort of thing happened in most of the other kingdoms and states of Europe although one or two places held fair inquiries – the archbishop and council of the papal state of Ravenna voted against the use of torture and recommended that the order should be preserved; and the archbishop of the Rhineland state of Mainz, with his council, gave his decision in favour of the Templars, although the pope later annulled it.

In Paris, in 1310, Philip IV had ordered that 54 Templars who had withdrawn their confessions should be burnt and this action broke down the resistance of most of the rest. He was then ready to take the next step. In 1312, at the council of Vienne, he brought pressure to bear on Clement V so that the pope abolished the order of the Knights Templar. Provision was made for its property to go to the Hospitallers but Philip found ways of taking 'necessary expenses' from the Templar estates before they were gradually handed over. Other rulers naturally did the same and much of the Templar property in England was still in the king's hands in 1338.

It is certain that the main and perhaps the only reason for the crushing of the Templars was the financial need and avarice of the French king. In this connection, and during the same years, he robbed other wealthy sections of the community – the Jews and the Lombardy bankers – which had no-one to protest on their behalf. Outside France most Europeans agreed with the contemporary poet, Dante, that he had 'lawlessly brought his greedy sails into the very Temple itself'. This is the opinion of most subsequent historians, one of whom, Henry C. Lea, has called the suppression of the Templars 'the great crime of the Middle Ages'.[1]

c. *The Hospitallers after 1312*

The Hospitallers must have watched the proceedings against their rivals with mixed feelings. Even the handing over of the Templars' possessions to their order was not made without a threat that the pope might reform it also 'both in its head and its members'. As late as 1343 Pope Clement VI wrote to Elyan de Villeneuf, the English Grand Prior, rebuking him for the misuse of funds on unnecessary luxuries. He also reminded him of the fate of the Templars – it was a pity their order had been dissolved, he said, as their zeal had kept the Hospitallers on the alert. The warning followed an improvement in the Hospitallers' fortunes, due to the acquisition of the Templars' lands and to the business ability of de Villeneuf. The order had been in financial difficulties in 1328, but by 1338, it had a surplus of income over expenditure of nearly £1,400,000. After deducting sums for living expenses and hospitality much of this was sent to Rhodes,[2] now firmly established as the new headquarters.

The augmented Hospitaller lands continued to be utilised as before.

---

[1] *History of the Inquisition in the Middle Ages* (1888), Vol. III, 238.
[2] Rhodes fell to the Turks in 1523. The Hospitallers made Malta their headquarters in 1530; this was surrendered to Napoleon in 1798.

To the serfs who worked on them the Hospitallers were only another kind of manorial landlord taking the produce that ought to have supplied their wants for the benefit of some vague foreign cause. After the end of the Crusades it is doubtful if many people knew or understood what the money was being used for, and, if they did, whether they would have approved.

SELECT BOOK LIST

The letters F and K denote that a book belongs also with those listed under the headings: 2. Friars, and 3. Knights of the military orders, respectively.

1. Monks, canons and nuns
COOK, G. H. *English Monasteries in the Middle Ages* (1961). F
CROSSLEY, F. H. *The English Abbey* (1943).
DICKINSON, J. C. *Monastic Life in Medieval England* (1961). F
KNOWLES, D. and HADCOCK, R. Neville. *Medieval Religious Houses, England and Wales* (1953). F. K.
KNOWLES, D. *The Monastic Order in England, 940–1216* (1963).
KNOWLES, D. *The Religious Orders in England*, 3 vols. (1948–1959). F.
MOORMAN, J. R. H. *Op. cit.* F.
PLATT, C. *The Abbeys and Priories of Medieval England* (1984). F.
POWER, E. *Medieval English Nunneries* (1922).
THOMPSON, A. Hamilton. *English Monasteries* (1913).

2. Friars
BOURDILLON, A. F. C. *The Order of Minoresses in England* (1926).
COTTLE, B. *The Triumph of English, 1350–1400* (1969).
JARRETT, B. *The English Dominicans* (1921).
MARTIN, A. R. *Franciscan Architecture in England* (1937).
MOORMAN, J. R. H. *A History of the Franciscan Order* (1968).
MOORMAN, J. R. H. *The Franciscans in England* (1974).

3. Knights of the military orders
ADDISON, C. G. *The Knights Templars* (1842).
BARBER, M. *The Trial of the Templars* (1978).
BRIDGE, A. *The Crusades* (1980).
PARKER, T. W. *The Knights Templars in England* (1963).
PARTNER, P. *The Murdered Magicians. The Templars and their Myth* (1982).
PERKINS, C. 'The Trial of the Knights Templars in England', in *English Historical Review*, XXIV (1909).
PERKINS, C. 'The Wealth of the Knights Templars in England and the Disposition of It after Their Dissolution', in *American Historical Review*, XV (1909–10).
RILEY-SMITH, J. *The Knights of St. John in Jerusalem and Cyprus, c.1050–1310* (1967).

THE PAPACY

1. EARLY DEVELOPMENT

The hierarchy in England, and in every other country of western Christendom, acknowledged the supremacy of the papacy. This was an institution which had developed in Rome, where the bishops (later known as popes) had accumulated certain overriding powers and were said to be the representatives (or Vicars) of Christ on earth. There was no biblical foundation for this, the main strength of the assertion lying in the former presence of the apostle Peter who was thought to be buried there. From him the popes claimed to have inherited total authority – 'the plenitude of power' – over all the Church. They saw themselves as the rulers of the whole of Christian society, deriving their authority from God, to whom they were responsible for the salvation of the world. Therefore they assumed that they were not merely the equals of kings but their superiors, and able, if need be, to make or break them. The constant reiteration of this theme resulted, by the eleventh century, in almost unquestioned acceptance of the papal monarchy throughout the western world.[1]

The popes wielded their universal authority with a firm and heavy hand, getting politically involved and interfering in disputes, whether between one country and another or between subjects and rulers. They made kings – the Norman conquerors in England and Sicily invaded with the blessing of the pope; punished them, in the way that Henry II was punished for the murder of Becket; excommunicated them – John of England, the emperor Otto IV and the kings of Portugal and Armenia were all at one time under Innocent III's sentence of excommunication;

---

[1] The Eastern Church was not in agreement with this and finally separated from Rome in 1054. Anathemas of each other, made by both sides at that time, were simultaneously lifted by the heads of both churches in 1965.

forced the hands of obstinate kings by putting whole countries under interdict (i.e. no church services were held), as was England under John from 1208 to 1213; raised up armies against them, like that of Philip II of France for the invasion of England in 1213; and released subjects from their oaths of allegiance – the people of England were freed in this way during the interdict. Laws were guarded – those of Ireland were preserved after Henry II's conquest of that country (made with the pope's approval) in 1171 – or annulled like Magna Carta in 1215. As a world ruler the popes could dispose of territories yet unknown and, in 1493, Alexander VI drew a line of demarcation giving newly-discovered lands to the east of it to Portugal and those to the west to Spain. These powerful earthly potentates even had influence beyond the earth for, from the twelfth century, they reserved to themselves the right to create saints, those holy ones in heaven on whom sinful humanity relied for intercession with Christ. The popes, then, were rulers to obey, to seek as allies, to appease, to fear and only rarely to oppose.

2. GOVERNMENT

The Church was governed by means of the papal curia (or court), which comprised all the administrative departments – financial, legal, etc. From Rome the orders and decisions went out and to Rome came petitioners and suitors from every country, bringing their cases and law-suits to the supreme law-giver, the pope, aided by his large staff of lawyers, clerks and judges.

The popes delegated much of their work to the College of Cardinals, an advisory body equivalent to the king's council in England. These senior clergy were the foremost dignitaries of the Church and their office carried special privileges: they lived in palaces, were known as princes of the Church, ranked with princes of the blood royal, governed the Church during a vacancy in the Holy See and, after 1059, had the sole right to elect a new pope. Religious qualifications were not necessary, for the popes liked to advance their friends and relations to this supreme ministerial role, a policy which guaranteed them support in personal matters, Church affairs and international politics. Cardinals made themselves useful as spokesmen to secular rulers who paid certain ones retaining fees: when Edward II was protesting to the pope in 1307 about trespasses on his royal rights he also wrote to 11 cardinals; similarly, Edward III wrote to 24 of them in 1329 in connection with the promotion of one of his civil servants to a bishopric.

Decisions taken by the pope and his cardinals were recorded in the chancery for distribution. Papal bulls took their name from the leaden seal or *bulla* which was attached to certain documents. They were reserved for the most important pronouncements such as the canonisation of a saint or a dispensation in favour of a royal marriage. Lesser items were sealed in red wax with the signet, depicting St. Peter fishing from a boat, known as 'the fisherman's ring'. All correspondence was carried far and wide by runners and riders, for there was a well-organised system of communications and the papal stables were the largest in Europe.

Sometimes more than the written word was needed and then the popes appointed a legate to go to a country as his representative on the spot. Legates possessed plenary powers so that they could make decisions on behalf of the pope and took precedence over archbishops and bishops. Their presence displeased both clergy and kings and in 1116 Henry I refused to allow a papal legate to enter the country. The difficulty was settled by an agreement that legates could only come in with the king's permission. During the first five years of the minority of Henry III (1216–21), England then being a papal fief following John's submission to the pope in 1213, the country was ruled by a regent in association with a legate from Rome. Future kings were determined to keep legates out or at least to restrict their rights. The height of legatine power was reached with Cardinal Wolsey, who was also Henry VIII's first minister. His double powers made him a figure both hated and feared. On his fall in 1530 everyone would have agreed with the Duke of Suffolk when he said, 'It was never merry in England while we had cardinals among us!' No further legate came until Cardinal Pole (d. 1558) arrived in the reign of Queen Mary I and he was the last to be appointed to England.[1]

The popes kept a firm grip on all the dioceses, for every bishop had to take an oath of obedience to the papacy. Regular episcopal visits to Rome were also necessary in order to report on and receive directions about diocesan affairs. It was permitted to send a deputy who sometimes became an almost permanent representative at the curia.

In all these ways the popes exercised their sovereignty and governed Christendom through the ecclesiastical law. The common faith in Christ and his earthly vicar ensured that, for the most part, this was accepted and the papal dictates were obeyed. Decisions, of course, did not satisfy

---

[1] From that time no papal representative was accredited to the English government until an Apostolic Pro-Nuncio was appointed in 1982.

everyone and there were sometimes undertones of disagreement as well as downright opposition.

3. PROPERTY AND INCOME

For income the papacy relied at first on the rents and dues it received from the Patrimony of St. Peter (i.e. the territory it had acquired in Italy) together with the contributions of Peter's Pence. As its influence extended and its administrative departments multiplied these proved to be insufficient.

Fresh means of raising money were looked for and a variety of sources was discovered over the years: an irregular income-tax on the clergy for 'the burdens and necessities of the Roman church'; an annual tribute demanded from rulers like King John who had surrendered their lands to the pope – in 1366 the English parliament declared this tax invalid, but the claims continued to be made; selling dispensations; exaction of heavy fees, fines and bribes from suitors and supplicants – a twelfth-century satirist wrote of the pope's advice to his cardinals on dealing with petitioners: 'For I have given you an example, that ye also should take gifts as I have taken them ... blessed are the wealthy, for theirs is the Court of Rome'; indulgences sold in a manner which amounted to commercial activity; and the sale of offices at court to clerks seeking advancement. These were the main financial measures which provided the bulk of the huge papal wealth.

The gathering-in of this was done by official collectors, able men appointed to each country from the ranks of archdeacons, abbots, rectors, papal clerks, etc. Theirs was a position worth having, with a definite stipend and permission to take necessary expenses from the funds collected. Faithful service might be rewarded by a bishopric. When the money was brought in it was kept for safety in a monastery or a church until ready for transport to Rome. Then it was sent under armed escort. The Templars, until their suppression, were often given this responsibility.

The enormous sums involved could never keep pace with the wasteful expenditure of most of the popes. Maintaining a majestic life-style, running state departments, playing a political role and even being involved in warfare soon used up the money available and there was a constant search for fresh supplies. By the beginning of the sixteenth century everything connected with the papacy was in some way made to yield money for the pope and his curia. Popular opinion, quoted by John of Salisbury to his friend, Hadrian IV (c.1100–59), the only English pope, did not change in four hundred years: then men had said that the pope was 'burdensome and oppressive to all', building palaces and going about 'not only in purple but in gold.' Such behaviour was very different from that of the Church's founder and people began to question its basis in Christianity.

4. PAPAL PROVISIONS

From the time of Innocent III (1198–1216) the popes claimed that all church posts were at their disposal. They exercised this new 'right' by 'providing' men to fill senior positions – bishoprics, prebends, canonries and the like – and its use became common in England after King John's submission in 1213.

The system was yet another means of raising money, for every dignitary who was provided by the pope had to pay a substantial sum for his appointment – a third of the first year's income (called the service tax) by bishops and abbots, and a half (called annates) by lesser members of the hierarchy. These were often referred to as first-fruits and were a great burden to the recipients who were often constrained to borrow large sums for their satisfaction. Failure to pay resulted in excommunication and suspension from office and this actually happened to Archbishop Pecham of Canterbury in 1279. Popes were not sympathetic towards defaulters, for this tax brought in an average of £2 million a year.

The use of provisions was also a means of rewarding the large numbers of officials at the curia with an income by giving them vacant benefices. Wherever they occurred the lucky holder could put in a vicar to do the work on the spot for a small stipend, while he himself remained in Rome in receipt of the larger part of the revenue. Such an outsider, intruded into an English rectory, might already hold an archdeaconry, an abbacy and a canonry in France, similar appointments in Italy and a cardinalate as well, so it was a case of the rich getting richer.

This went on almost without check until the mid-fourteenth century, although not without criticism from both Church- and lay-people. Matthew Paris wrote about the servants 'of the Romans, seizing whatsoever in the country is precious and serviceable and sending it away to their lords living delicately out of the patrimony of the Crucified'. At a time when hundred of livings were in the possession of foreigners many

Englishmen would have echoed this and some rebelled.

In 1231 Sir Robert Tweng, a young Yorkshire knight, protested when, for the second time, an Italian was put into Kirkleatham, a living in his own gift. With his band of supporters he told people not to pay rent to aliens and gave out grain already gathered into barns for them. The anti-foreign movement spread to other parts of the country, papal messengers were attacked and the documents they carried trodden underfoot. There was widespread sympathy for the disturbers of the peace and little was done to stop them. Indeed, some of those in high places, both clergy and royal officials, were themselves involved. After inquiries made in 1232, at the command of the pope, it was decided that punishment of the offenders might bring about a civil war and so most people were treated leniently. Sir Robert Tweng was sent to Rome to explain his behaviour. He also got off lightly and even received back the patronage of his church. Furthermore it was conceded that the consent of lay patrons like himself was necessary for future appointments to any of their benefices. Apart from that, matters went on much as before and protests continued to be heard.

In 1245 a royal inquiry estimated that the Italians took out of the country 'a greater revenue than that of the king himself'. The following year a great council was held in London and from it letters were sent to Rome from king, nobles and bishops, complaining about provisions. The pope then promised amendments to everyone's satisfaction but these proved to be too easily set aside.

Bishops were never happy about the situation but they found it difficult to dissent because of their oath of obedience to the papacy. In 1253 Robert Grosseteste, the aged bishop of Lincoln, dared to state his objection. He was one of those rare bishops who cared for his diocese and the people in it, and an Italian, whether present or absent, was useless for the tasks to be done. When required to present the pope's nephew to a canonry at Lincoln, Grosseteste wrote, 'As an obedient son I disobey, I contradict, I rebel.' On receipt of this the pope was at first inclined to order the king to put the 'old dotard' in prison, but in the end he took the advice of his cardinals who said, 'We cannot condemn him. He is a catholic and a holy man, a better man than we are ... an active enemy of abuses.'

Matters became worse when the popes went to live in Avignon. This residence coincided with the first part of the Hundred Years' War with France which started in 1338. Then English people felt that they had an additional grievance because their dues and rents, paid to foreign (mainly Italian and French) provisors were being sent out of the country to people who supported their enemies. Feelings were stronger than ever and were voiced in high places: Edward III pointed out to Clement VI (1342–52) that 'the successor of the Apostles was commissioned to lead the Lord's sheep to the pasture, not to fleece them'; and the 'Good' Parliament of 1376 named the pope as 'the cause of all the plagues, murrain, famine and poverty of the realm', and complained of the drain of English money out of the country to 'the sinful city of Avignon'.

This state of affairs was only relieved by the passing of the Statute of Provisors in 1351 (re-enacted in 1390), which denied the right of the papacy to provide to English benefices. While not totally doing away with provisions there was a great reduction in them and in the appointment of foreigners. At Lincoln, in 1344, out of 68 members of the cathedral chapter 25 held their benefices by papal provision, but in 1444 not one of them did. The popes objected to the Statute but successive parliaments refused to repeal it.

A new method was soon found of partly replacing the lost revenues. When a bishopric became vacant, instead of promoting a man to fill it the popes often translated an existing bishop to it, thus leaving another vacancy to be filled. They then claimed the right to provide the incumbent for this new vacancy. In 1388, for instance, the promotion of the bishop of Ely to the archbishopric of York was followed by the moves of three other bishops. Every time this was done, of course, the provision fees went to the pope.

Kings and popes generally tried to keep on good terms and to reach a compromise over provisions. This often meant that the king chose his own man while the pope provided him as a personal act of grace (and received the fees). Because it often suited both parties some provisions continued to be made in the fifteenth and early years of the sixteenth centuries and were still giving rise to criticism. 'There are three things today, that make a bishop in England', wrote Thomas Gascoigne (1405–58), Chancellor of Oxford, 'the will of the king, the will of the pope or of the court of Rome, and the money paid in large quantities to that court'.

In 1524 Henry VIII allowed Cardinal Campeggio to be provided to the bishopric of Salisbury, but ten years later he abolished the popes' rights in the appointment of bishops. Campeggio was then deprived of his bishopric by act of parliament because he was an alien and a non-resident. So ended the 'election of the pope which is called provision', which had irritated Englishmen for more than three hundred years.

5. SOJOURN IN AVIGNON

In 1305 the archbishop of Bordeaux was elected as pope and was known as Clement V. Although he was a Gascon subject of the English king his background and outlook were French and he was almost totally in the power of the French king. He delayed his departure for Rome and his coronation took place at Lyons. In 1309 he chose Avignon as his residence and he and his successors lived there until 1376. As the papal capital, the little town became one of the most important places in Europe, with a newly-built papal palace which still dominates the district. Extravagant living and immoral ways were typical of the Avignon popes. Many visitors were shocked by what they saw and took away with them descriptions of a leadership lacking in spiritual authority.

To everyone except the king of France the pope's establishment at Avignon was nothing short of a scandal – the 'Babylonish Captivity', according to the Spiritual Franciscans. Anyone with business at the papal court had to go into this sphere of French influence, a venture not conducive to success for Englishmen. With the beginning of the Hundred Years' War anti-French feeling in England became also anti-papal. It was during this time that the Statute of Provisors was passed and also, in 1353, the Statute of *Praemunire* which forbade appeals to the pope.

As the fourteenth century wore on French influence weakened owing to English victories. At the same time the papal states were rebelling and the pope's presence in Italy was urgently needed. The return was decided upon and Gregory XI entered Rome in 1377 taking up his residence in the Vatican, which thereafter became the official seat of the papacy. Everyone must have thought that the pope was now in his proper place and the Christian world would be the better for it. A year later Gregory died and the situation immediately became worse.

6. THE GREAT SCHISM

An Italian pope, Urban VI, was elected by an almost unanimous vote. The French cardinals soon regretted this and chose another from among themselves as Clement VII. He returned to Avignon and a state of schism began, Urban excommunicating Clement who responded in the same way. When they died successors were elected to each and rival popes continued to rule from Rome and Avignon for nearly forty years. Each maintained his own curia and the whole apparatus of papal organisation was duplicated.

In a Church which had always been autocratic the element of choice was new and strange and caused people to wonder which pope, if either, was really the Vicar of Christ. Secular rulers upheld their own political favourite, France and her allies accepting the Avignon line, while England, Germany, Poland, Scandinavia and most of Italy supported the Roman popes. Hungary was drawn into the latter group and the new alliance was cemented by the marriage of Richard II and Anne of Bohemia.

The existence of two popes discredited the Church and eventually both sides called on each of them to abdicate. When neither would do so the university of Paris suggested that a general council of all the religious leaders should be held and this met at Pisa in 1409. Both popes were deposed and another was chosen. Unfortunately neither of the existing popes recognised this decision and Europe now saw the spectacle of three popes.

Another council was summoned to Constance and it met from 1414 to 1418. During this time one pope abdicated and the other two were deposed. Finally, in 1417, a conclave of the cardinals chose Martin V as the new pope. He was accepted by all and in 1420 he established himself in Rome. The Great Schism was over.

7. THE LAST CHANCE TO REFORM

The council of Constance had enacted a decree calling for 'the reform of the Church in its head and members'. The new pope and his successors failed to grasp this opportunity for amendment because they were more concerned with the recovery of lost papal supremacy. By the middle of the fifteenth century the popes had made themselves a force to be reckoned with again. This was the time of the renaissance popes who built new palaces, renovated basilicas and became patrons of the arts, all at enormous expense. Living in earthly splendour, these men were amongst the worst of those who had ever called themselves the Vicars of Christ. Their example could not be admired by right-thinking

Christians. As the popes forfeited respect a ground-swell of criticism began to be heard and the call for reform grew louder. If the popes would not admit the need for reform then the need itself would bring forth the reformers.

SELECT BOOK LIST

BARRACLOUGH, G. *The Medieval Papacy* (1968, reprinted 1979).
BARRACLOUGH, G. *Papal Provisions* (1935).
BINNS, L. E. *The Decline and Fall of the Medieval Papacy* (1934).
BURN-MURDOCH, H. *The Development of the Papacy* (1954).
DEANESLY, M. *Op. cit.*
LUNT, W. E. *Papal Revenues in the Middle Ages*, 2 vols. (1934).
MacKENZIE, H. 'The Anti-foreign Movement in England, 1231–1232', in *Anniversary Essays in Medieval History by Students of C. H. Haskins* (1929).
SMITH, J. H. *The Great Schism* (1970).
SOUTHERN, R. W. *Western Society and the Church in the Middle Ages* (1970).
THOMPSON, A. Hamilton. *Op. cit.*
ULLMAN, W. *The Growth of Papal Government in the Middle Ages* (1955).
ULLMANN, W. *A Short History of the Papacy in the Middle Ages* (1972).

ECCLESIASTICAL AUTHORITY AND NON-CONFORMITY

1. HERESY

Membership of the Church was compulsory for all baptised Christians and the majority were satisfied with it. They might mutter in corners about such vexations as archdeacons' courts, the morals of parish priests and the unceasing demand for tithes, but they accepted that the Church's ministrations were necessary for salvation. More thoughtful people questioned the dictatorial power of the Church, its unashamed wealth and its unbiblical doctrines. In twelfth-century Europe they preached a return to a simple religious life based on that of the apostles. Since this implied criticism of the Church, steps were taken to combat it. The dissidents, called heretics (or choosers), had to be brought back to the fold or else punished.

Persuasion was tried at first but, when that failed, more vigorous action was taken. In the years following 1233 papal agents from the Dominican and Franciscan orders were empowered to inquire into heresy and to extirpate it. Their organisation was called the Inquisition. Thereafter, heretics were excommunicated, tortured (if necessary to force confession) and tried, all for the good of their souls. The primary aim of the inquisitors was to convert the heretics, and those who recanted were accepted back into the Church and given penances. The most stubborn were handed over to the secular authorities for the death sentence because, as Aquinas stated in the thirteenth century, 'heretics must be compelled to hold the faith' and, if they did not, could 'justly be killed'. Execution was by burning, a method which had existed in Roman law for parricide, arson and sorcery.

Persecution on this level succeeded in wiping out all the early heretical sects except the Waldensians (followers of Valdes) of southern France and northern Italy. These determined people led a life of non-conformity in remote valleys and mountain fastnesses. They maintained their beliefs in secret through the medieval period and their independent Church has remained in being to the present day. There would have been other separated groups of Christians but for the repressive measures of the Inquisition. The Western Church only survived as a seemingly united institution by driving contrary religious beliefs underground or extinguishing them altogether.

For a long time, England was spared all this. Situated on the edge of Europe, far from the main centres of heresy, with the English Channel presenting difficulties to evangelists, she remained virtually free from contact with heretics. The challenge, when it came, was proclaimed by one man, whose radical and original ideas reached and inspired a host of committed followers.

2. JOHN WYCLIF

a. *Oxford*

John Wyclif was a Yorkshireman, probably from a minor landed family that had its seat at Wycliffe-on-Tees. Born about 1330 he entered Oxford university as a youth and obtained his B.A. and M.A. degrees. He stayed on to study and took his doctorate in divinity in 1372. During this time he was connected with three of the colleges, being, in turn, a fellow of Merton, the master of Balliol and a resident at Queen's. As a university don he was, according to a contemporary chronicler, 'the most eminent doctor of theology of those times'; even a later critic admitted that he was the 'flower of Oxford scholars'. But it was not so much his learning that pushed him into the public eye as the use he made of it to call attention to the defects of the Church.

His study of history and theology, as well as his observations of religious practices and the hierarchical organisation, brought him to the conclusion that the Church had deviated from its biblical roots. So strongly did he feel about it that, between the years 1372 and 1382, he made his criticisms known at Oxford lectures and in a series of books. In effect he courageously and single-handedly took on the might of the medieval Church, attacking its wealth and worldliness, exposing its corrupt methods and protesting against its doctrinal errors. Such ideas had never been spoken openly before and they were acclaimed enthusiastically by the students and masters who flocked to hear him.

Every aspect of the Church came under Wyclif's stinging rebukes. It was nothing less than a complete reformation that he called for and he pursued this aim energetically for the rest of his life.

Wyclif's authority was the bible. He contrasted the humble life of Christ with that of the luxury-loving Vicars of Christ. The unscriptural office of pope, he said, was unnecessary, for Christ was the only head of the Church. This opinion was reinforced by the general uncertainty induced by the Schism. Over the Church in each country Wyclif wanted to place the national rulers, who would see that the clergy led more spiritual lives; they themselves would no longer employ bishops and other higher clergy as their political advisers and civil servants, but would order them to serve the people in their religious posts.

Wyclif objected to the fact that the Church held one-third of the land of England, especially when he saw the great wealth it brought in being misused on all sides. He therefore suggested that some of this might be confiscated by the State. His main target was the monasteries, which reaped a goodly crop of endowments and whose monks – the 'possessioners' – lived on the fat of the land, forgetting their charitable concerns and their spiritual functions. All orders, said Wyclif, should be disbanded and their houses closed, the money so gained being used to help the poor. The most capable monks should become parish priests or else teachers and artisans. Wyclif later included the friars in this reorganisation for, with the exception of the Spiritual Franciscans, they had abandoned their early ideal of poverty.

Apostolic succession and ordination by a bishop meant nothing to Wyclif. He thought it more important that priests (who need not be celibate) should set an example of Christian living. They ought, he wrote, 'to be holy ... strong in every sort of virtue' (and these were the words of one who was himself acknowledged by Archbishop Arundel to be 'a perfect liver'). Tithes should be given for their support, if they were worthy, and freely-given alms might be offered also. The holding of more than one benefice would not be allowed and rectors would have to reside in their parishes – a blow also to papal provisors.

Various teachings and practices came within Wyclif's disapproving gaze and he wished the Church to be purged of them: confession to a priest was not necessary, for Christians could confess their sins directly to God; the entire system of purgatory, chantries, indulgences, prayers and masses for the dead was irrelevant and only a means of making money out of the gullible; the worship of saints, their relics and images, and also pilgrimages to their shrines, was dangerous, for it might prevent people from worshipping God – although Mary and certain others should be treated with reverence; excommunication was unimportant, for it was man's curse not God's; the right to give sanctuary protected criminals to the detriment of the realm; and the over-elaboration of church decoration and ceremonies were obstacles to worship.

Wyclif's words were like a gale-force wind raising the ecclesiastical dust of ages and giving his audiences a different view of their so-far-unquestioned religion. The obvious sincerity of the outspoken Yorkshireman was an inspiration to many of his hearers and gained him dedicated disciples among the Oxford scholars.

Although Wyclif spoke and wrote in Latin, such novel opinions were soon heard far beyond the walls of the university and struck an answering chord in the hearts of patriotic Englishmen. They would have welcomed his picture of an ideal England free from the trammels of a grasping clergy: 'Oh! how happy and fertile would England be if every parish church had as of yore a saintly rector residing with his family ... . For if they would teach efficiently in word and deed the law of Christ, as in old times, abuses of this sort [a sumptuous way of living] would cease.'

It was to the king that Wyclif looked to put his reformatory scheme into effect, for he realised that only the ruling body could do anything so drastic. He had high hopes that this might happen, for John of Gaunt, virtually the ruler of England during the declining years of his brother, Edward III, and in the boyhood of his nephew, Richard II, wished to secure greater control of the clergy and their wealth. The prince employed Wyclif over a period of years to give him theological backing for various anti-clerical and anti-papal measures. As a politician he was more concerned with the stability of the country than a thorough-going re-organisation of the Church, with all its attendant disturbances. He therefore used Wyclif's scholarship but put him off with the politician's argument that the time was not yet ripe.

In the autumn of 1376 Gaunt invited Wyclif to denounce the ill-used riches of the higher clergy from the pulpits of several London churches. Wyclif seized the opportunity to meet a wider public and the citizens crowded to hear his rousing sermons. He became a popular figure with the Londoners, as he boldly voiced the complaints they had long secretly held themselves.

This open offensive by an unlicenced[1] priest provoked the wrath of William Courtenay, bishop of London. When the southern convocation

---

[1] A priest could only preach in a diocese if he held a licence from the bishop.

met at St. Paul's in February, 1377, he persuaded the milder Simon Sudbury, archbishop of Canterbury, to call Wyclif to appear before the bishops. John of Gaunt considered this action to be an indirect attack on his own power. He provided Wyclif with four Oxford friars (one from each of the mendicant orders) for his defence and himself accompanied the party to the cathedral. The trial never got under way, for the citizens of London burst in upon it in fury at a totally separate action of Gaunt's concerning the government of the city, and the proceedings broke up in uproar. Wyclif retired to Oxford uncondemned, remembering with gratitude the friars who, he wrote, '... stood by my side fearlessly in the cause of God'.

Wyclif's Benedictine enemies brought his writings to the attention of Pope Gregory XI, who denounced eighteen errors in them. The pope then sent bulls to Edward III, Sudbury and Courtenay, requiring them to check whether Wyclif indeed taught these. If so, they were to arrest him, obtain his confession and keep him in chains until the papal pleasure was known. If he should escape he was to be caught and sent to Rome. The royal council paid no attention to these demands and even consulted Wyclif on whether England might 'keep back the treasure of the kingdom' from being sent abroad to foreign papal provisors. (Wyclif reckoned this to be £20 million annually, in cash or in kind).

The chancellor of Oxford was ordered to deliver Wyclif to Sudbury and Courtenay. This put the university in a quandary for Gregory threatened it with the loss of its privileges. The chancellor made a gesture towards obedience and, at the end of 1377, got its greatest scholar to agree to 'house-arrest' in one of the university halls. He then declared that he and the other masters of divinity considered that Wyclif's theses, 'though they sounded ill to the ear, were all the same true'.

At length, in March 1378, Sudbury and Courtenay summoned Wyclif to an examination in the chapel of Lambeth palace. They must have known that popular opinion was against them. Not only were they obeying a papal order, but the subject of their investigation was an influential government adviser who had the protection of the royal family and the good-will of the people. Just before the trial began a message from Princess Joan, widow of the Black Prince and mother of Richard II, warned them that no judgement was to be pronounced. Wyclif began his defence but was interrupted by a noisy crowd of applauding citizens. The bishops felt it best to bring matters to a speedy close, cautioning Wyclif to refrain from discussing his disputed theses. Once again Wyclif walked free from a trial, his opinions still uncensured.

He was saved from further papal prosecution by the beginning of the Schism at the end of the year. While there was a rival in the field, Urban V, the 'Roman' pope, could not risk losing the support of the English government by further interference.

After the Lambeth inquiry Wyclif went back to Oxford and turned his attention to the doctrine of transubstantiation, which stated that the consecrated bread and wine changed into the actual body and blood of Christ. This had not been among the beliefs of the early Church and had only become necessary dogma since 1215. Wyclif now refuted it. He considered that God had created the best possible universe, therefore to destroy a part of it, as the bread and wine were said to be destroyed, or 'annihilated', in the consecration, was to annihilate something that had an existence because of the will of God. According to Wyclif, it was impossible for man to do this. It followed that the world (and its contents) was a rational creation and things observed in it were what they seemed to be. Convinced of this, Wyclif could not then believe that a priest could 'make the Body of Christ'. Such an action would confine the Creator of the universe to an earthly object which was subject to everyday mishaps, an inconceivable situation. This same object had been grown in the field by man and it did not make sense that he who was made in the image of God, should later worship as God the work of his own hands. This was nothing short of idolatry.

Wyclif believed that Christ was, in some unexplained way, present in the unchanged bread and wine in a spiritual manner, as the sun shines through glass, and could thus be received by faith. Far from advocating disrespect for the bread and wine, Wyclif actually recommended taking communion and not merely being present at mass. He was probably the first person to suggest this for the laity, since the Lateran council of 1215 had stipulated that they should receive it once a year.

In discussing transubstantiation Wyclif had touched upon the central point of the Church's faith on which all the rest – the cult of saints, pilgrimages, indulgences, masses for the dead, etc. – depended. As the host was elevated every Sunday it focused the attention of the faithful, not only on 'the Body of Christ', but also on the mystical body of the Church. To diminish it was to strike at the very foundations of that Church. Wyclif's lectures on this subject and his book, *On the Eucharist*, therefore, brought a storm of protest from the clergy and lost him many previously-staunch supporters at Oxford, like the friars. Objections were made because Wyclif's opinions, if put into practice, would have removed the priestly power to bring about the 'miraculous' change in the bread and wine, with the consequent possibility that the priest might then seem to be irrelevant, in the eyes of the laity. The power of the Church itself depended on the acceptance of this doctrine.

The chancellor of Oxford, William Barton, appointed a commission of twelve doctors of divinity to consider this new controversial teaching of Wyclif's. The result was that, during the winter of 1380/81, his views were condemned as erroneous by 7 votes to 5. This majority declared that the doctrine of transubstantiation 'must be believed, taught and manfully defended against all gainsayers'. Wyclif was told not to teach his mistaken ideas again under pain of suspension from the university, imprisonment and excommunication. After listening to this he was heard to say that 'neither the chancellor nor any of his accomplices could weaken his opinion.'

Always a fighter, Wyclif appealed to John of Gaunt, who realised that this time his learned servant had gone too far. He himself was willing to conform to the orthodox practices of the day and he did not relish offending the entire English hierarchy on this point. In April, 1381, he rode to Oxford to try to persuade his ally not to press these dangerous opinions. Wyclif knew that he had to choose between keeping his high-born patron or leading a lowly life devoted to his ideals. Even for the 'uncrowned king'[1] of England he could not agree to be silent where he felt that he ought to speak. So the two friends, the great man of affairs and the dedicated reformer, came to the parting of the ways, the one returning to the royal court, the other preparing to leave for more obscure surroundings. It is likely that John of Gaunt continued to protect Wyclif from the hierarchy and, for his part, Wyclif trusted the duke to the end of his days.

The Peasants' Revolt began in May of that year. Faced with possible overthrow Church and State united to deal with this sudden threat. After that, any likelihood of the State confiscating the Church's endowments was removed and henceforth the two stood together against any possibility of change. There was no understanding of the plight of the peasants. Wyclif was the first member of the Church and upper classes to criticise the near-slavery in which they were held by the feudal system and he asked that the rebels should be treated mercifully. He himself was most affected by the murder in the Tower of Archbishop Sudbury, for the new primate was the more antagonistic Courtenay.

By the end of that troublesome summer Wyclif had left Oxford

---

[1] So-called by the hostile chroniclers of St. Albans abbey.

forever. It must have been a wrench for him to leave the place that had been his home ever since youth. It had nurtured his perceptive understanding, rewarded his learning, honoured his free-thinking and defended him when in danger – but now it had silenced him. He remembered it fondly as 'a place gladsome and fertile, so suitable for the habitation of the gods that it has been rightly called the house of God and the gate of heaven'.

Oxford must have mourned the departure of its chiefest ornament for, according to William Thorpe, a former pupil, a 'great many communed oft with him and they loved so much his learning that they writ it and busily enforced them to rule themselves thereafter.' For them he was 'the greatest clerk that they knew then living', a description with which Archbishop Arundel later agreed. His was a powerful influence and he attracted followers by his scholarship, his resolution and his charm. He was 'an innocent in his living' and an ascetic, yet he confessed to once being partial to good food and raiment. His quick temper was well-known and he admitted that, as a young man, he had been arrogant in debate. He wielded his pen like a sword in his attacks on the Church and did not refrain from using the strongest language in his criticisms. He gave himself wholly to the enormous task of reforming the Church and never faltered when he raised up a mighty opposition. His courage was beyond question – it was shown in his lectures and his books and demonstrated at official inquiries. No one doubted that he was ready to face the ultimate punishment for his cause. His withdrawal removed an irreplaceable pioneer and left an aching void in the hearts of his students and erstwhile colleagues.

b. *Lutterworth*

In 1374 Wyclif had become rector of Lutterworth in Leicestershire, a benefice in the gift of the Crown. According to the custom of the day the income from this was meant for his support at Oxford. During his absence he would have provided 'a suitable substitute' and probably visited his parishioners 'at appropriate times in the year'.[1] Now he made the eighty-mile journey there for the last time to take up permanent residence in his parish. He was not in good health and his enemies expected that they had heard the last of him.

John Purvey, an Oxford scholar who had recently obtained his

---

[1] This is assumed from his own statement on the duties of a rector in *On the Truth of Sacred Scripture.*

doctorate, also went to Lutterworth. He lived in the rectory with Wyclif, 'toiled unweariedly with him as his inseparable companion' and 'drank in his most secret teaching.' Purvey acted as Wyclif's secretary, translating his Latin sermons into English and assisting in other projects. He must have been a strong prop for his master to lean on, for it was about this time that Wyclif suffered a stroke. Although he was partially paralysed his brain was not impaired and the work went on, but he no longer had the same physical strength as formerly. William Thorpe knew him at this time as a 'spare, frail, emaciated figure'. While Wyclif pursued his high calling, perhaps with a sense that time was running short, the parish was cared for by a young curate, John Horn, and the usual parochial staff.

Archbishop Courtenay received his pallium in May 1382 and he immediately called a specially-selected committee of bishops, graduates in theology and canon lawyers – all opposed to Wyclif – to meet in Blackfriars hall in order to examine 24 'propositions' taken from Wyclif's writings. After four days of study it was decided unanimously that 10 of the propositions were heretical and the remainder were erroneous. Hardly had this been read out when an earthquake terrified everyone. As this was a rare occurrence in England it was claimed by Wyclif and his followers as a sign of God's displeasure at the verdict, especially when it was learned that Courtenay's see church of Canterbury had been damaged at the same time. Wyclif himself was not called before the council, possibly because of illness and also because he was still a well-loved personality and Courtenay remembered the behaviour of the Londoners at St. Paul's and Lambeth. It was enough for the archbishop to get an official description of Wyclif's tenets as heretical, for then he could strike at the master through his adherents.

About this time a Cistercian monk at Oxford referred to the Wycliffites contemptuously as 'Lollards.' This was a Flemish term for heretics because they were heard to mumble (Old Dutch *lollen*) their prayers. It became the usual name for followers of Wyclif.

Courtenay now moved against Oxford university, ordering the new chancellor, Robert Rigg, to publish the Blackfriars decrees there. Rigg responded by having the university sermon for Corpus Christi day preached by one of Wyclif's disciples. This was an occasion for a demonstration of support for the absent teacher. Courtenay immediately sent for Rigg and demanded the suspension of known Wycliffites and the confiscation of the master's books. When Rigg agreed to this two other leaders, Philip Repingdon and Nicholas Hereford, rode to John of Gaunt for help. The duke listened to them sympathetically but, in the end, advised them to make their peace with the archbishop. This was the end of Gaunt's public support of the followers of Wyclif, although he probably continued to give some protection behind the scenes. Without him they were helpless.

In the ensuing months there were moments of defiance from individuals but, by means of enquiry, expulsion, excommunication, search, imprisonment and threats, Courtenay eventually persuaded most of them to abjure their heresies. During Convocation, deliberately held at Oxford, the place that had taught them their errors, they were forced to read their recantations. Then they were absolved and reinstated. When John Aston, an energetic preacher, made his submission there were crowds of undergraduates at the door but none dare show their feelings; freedom of speech had been banished. Through the heavy hand of the zealous archbishop, the university of Oxford, which had been the first to welcome the early dawn of religious liberty, now ceased to fight against the arbitrary rule of the, as yet, unassailable Church.

There were still occasional pockets of resistance and Arundel continued to seek them out. His Constitutions of 1407 banned the unauthorised reading and teaching of Wyclif's works; they also ordered a monthly inquiry into the theological opinions of members of the university, specifying measures to be taken to stamp out heretical tendencies. These cannot have been entirely successful for, in 1410, fourteen of Wyclif's books were burnt at Carfax in the centre of Oxford.

Wyclif must have grieved at the fate of Oxford and the fall of his colleagues. His own presence had not been required, perhaps because of his physical disability, but probably mainly because Courtenay judged it wiser not to touch an already persecuted figure, popular with royalty and with rich and poor alike. An appearance before the Oxford Convocation would not have brought submission – 'What! I should live and be silent?... Never! Let the blow fall, I await its coming' – and his imprisonment might have led to widespread disaffection and perhaps even to the triumph of his views. So Courtenay left him to ponder on his failure.

Wyclif did not think that he had failed. Still burning with a sense of mission he adapted to the change – he could still work for his cause from Lutterworth. Even before he had left Oxford he had formed some of the keenest scholars into a group of 'poor priests' (or 'true men', 'faithful priests' or other similar title). He had sent these fervent evangelists out on preaching tours to spread his ideas and beliefs among townsfolk and villagers, merchants and knights. With this preparation, he expected that an informed people would be ready to welcome the desired reformation when it was begun by the king. Although he now realised that the great rebirth of the Church, starting at the top, was not going to happen in his lifetime, he never lost hope that one day there would be a national demand for reform.

When the Oxford scholars succumbed to Courtenay's pressure the task was taken over by others, probably unbeneficed clerks and some friars. They were not formed into an order, for Wyclif disapproved of orders, nor did they have a rule or a special habit. Rather like the first Franciscans, they went forth from Lutterworth to attempt the nearly-impossible. They taught on village-greens, in churchyards, in churches (when invited by patron or parish priest), as well as in the houses of peasants, merchants and gentry alike. They were constantly on the move because of Wyclif's fear that they might become 'possessioners' if attached to one particular place for long, and also because they could the more easily avoid being caught. They knew that theirs was a dangerous occupation for the Church authorities were determined to eradicate those who spread Wyclif's doctrines. A few of the preachers ended up in prison, many found local friends to hide them and some were protected by John of Gaunt himself, who, in Wyclif's words, 'was unwilling to punish faithful priests'.

Wyclif himself was not idle. He wrote of using 'the leisure I now enjoy from scholastic exercises in the end of my days for the special edification of the Church, by collecting together my plain sermons for the people.' These sermons, and other papers, were translated into English by their author and others and carried by the Poor Priests with the instructions that they 'must be adapted according to time and place.' Wyclif attached great importance to them, considering that preaching the gospel – a rare event in a parish church – was of more value than saying mass.

The gospel itself was a closed book to lay-people, for it was written in Latin and very little was passed on to them by a generally ignorant parish clergy. Wyclif wanted them to know for themselves about the life of Christ and the apostles and to understand which Christian traditions were (or were not) rooted in the scriptures. He himself knew the whole of the Latin Vulgate bible thoroughly and often illustrated his lectures and books by copious quotations from it. Now he decided that it must be translated into English for all, 'clergy or laity, male or female,' to read. He had an unusually high opinion of the laity and declared that the New

Testament was 'open to the understanding of simple men,' and that 'no man was so rude a scholar but that he might learn the words of the Gospel according to his simplicity'. Ordinary, uneducated English people had never been so praised by a distinguished university teacher before.

Up to this time there had been a few European translations of parts of the bible made for kings and monasteries. Anne of Bohemia brought German and Czech copies of the Gospels with her to England and some members of the English nobility had French translations. While these remained in monastic libraries or aristocratic closets the Church allowed their possession. It did not approve of translations for the common people made by the Waldensians and other heretical sects. This was just what Wyclif planned to provide – a translation of the entire Vulgate, not only for the wealthy but for the lower classes as well.

With Wyclif to inspire them the enormous enterprise was undertaken by a group of Oxford scholars. There were two versions. The first was a word for word translation, perhaps meant to help parish priests to interpret the meaning of the Latin gospels that they read at mass. It was begun under the direction of Nicholas Hereford who worked through the Old Testament and part of the Apocrypha. A note in the middle of a chapter, 'Here ends the translation of Nicholas Hereford', may mark the point which he had reached in the summer of 1382 when he fled the country. The work was completed in the next two years, probably by John Purvey with others.

Afterwards a second translation into easily understood English was made, which is usually attributed to Purvey. With the help of 'many good fellows and cunning' this was finished by 1397. It was a faithful, unbiased translation that even opponents could not criticise. Published with it was a lengthy General Prologue, making clear the author's heretical beliefs, which earned orthodox disapproval. It was welcomed by all except the Church hierarchy, being bought by the wealthy and read to less well-off people by the Poor Priests. For the followers of John Wyclif it possessed an absolute authority which displaced that of the authoritarian Church. It was copied and re-copied in part or whole and remained the only English bible for the next 150 years. More than 235 manuscripts are known to survive, in spite of many vicissitudes, mostly without the Wycliffite prologue. John of Gaunt's younger brother, the Duke of Gloucester, owned an illuminated copy of the first version which is now in the British Museum. Part of the second version (also illuminated) can be seen in the St. Peter Hungate Church Museum at Norwich. Queen Anne (d.1394) herself received a copy of the gospels, probably presented to her by a Lollard sympathiser at court. Arundel had sanctioned her possession of this, and other bishops gave similar permission to the wealthy. (This did not extend to the prologue, which was considered heretical). In later years, after the condemnation of the Wycliffite bible, it was wrongly assumed that such copies were of a pre-Wyclif translation (and therefore allowable), as Sir Thomas More did in 1528.

Wyclif spent two and a half very busy years at Lutterworth, continuing to write, encouraging the translators and the Poor Priests, talking to visiting disciples and never letting up on the urgent work he felt compelled to do. He knew that the end was approaching and on 28 December 1384, while hearing mass in his parish church, he had a second stroke. He died three days later without having spoken again. He had never been excommunicated or declared a heretic and so was buried in the churchyard at Lutterworth, the grave being marked by a stone slab. He died sure that he had started a movement that could not be halted, that many men and women would uphold his teachings and that one day these would prevail. England had to wait a century and a half for this, because the fundamental changes desired by thoughtful religious people could only be brought about if the king also, for whatever reason, wanted them, as Wyclif had foreseen.

Strangely enough, it was not in England but in a foreign land that Wyclif's ideas first gained national acceptance. This came about through the marriage of Anne of Bohemia to Richard II in 1382. The alliance brought Bohemian students to Oxford, where they drank in Wyclif's ideas and returned to their own country carrying manuscripts of his theological works.[1] Scholars at Prague university, townspeople and villagers responded so that a great movement under the leadership of John Hus demanded reform. In 1415 Hus was summoned before the council of Constance and, although he held the emperor's safe-conduct, he was condemned as a heretic and burnt, his ashes being cast into the Rhine. His followers immediately rose in rebellion and eventually, with the co-operation of their king (because it happened to suit him politically) achieved their desires – confirmed reluctantly by the pope in 1435. One of their leaders was the Englishman, Peter Payne, former principal of St. Edmund's Hall, Oxford, who had fled to Prague for safety in 1416 taking with him many of Wyclif's works.

---

[1] Because of the later burning of his books, many of Wyclif's Latin works survived only in Bohemia.

At Constance Wyclif also was declared a heretic and his bones were ordered to be dug up, removed from consecrated ground and burnt. Lutterworth was in the diocese of Lincoln, whose bishop was then Philip Repingdon, the former adherent of Wyclif, and he refrained from obeying the order. Not until a new bishop was enthroned were Wyclif's remains disturbed. In 1428 the burnt ashes were thrown into the nearby little river Swift, supposedly 'to the damnation and destruction of his memory'. But, through this act, Thomas Fuller, the seventeenth-century churchman and historian, saw a glorious remembrance for the great heresiarch: 'Thus this brook hath conveyed his ashes into Avon, Avon into Severn, Severn into the narrow seas, they into the main ocean. And thus the ashes of Wyclif are the emblem of his doctrine, which now is dispersed all the world over'.

Fuller's comment proved correct, for the Protestant churches of the sixteenth, seventeenth and eighteenth centuries put into practice most of Wyclif's precepts. These seem so normal now that it is astonishing that anyone ever had to fight for them. The Roman church, too, has accepted some of his suggestions: as early as the council of Trent (Session XIII, 1551) more frequent communion was recommended; the vernacular bible was made available, first to the clergy and later to the laity; the clergy are now supported by freely-given alms; services are simpler; excommunication is a weapon little used; and popes are seen to serve the servants of God and not themselves.

The far-seeing fourteenth-century reformer looked back to the life of Christ and his apostles and forward to a Church shorn of its complexities. The churches that inherited his principles and the Church that once denounced them can all admire his constancy and acknowledge the benefits they have derived from the ideals of Christian worship that he so tenaciously advocated.

3. THE LOLLARDS

a. *The missionaries*

Although Oxford university was no longer the home of Lollardy the ideas which had first been proclaimed there had long since found a sympathetic reception among thoughtful members of the lay community. They had spread, as a hostile chronicler put it, 'like the overwhelming multiplication of seedlings.' To prevent these taking root, in 1382 Archbishop Courtenay obtained from the king in parliament the right to arrest and imprison heretics. Thereafter Lollardy was driven underground and those who continued the work of evangelism did so knowing the danger.

The early leaders were some of Wyclif's academic colleagues who still refused to abandon their unorthodox opinions. After his master's death John Purvey went to Bristol and taught there and in the surrounding area. John Aston repented of renouncing his Wycliffite beliefs and went on preaching tours of the west country. He died about 1388, constant 'right perfectly unto his life's end'. He had been joined by Nicholas Hereford who was caught in Nottingham in 1387 and kept in the castle there; by the end of 1391 he had recanted and was rewarded with the chancellorship of Hereford cathedral. Purvey remained at large until 1400 and the following year this dedicated evangelist was obliged to make his recantation in public at St. Paul's Cross (a pulpit in St. Paul's churchyard). He was given a benefice in Kent but resigned it after three years. Presumably he went back to preaching the gospel, this time remaining successfully out of the Church's clutches. He was remembered as 'one of great authority' among the Lollards. The work of these men (and Repingdon's also) was not undone by their recantations. They had laboured long and hard in the field and passed on to others a living faith that could not be extinguished.

Even without the Oxford theologians the Lollards were not short of enthusiastic teachers. Many of these were chaplains and unbeneficed priests who had little in common with wealthy senior clergy. Unattached to particular parishes, they were free to move about as they wished, talking to people of their own sort and so spreading Lollard opinions far and wide. As they considered the laity to have an equality with the priesthood it was not long before self-appointed lay preachers followed in their footsteps. The first one known to us was William Smith, a blacksmith, who, with Richard Waytestathe, a chaplain, and William Swinderby, an unbeneficed clerk, formed a team with its headquarters in a deserted chapel outside Leicester. In Wyclif's lifetime they created a strong Lollard presence in the district, which included the mayor and some of the clergy.

Swinderby was a stirring preacher and among the earliest to interpret Wyclif's ideas to the uneducated majority, who welcomed them as people hitherto starved of the truth. 'One of the greatest... of Lollard evangelists'[1], to the Church authorities he represented danger. In 1382

[1] McFarlane, K. B., *Wycliffe and English Non-Conformity*, 120.

he was summoned before the bishop of Lincoln's court, where he was persuaded to recant by the threat of death by burning, although he denied the legality of this. During the next few years he continued his work in Coventry and the western border of Herefordshire. In 1389 the bishop of Hereford pronounced him 'a heretic...and seducer of the people and as such to be avoided by those faithful to Christ'. After that Swinderby retreated into Wales and was heard of no more. Proclamations were made threatening those who sheltered him with forfeiture of goods, but his presence was never betrayed.

A runaway London apprentice brought Lollardy to Northampton where he entered the household of the mayor, John Fox, then in his third term of office. Fox gave encouragement to Lollard converts until a rival merchant informed on him and in 1393 he was deposed by the government. The bishop of Lincoln thought that the greater part of the town was infected by heresy and a group of Lollards was arrested and imprisoned, although details of any trial are not known. Fox was elected for a fourth time in 1399, but nothing more is heard of Lollardy at Northampton.

Other missionaries journeyed to distant parts of the country – William Thorpe 'travelled about busily in the north country and in other diverse countries of England,' in the 'twenty winter and more' before his trial in 1407; Richard Wyche founded a Lollard cell in Newcastle, although it was discovered and, after his trial in the winter of 1402–3, he spent some time in the bishop of Durham's prison; some even went over the border into Scotland. The main Lollard areas, however, so far as may be judged from surviving records, were the Midlands, East Anglia, Kent, the Thames valley and the Bristol area.

In the fifteenth and sixteenth centuries itinerant preachers were often men, such as textile workers, whose jobs took them away from home and so gave them 'cover' for their evangelistic work. Others, like John Hacker, a London water-bearer, went when they could: in the 1520s, two of his group, Lawrence Maxwell and John Stacey 'once a year at their own costs went abroad [i.e. distant parts of England] to visit the brethren and sisters scattered abroad.'

The Lollard travellers provided a forum for all those who had at any time found fault with the behaviour of their parish priests, resented paying tithes, disliked having to confess their secret peccadilloes, questioned the value of images and pilgrimages and wondered about purgatory, indulgences and the efficacy of prayers for the dead. Listeners heard for the first time that none of these things was mentioned in the gospels and that no-one stood between themselves and God. This new-found knowledge appealed to discerning men and women of all social classes and they joined the growing band of earnest seekers after truth.

b. *The language of the people*

One of the main criticisms of the Church was its attitude to lay people in excluding them from the chancel, the language of the mass, taking communion (except once yearly at Easter) and the direct knowledge of the gospels. This would not do for the Lollard leaders who were determined that every member of the sect should be as well-prepared as themselves. As the prologue to the Wycliffite bible stated, 'God both can and may, if it liketh him, speed simple men, out[side] of the university, as much to know holy writ as masters in the university'. In order to bring this about, the training of preachers and the education of the fellowship was taken in hand. Naturally, English, the language of the people, was used, so that there was no impediment to understanding. So successfully was this done that a contemporary chronicler complained that 'both men and women were suddenly transformed into doctors of evangelical doctrine by means of the vernacular'.

Schools (or short courses) were held at which instruction was given on the bible and doctrine by experienced teachers. In 1424 Richard Belward, of Earsham, Norfolk, was accused of holding 'schools of Lollardy in the English tongue' at Ditchingham. In 1430, Hawise Moone, of Loddon, in the same county, remembered going to 'schools of heresy in privy chambers and privy places of ours'. There was much to learn and, in 1485, one student said, ' ... it is essential to attend the schools for a whole year before you will know the right faith'.

Study was based on the second version of the Wycliffite bible, sermons by Wycliff and other Lollard leaders and treatises on Lollard beliefs. One useful handbook contained information on canon law, notes for sermons, extracts from Wyclif's writings and translations of the Sunday gospels and epistles. Armed with knowledge from the schools and some personal scripts, the missionaries were well able to disseminate their message and to answer any questions that might be put to them.

The purchase of parchment and the time spent in copying literature would not have been possible without funds provided by gentry sympathisers, as well as safe houses in which to operate. Surviving manuscripts suggest that the reproduction was closely supervised and carefully executed. Because of the secret nature of the work little is known about where it was done, except for Braybrooke in Northamptonshire and Kemerton in Gloucestershire, parishes associated with the Lollard knight, Sir Thomas Latimer. The collection of texts at both these places brought two Bohemian scholars there in 1407 in order to copy some of Wyclif's Latin works to send home to Prague.

The documents produced were in easy-to-carry rolls and quires besides full-scale books. In these various forms appeared the bible (often separate gospels and epistles), sermon cycles, commentaries and shorter tracts. Apart from the bibles, many of these manuscripts survive and, as more must have been destroyed, they point to a large production and distribution. The lighter-weight manuscripts, in parchment covers, were carried by the teachers on their journeys and sometimes left for the further study of their congregations. One preacher wrote at the end of his treatise, 'Now sirs, the day is over and I may keep you no longer.... Nevertheless, I intend to leave [my sermon] written among you, and whoever likes may look over it....'

The Church authorities realised that an attack on the English language was necessary to stop the spread of heretical ideas culled from personal reading of the bible. Arundel's Constitutions of 1407 forbade, among other things, the ownership of the Wycliffite bible without his permission. From that time onwards the mere possession of the bible and related texts in English was sufficient to incriminate the holder.

This ban on the native speech extended to the basic elements of the faith: the first two Commandments might prevent people from worshipping the consecrated host and also images; even the Lord's Prayer might be construed as heretical because of its direct approach to God without the need for saintly intermediaries – a God to whom sins could be confessed and whose forgiveness did not depend on the absolution of a priest. Whereas in 1238 Bishop Grosseteste had wanted these taught in English and, in 1400, Mirk had advised parish clergy to do so, in the years following the Constitutions it was decreed that they be taught in Latin. Henceforth to know them in English was to risk being accused of Lollardy and in 1426 this happened to John Burrell, of the Norwich diocese, who had been taught them by his brother. This requirement seemed so ridiculous to William Wakeham of Devizes that, in 1437, he asserted that it was 'no better for laymen to say the *paternoster* in Latin than to say "bibble babble".'

In spite of the prohibition the missionaries went on proclaiming the gospel in English. When they arrived at their destinations they made contact with like-minded people (probably known through their families or trades) with whom they stayed. Meetings for local Lollards and possible recruits were held in private houses or work-places, disguised as family parties or business associations. They consisted of readings, instruction, explanation and discussion. After the itinerants had moved on, the study-groups continued to assemble together as opportunity occurred. They obtained the books which they needed from such centres as Braybrooke or professional stationers who were involved in Lollardy. Separate gospels or epistles might be afforded by even the humbler Lollards and the wealthier ones were prepared to pay a lot of money for larger volumes. A Norfolk man, Nicholas Belward, paid a high price, before 1429, for a copy of the New Testament, which he had bought in London and used for teaching purposes. The 'beautiful books of heresy' that William Pysford[1] of Coventry, and his son-in-law, William Wigston of Leicester (both wealthy merchants), were known to possess in 1511, must have been equally expensive. Sometimes goods were exchanged – 'a load of hay for a few chapters of St. James, or of St. Paul in English', or 'a tick of a featherbed'. The epistle of St. James and also the book of Revelation were particularly in demand for the support they gave to people suffering persecution. Some books were kept as personal property and others were loaned out from a 'library', like that of Robert Silkby in Coventry at the beginning of the sixteenth century.

To reach their buyers the books and pamphlets were hidden in capacious sleeves or among other merchandise. On arrival they were carefully concealed, like the books that John Stilman had hidden 'in an old oak' near Salisbury from 1505–7, and were brought out at suitable moments. William Wakeham said that he 'with other heretics and Lollards was accustomed and used to hear in secret places, in nooks and corners, the reading of the Bible in English, and to this reading gave attendance by many years'. In 1511 James Brewster, a carpenter of Colchester, said that he and others had 'been five times with William Sweeting in the field keeping beasts, hearing him read many good things out of a certain book'. Naturally also, readings occurred at home – in 1425 Margery, the wife of William Baxter, a wright of Martham in Norfolk, admitted that her husband had read a Lollard book to her when the day's work was done and had also held readings for groups who came to hear him.

---

[1] Executor of William Ford, who founded Ford's Hospital, Coventry, in 1508. He himself contributed money for the building and upkeep of this almshouse, which survives and is still in use today.

Many people learned long passages from the scriptures by heart, probably because they did not have their own copy and possibly also to avoid the danger of being found in possession of one. Some time before 1521 Alice Ashford of Chesham helped her nephew, James Morden, to learn part of the Beatitudes. After five visits to her he had it by heart and then went on to another section, the learning of which needed only two visits. At about the same time Alice Collins was noted for her good memory and used to be sent for to recite the scriptures at conventicles held in Burford.

The fact that there were already readers outside the ranks of the clergy and among the Lollards in the fourteenth and fifteenth centuries was due firstly to the necessity for literacy in business. Merchants, tradesmen and craftsmen needed to make orders, keep records and write letters, and to this end they had their apprentices and families taught to read and write. There were thus plenty of literate people able to read the bible and other works in English to any non-readers who were interested. Almost certainly among their listeners were some who were determined to learn to read for themselves. William Smith, one of the very first Lollards at Leicester, had taught himself to read and write and had become a noted teacher.

The result of all this searching of the scriptures was that a large number of knowledgeable people withdrew their allegiance from the catholic Church. They formed a separate sect which was the converse of the hitherto unchallenged dictatorial institution. Their beliefs were those of Wyclif, based on the bible which they had in their hands. They rejected Church rites and doctrines which were not mentioned in it – the papacy; the division placed between priests and people, because the bible said that *all* Christians were a 'holy priesthood' (1 Peter 2. 5, 9; Rev. 5. 10); the power of priests to 'make God' in the eucharist or to give absolution; confession to priests; the intercession of saints, the worship of them and their images, pilgrimages to their shrines and the indulgences which might be bought there (they especially disliked Thomas Becket, who had fought against English justice for the material interests of the Church); and the rites and ceremonies of the dead, which they saw as both mistaken and a means of making money out of the ignorant and gullible.

For the Lollards, English was the key to religious belief. Through it they could understand so well that an apprehensive cleric wrote, 'Every lewd [i.e. lay] man is become a clerk and talks in his terms'. The ordained clerks realised that there was an informed force in their midst that had to be reckoned with – and removed.

c. *Women Lollards*

As Lollards considered the laity to be the equals of the priesthood, so they also thought that women were the equals of men. Lollardy being essentially a family movement, the position of women within the family circle gave them opportunities for participation that were not available to them in the Church. In the privacy of the home they were able to teach children and servants to read and to understand Lollard beliefs. The arrangements for conventicles in their houses would often devolve upon them, as well as the provision of hospitality for travelling teachers. One housewife known to have done this was Hawise Moone, for she confessed that she and her husband had harboured heretics, saying, '... and them I have concealed, comforted, supported, maintained and favoured with all my power.'

When books were brought their distribution was often undertaken by women, as Alice Rowley of Coventry admitted doing prior to 1511. Many had collections of books themselves, like Mrs. Dolie (at Amersham in 1521) who kept them in her own room and set great store by them. Such women, especially mistresses of large households, had the time to study and it is not surprising that they were consulted on the meaning of certain texts and rites. In 1522 William Rayland, while dining with Mrs. Girling, a refugee in Essex, asked her about the meaning of 'the sacrament of the altar'. Several of these scholarly women became notable preachers, a fact deplored by a late-fourteenth-century critic in a sermon. '... simple men and women ... teach and scatter the word of God.' Some married couples formed active partnerships and made long missionary journeys together, sustaining Lollard friends and converting others – William and Joan White in Norfolk and Suffolk at the beginning of the fifteenth century, for example, and Thomas Man and his wife in extensive campaigns in the south and east of England a century later.

The senior clergy, subjected as they were to the Church's view of women as inferior beings, tended to underestimate the female influence in the spread of Lollardy. This may have been encouraged by the women themselves, some of whom attempted to hide their qualifications, like Juliana Young in Coventry in 1511, who denied that she could read until Robert Silkby's testimony betrayed the fact.

Much of the women teachers' work was done within the domestic scene – Margery Baxter talked while she was 'sitting and sewing in her chamber by the fireplace' – and was only brought to light during heresy hunts. Even then, very often, the women were seen merely as appendages of their menfolk, involved through family circumstances. To bishops it was beyond consideration that they might have a better understanding and experience of the Christian faith than themselves. Yet these same women played a memorable part in helping to preserve and continue a religious movement in which they firmly believed and for which they were ready, if called on, to die.

d. Persecution

As members of a persecuted sect it behoved the Lollards to walk warily. They laid low and lived a secret life of codes – perhaps 'May we all drink of a cup' was one –, signs, aliases, pretended reasons for meetings and identifications of each other as 'known men'[1] and 'known women'. Priests who tried to delve into the minds of suspect parishioners were met with defensive answers. Such resistance could be taught and, in 1511, Alice Harding of Amersham advised Richard Bennett how to conceal his true opinions when the priest called.

The majority of the Lollards lived at home and, in the interests of peace and quiet, made some attempt to conform to the minimum requirements of the Church. On the whole, they went to their parish church every Sunday and complied with what went on there; indeed, the Coventry Lollards, who were tried in 1511–12, 'pretended most show of worship and devotion at the holding up of the sacrament'. Each year they kept up appearances by confessing in Lent and receiving communion at Easter. This effort to remain inconspicuous was expressed by seven Reading Lollards, who, in 1499, had received the sacrament 'only for dread of the people and to eschew the jeopardy and danger that we dread to fall in if we had not done as other Christian people did'. Refusal to keep these compulsory observances was noted as heretical behaviour. Margery Baxter gave herself away when she was seen to be simmering bacon on the fire during Lent. Simon Ward, a London paviour, was noticed because he had not been to the Lenten confession nor the Easter Communion in 1491.

Lollards could also be spotted by their failure to give reverence and make donations to images. Towards the end of Richard II's reign William Dynot and three other tradesmen of Nottingham who were guilty of this, were taken to London and examined before the archbishop

---

[1] First recorded about 1450.

of York. They were forced to repeat this oath: 'I, ... swear to God ... that from this day forward I shall worship images, with praying and offering unto them in the worship of the Saints that they be made after, and also I shall no more despise pilgrimage.' It went against the grain for any Lollard to behave in this way and Robert Hatchett so far forgot himself as to say to someone making an offering to the statue of the Virgin in the Carmelite convent at Coventry in 1486, 'May God help thee. Thou art a fool'. Similarly, Mrs. Dolie refused to allow her maid to make a proxy pilgrimage to the statue of Our Lady of Walsingham on behalf of her dead husband, saying that images were only carpenters' chips. In 1528, Marian Westden of Colchester tried to disguise her true beliefs by giving the smallest number of candles to images that she thought necessary to baffle prying eyes.

The dislike of oaths was a sure sign of a Lollard. When Chaucer's Poor Parson remonstrated with the Host for swearing 'for god's bones' and 'by god's dignity', the inn-keeper knew him for what he was and responded, 'I smell a loller in the wind'.

A wedding would be an ideal opportunity for Lollard teaching. At the reception of Nicholas Durdant's daughter at Henley, prior to 1521, the guests assembled in a barn to hear an epistle of St. Paul. Those who were not Lollards would realise what was going on and may even have been present, out of curiosity, at the reading.

For a man to die in his heresy, without the last rites of the Church, argued a firm conviction in his faith. Such a person was John Morden of Chesham. In 1514, when he was dying, he sent for his son-in-law, Richard Ashford, and asked him about his religious opinions. After listening to a statement of orthodoxy, he said, 'Thou art deceived,' and proceeded to tell him of his own beliefs. As a parting gift he handed over a book and died knowing that his last action was to bring another convert to Lollardy.

Even in their wills the Lollards could be recognised. Not for them elaborate funeral obsequies. Edward Cheyne, son of a Lollard knight, directed by his will, dated 1415, that his funeral pall be made not of 'cloth of gold neither of silk but a russet cloth'; Sir Thomas Broke (in 1439) wanted only a simple funeral attended by poor men in white; and Sir Thomas Latimer (in 1401) and his wife, Anne (in 1402), did not desire the usual memorial masses. Instead of bequests to churches and images, monasteries and mendicant orders, their money went to 'the poor blind, the poor halt, and the poor feeble', according to Wyclif's reminder of Christ's teaching. From a will and funeral of this sort it would be obvious to onlookers that the deceased had been a Lollard and that probably most of the mourners were also. It was enough to make men think again about the moral and spiritual claims of both Lollardy and the Church.

These and other more overt actions by bolder spirits would make it difficult, if not impossible, for Lollards to go unnoticed among more obedient parishioners. For the most part they were left to mind their own business and even archidiaconal visitations did not always reveal their presence. Their discovery depended on particularly zealous bishops stirring their subordinates into action. Then the unpleasant process of questioning everyone was set in motion to persuade people to inform on their neighbours until the unfortunates were exposed.

Those who could, especially the teachers, tried to flee from probable arrest. John White of Chesham, in 1464, was warned by a friend that the bishop's officers were coming to Amersham and so was able to get out of harm's way. People living near diocesan boundaries were able to leave a diocese where persecution threatened for an adjacent one whose bishop had not yet taken action. Several communities survived in this way. There were connections between Lollard groups in different parts of the country so that people on the run knew where they might find a refuge. Henry Miller fled from Amersham to Chelmsford and Thomas Geoffrey from Uxbridge to Ipswich in 1521. About the same time Alice Johnson and her husband arrived in Boxstead, Essex, evading persecution in Salisbury. Thomas Man and his wife, who had taught for nearly forty years, helped five families to escape from the Chilterns in 1511 to safe places in Norfolk and Suffolk. A few years later Thomas himself sought refuge in the house of Marion Randal and her husband in Rickmansworth. Some must have travelled at night by field paths and country lanes, others went more openly, perhaps assuming a different identity – Robert Silkby took the alias 'Dumbleby' when hurrying from Coventry.

Those who were unable to escape were arrested on a charge of suspicion and their houses were searched for heretical books in English. If there had been enough time they would have tried to get rid of this incriminating evidence – Alice Rowley was able to burn her books; and when Thomas Watts of Dogmersfield, Hampshire, was arrested in 1514, his wife burnt one of his books and hid two others in a ditch. The captured Lollards were taken to the bishop's prison and eventually came before the bishop's court. Overawed by the trappings of ecclesiastical authority, at the mercy of canon lawyers and without any legal assistance, it is little wonder that most of them recanted. If they admitted their guilt they then took an oath renouncing their former beliefs and promising to give the names of their associates. This was followed by the performance of a penance – usually appearing bare-foot and bare-headed in the nearest market-place on market-day and also in the Sunday procession at the parish church, offering a candle and enduring a beating.

If the charge of suspicion was denied the accused was interrogated, with the help of witnesses, in order to force a confession. Stubborn ones might hold out for a time for, as Bishop Blyth of Coventry and Lichfield wrote in 1511, 'They will not confess but by pain of imprisonment'. He was proved correct by Alice Rowley, then languishing in his prison. During examination she said stoutly, 'My belief is better than theirs, save that we dare not speak it ... I care not, they cannot hurt me, my Lord knoweth my mind already'. But the spell in the bishop's prison did its work and seven weeks later she abjured.

One wonders if the harsh conditions of the prison alone were enough to break her will or if some sort of physical pressure might have been used. There are certain dark hints that torture may have induced some victims to confess or abjure. Arundel himself said to William Thorpe, then a prisoner in his castle of Saltwood, ' ... thou shalt go thither where Nicholas Hereford and John Purvey were harboured, and I undertake, ere this day eight days, thou shalt be right glad for to do what thing that ever I bid thee do.'

e. *Death by burning*

In the years following Wyclif's death his disciples continued to work for the reforms that he had planned. In 1395 they nailed a manifesto concerning 'the reformation of holy church in England' to the door of Westminster hall when parliament was sitting.[1] Since the temporal possessions and offices of the clergy were criticised in this the Church authorities were alarmed and they petitioned the king for the introduction of the death penalty for heresy. Their request was not granted although Richard II disapproved of the Lollards – his description of himself can still be read on his tomb in Westminster abbey: 'He overthrew the heretics and laid their friends low.' However, Richard was deposed and dead by the end of 1399 and the new king, Henry IV, having come to the throne with the help of Arundel, agreed to the Church's

---

[1] A more detailed Lollard proposal for the redistribution of the Church's wealth was addressed to Henry V and parliament in 1410. This is referred to in Shakespeare's *Henry V* (I, i).

request.

In 1401 the statute *De Heretico Comburendo* (On the Burning of Heretics) was passed. This declared that, after guilt had been established in the Church courts, obdurate and relapsed heretics should be sent to the civil power which was obliged to carry out the punishment. William Lyndwood, in his *Provinciale*, makes it quite clear that this meant 'handed over for the fire'. England was thus brought into line with the rest of Christendom so that, as Pope Boniface IX had written to Richard II and the two archbishops, ' ... not one spark [of heresy would] remain hid under the ashes, but that it would be utterly put out'.

Only one member of the hierarchy, Reginald Pecock, bishop of Chichester (c.1390–c.1461), ever suggested that reasoned argument should be attempted in order to bring the Lollards back to the fold, before 'fire or sword or hangment' were thought about. Otherwise, he wrote, the clergy would be blamed at the Last Judgement. For this and other novel ideas this enlightened prelate was himself sentenced as a heretic and given the choice of abjuration or becoming 'the fuel of the fire as well as the food of the burning.' As he always acknowledged the authority of the Church he chose the former, was then deprived of his bishopric and thereafter confined to Thorney abbey, Cambridgeshire, Tolerance had been rejected.

Even before the statute of heresy became law the first martyr was burned at Smithfield in London. He was William Sawtry, a Norfolk chaplain who had previously abjured and was now condemned as a lapsed heretic, although the death penalty had not existed when his faults were committed. There is no doubt that the fearsome fate of being roasted alive acted as a deterrent. The very week that Sawtry died John Purvey was reduced to making his recantation; and a hundred years later Thomas Houre of Amersham told Alice Sanders that, because many people were being arrested for heresy, he 'would lean that way no more.'

To the former penances for abjured Lollards was added another – the carrying of a faggot in church and market-place. Afterwards the life-long wearing of an embroidered faggot-badge served as a reminder of the fate that would await them should they forget their oath. This was a sign of disgrace and, in the reign of Henry VIII, John Hig of Cheshunt asked his bishop for permission to remove it as no-one would give him a job while he wore it.

The second person to be burned was John Badby, a tailor of Kemerton, who was arrested in 1409 and sent to London. Faced with the might of Church and State in St. Paul's this ordinary subject refused to budge from his opinions, so he was condemned to be burnt. As the stake was being prepared at Smithfield the young Prince of Wales, the future Henry V, promised him freedom and a pension for life if only he would forsake his heresy. Nothing could shake Badby's fortitude and the pile of wood was lit. His screams caused Henry to think that he had changed his mind and water was thrown on the flames. When the suffering Badby understood why, he remained adamant in his convictions so the fire was relit and the martyr died. In five years time Henry V would 'beat the French at Agincourt, but there was something here beyond his understanding and beyond his power'.[1]

Henry V had to do with a more highly-placed Lollard than Badby. This was Sir John Oldcastle (Lord Cobham, by marriage), a member of his own household, who had probably been converted as a youth by William Swinderby. When heretical tracts of his were found in an illuminator's shop Arundel informed the king that he 'was and is the principal harbourer, promoter and defender' of heretics, especially in the dioceses of London, Rochester and Hereford. At first Henry tried personal persuasion but, when that failed, he allowed the arrest and trial of his courtier. Oldcastle refused to abjure and was handed over to the secular arm. Henry postponed the final penalty for forty days and during that time Oldcastle escaped from the Tower. In his anger at being persecuted he organised a Lollard rising in order, presumably, to make reforms. The government got wind of it so that, when the small rebel band arrived at the gates of London, it was easily overwhelmed. Many were captured, some of whom were hanged, but Oldcastle himself got away. There was a price on his head but he was not given up and was only captured after two and a half years on the run. At the end of 1417 he was burnt, suspended by the waist over a fire in London, where his plan had failed. To the king he was a traitor, to the Church a heretic, but to his fellow-Lollards an unflinching leader and a martyr.

Although most Lollards did not take part in the revolt it did their cause much harm as, from that time, Lollardy was often linked in the official mind with treason. The State as well as the Church became their enemy. In future, there were no knights or nobles who would risk losing life and lands for what was looked on as a subversive movement. Without protectors of this sort Lollardy could only survive by trying to keep out of sight.

---

[1]Trevelyan, G. M., *England in the Age of Wycliffe*, 335.

At intervals during the next hundred or more years there were prosecutions by heresy-hunting bishops and one or more burnings usually followed. Between the years 1401 and 1525 nearly 100 men and women were destroyed in this way. Their names, where known, make a roll of honour of lowly, heroic, bible-loving Christians, who went to their deaths believing steadfastly that 'the word of God sufficeth to man's salvation,'[1] without any need of the mediation of a materialistic and repressive Church. John Claydon welcomed a reading-group into his London house and in 1415 his books were burned with him. William White, on his way to the stake in the Lollards' Pit at Norwich[2] in 1428, was struck on the mouth by one of the bishop's servants to prevent him from preaching to the people for the last time. John Goose, from the Chilterns, was taken home by the sheriff of London in 1474 for a little kindly persuasion; he asked for meat and, while eating it, said to those present, 'I eat now a good and competent dinner, for I shall pass a little sharp shower ere I go to supper', and, when he had finished, he asked to be taken to his execution. In 1494 Joan Boughton, who was more than eighty years old, was burnt at Smithfield, and possibly also her daughter, Lady Young. The latter was the widow of a former Lord Mayor and it may be that the killing of such socially important people at a time when there was an upsurge in Lollardy, was meant to be a deterrent to possible recruits.

The slaughter of the helpless went on into the sixteenth century. In 1511 two leaders of the Kentish Lollards, William Carder and Agnes Grebill (then aged sixty), both of Tenterden, were burnt in Canterbury; other active members of the group were forced to witness the burning of Carder, among whom were Agnes Grebill's husband and two sons. At Coventry, during the winter of 1511–12, 74 people, of whom a third were women, were arrested and tried for heresy; the trials ended with the condemnation and burning of Joan Washingby (or Ward), whose twenty-year involvement with the movement had at last been uncovered. Thomas Man, who claimed at his trial that he and his wife had made between 500 and 700 converts, was burned at Smithfield in 1518. In 1520 'Seven Godly Martyrs' (including Widow Smith) were burnt at Coventry, mainly because they had taught their families the Lord's Prayer and the Ten Commandments in English, facts which had been checked by questioning the children concerned. Two years later one of

---

[1] William Thorpe said this to Arundel during his examination at Saltwood castle.
[2] A commemorative plaque on Bridge House, Riverside Road, is near the site, to which Lollards' Road leads.

their leaders, Robert Silkby, was captured and was burnt there also.[1]

Great crowds attended the burnings and some fervent observers must have approved – in 1463 a London goldsmith made a bequest of about £60 to pay for faggots for the burning of heretics. It cannot be supposed, however, that everyone enjoyed the spectacle of otherwise harmless and even respected fellow-countrymen and -women being consumed by the flames and sometimes they dared to make known their aversion. Richard Wyche, burnt in 1440 after forty years missionising, was considered a holy man by the common people; his death was followed by disturbances at Smithfield, so that the lord mayor and aldermen had to take precautions in order to preserve the peace.

A condemned heretic died knowing that his heirs suffered also, for his property was forfeit to the crown. A Bisham woman who abjured in the winter of 1502-3 remarked on the unfairness of this, saying that the people who had been recently burnt at Wycombe had been put to death for the sake of their goods. Similarly there were mutterings among the citizens of Coventry about the cruelty of the sheriffs who took all the possessions from the families of the dead heretics, leaving them destitute. Their behaviour compared ill with that of the victims, of whom a contemporary said, 'This is certain, that in godliness of life, they differed from all the rest of the city'. Perhaps these words may express the opinion of the mass of ordinary English people concerning the Lollards in their midst who only wanted to follow the commandments of Christ.

f. Richard Hunne

Richard Hunne was a wealthy merchant-tailor and a freeman of the city of London, known as 'a fair dealer among his neighbours' and 'an especial father of the poor'. In 1511 his baby son died and the rector of his parish church, St. Mary's Spittle, Whitechapel, claimed the bearing-sheet[2] as a mortuary. Hunne could easily have afforded to part with the robe – he was 'well worth a thousand marks' (say £100,000 in modern money), according to Sir Thomas More, – but he objected on principle. His reason was that, while mortuaries were supposed to be taken from the property of deceased persons, the dead child had not owned the bearing-sheet. The rector took the matter to the ecclesiastical court at

---

[1] The names of these men and women, together with those of later Protestant martyrs, are commemorated on the Martyrs' Memorial, erected in 1910 near the former Martyrs' Field, the site of the burnings.
[2] See Chapter Two lc.

Lambeth which, in 1512, found, not surprisingly, in his favour.

Hunne was not disposed to accept this without a fight and, in 1513, under the Statute of *Praemunire*, he sued the rector in the king's court. This statute had been interpreted in 1496 as giving people the right to take ecclesiastical law-suits concerning temporal causes to the civil court. Even so, it required strong nerves to challenge the power of the Church courts and no-one had yet done so. Only a rich man who could risk losing would dare to take on the age-old rights of the Church. Hunne was hopeful of the outcome and told his friends that it would make legal history as 'Hunne's Case'.

It became a test-case affecting all minors and married women, none of whom possessed any property in law, yet from whose families a mortuary would be sought on their deaths. Church officials were alarmed for, if Hunne were successful, thousands of such cases would follow, and rectors, vicars and monasteries owning appropriated churches would lose a useful part of their income. It was essential that action be taken before the case was settled, and the Church used its one sure weapon. Towards the end of 1514, on the orders of William FitzJames, bishop of London, Hunne was arrested on a charge of heresy and incarcerated in the bishop's prison near St. Paul's, known, from its usual occupants, as the Lollards' Tower.

Hunne had been heard to defend Joan Baker, a known Lollard who had abjured in 1511. Nevertheless, he was a devout man, going to mass daily and, on one occasion at least, attending vespers. Although a Lollard sympathiser, he may not actually have been a member of the sect. Londoners thought that he 'was made an heretic for suing a *praemunire*', that is, as an act of reprisal.

On 2 December he was taken to the bishop's palace at Fulham for interrogation. The most serious charge was that he had epistles, gospels and other books in English. Hunne admitted that he may have behaved unwisely, said that he was sorry and submitted to the bishop's correction. He was then taken back to the Lollards' Tower. The next step should have been his abjuration and public penance, but this would not have settled the *praemunire* case about which the Church was so apprehensive. The turn of events brought new problems for, on the morning of Monday 4 December, Hunne was found hanging in his cell. Nothing was disturbed until a coroner's jury of 24 citizens met there the next morning. From the state of the body and the cell it was obvious to them that Hunne had been murdered.

Interviews of witnesses went on during the next few weeks, including that of Charles Joseph, the bishop's summoner and gaoler, who was removed from sanctuary to the Tower. After attempting an alibi he at length admitted that he, together with Dr. William Horsey, the bishop's chancellor and the custodian of the Lollard's Tower, and John Spalding, the bell-ringer of St. Paul's, had strangled Hunne and then hanged the body, intending to give the impression that Hunne had committed suicide. The verdict, probably given towards the end of February, 1515, was of wilful murder by Dr. Horsey, Joseph and Spalding, who were immediately arrested to stand trial at the next assizes.

In the meantime the bishop, who may, or may not, have been implicated, had to decide what to do about the body. If Christian burial was allowed it would be admitting that Hunne had not been a heretic and had been wrongly arrested and imprisoned. A post-mortem trial was held in the lady chapel of St. Paul's, presided over by FitzJames assisted by three other bishops and some thirty senior clergy, in the watchful presence of the lord mayor, aldermen and sheriffs. For this, new witnesses and evidence not mentioned at Fulham were produced, the result being that Hunne was declared a heretic. Four days later, on 20 December, his body was burnt at Smithfield. This sentence meant that his considerable property was forfeit to the crown and that his widow and two young daughters were reduced to poverty.

A newly-elected parliament met in February and the Commons showed that they were behind the Hunne jury. They promoted a bill for the restitution of Hunne's property to his family, which was thrown out by the Lords of whom the majority were churchmen.[1] Feelings were running high and FitzJames, anxious about his chancellor, exclaimed in the Lords that the Commons were trying to make out that the Hunne jury were 'true men', when they were really 'false perjured caitiffs.'

The bishop was fearful of the coming trial and in desperation he wrote to Wolsey for help, saying that he was sure that if his chancellor were 'tried by any twelve men in London' they would 'condemn [his] clerk though he was as innocent as Abel'. Wolsey arranged that, after pleading not guilty, Horsey should be fined and discharged. The chancellorship had to be given up and the former holder sought future preferment in the provinces. Joseph and Spalding were also discharged.

The whole affair had London in a turmoil and brought to the fore so

---

[1] The 1523 parliament succeeded in obtaining a grant of all Hunne's property to his daughter Margaret and her husband, Roger Whaplod. Obstacles must have been put in the way of this, for the Whaplods were still petitioning for help some time after 1536, because they had 'seven small daughters to support'.

many Lollard and anti-clerical sentiments that the bishop told the Lords that, unless something was done, he 'dare not keep [his] own house, for heretics.' At the same time, the papal collector and later historian, Polydore Vergil, wrote to a cardinal in Rome that the people would be raging against the clergy but for the king's peace-making efforts. (All this happened long before Martin Luther's name was known or Henry VIII had clapped eyes on Anne Boleyn).

The discord remained. When the lawyer, Simon Fish, in his *Supplication of Beggars* (1529), wrote, 'If poor Richard Hunne had not sued a priest, he would have yet been alive', no-one needed to ask who Richard Hunne was; and his question to the king, 'Did not Dr. Horsey murder Richard Hunne when he sued for your writ of *Praemunire?*' would have found a similarly knowledgeable reader.

The injustice of it all rankled with the Londoners, who waited for their chance to right the wrong. It came with the parliament of 1529 when 'men began charitably to desire a reformation, and ... to show their grudges.' The king, by then wanting a divorce, wished to put pressure on the pope and was not averse to a Commons attack on ecclesiastical privileges. The first thing the lower house did was to introduce a bill limiting mortuaries and this the Lords passed, although it 'sore displeased' parsons and vicars. After that, no longer could mortuaries be demanded from the relatives of minors and married women. The abuse that had cost Richard Hunne his life was at last forcibly removed, fifteen years after he had been foully done to death in the Lollards' Tower.

g. *The Lollards and the Reformation*

In 1511 Erasmus joked that the price of fuel was rising because 'the heretics cause so many holocausts, and yet their numbers grow'. This comment bore witness to the fact that, in the early years of the sixteenth century, despite all attempts to subdue it, Lollardy was a force to be reckoned with. It was attracting newcomers from the higher ranks of society and even from within the Church itself: in 1506 the prior of St. Osyth, Essex, who had been converted by William Sweeting, was forced to abjure, as was the prior of a Rochester hospital in 1525; and Richard Bayfield, a monk and chamberlain of Bury St. Edmund's, left his wealthy abbey and became an active Lollard, standing trial and abjuring in 1528, but relapsing and being burnt in 1531.

As 'a man sorrowing the decay of the Church,' John Colet, Dean of St. Paul's, dared to address Convocation in 1512 on that Church's failings. He spoke in Latin, but later, when he preached in English on the reforms that he thought ought to be made, great crowds of lay-folk came to listen. The fame of his sermons brought two Lollards, Thomas Geoffrey and John Butler, from Uxbridge on several Sundays to hear some of their long-held beliefs spoken of publicly in the pulpit. Colet certainly had Lollard inclinations: he had read Wyclif's books and was referred to by Erasmus, with some amusement, as 'some Wycliffite, I suppose'; he had also translated the paternoster into English and spoken against the veneration of images. For these reasons he was charged with heresy by FitzJames and only rescued by the efforts of the more equitable archbishop of Canterbury.

The authorities were worried and Convocation, meeting in 1514, declared that the suppression of heresy was its chief task. A series of persecutions between the years 1510 and 1528 in the dioceses of London, Lincoln and Salisbury, was on a greater scale than ever before and accounted for the arrest of a thousand Lollards with the usual consequent abjurations and burnings.

Help was now at hand from a foreign source. In 1517 Martin Luther challenged the Church by nailing his ninety-five theses to the door of the castle church at Wittenberg. Copies of these and other writings were quickly distributed by means of the printing-presses[1] and very soon Lutheran ideas percolated into England. They were discussed at Cambridge university and more and more educated voices began to be heard in criticism of the Church and its doctrines. In 1525 Thomas Bilney left Cambridge for a preaching tour of East Anglia and some Essex Lollards made a special journey to Ipswich to hear him.[2] Lollards welcomed the new Protestants and, in fact, gradually merged with them because they shared similar religious beliefs – on the reading of the bible in English, the veneration of saints, image-worship, pilgrimages, transubstantiation, clerical endowments and the unbiblical office of the pope. As Tunstall, FitzJames's successor as bishop of London, wrote to Erasmus in 1523, 'It is no question of pernicious novelty; it is only that new arms are being added to the great crowd of Wycliffite heresies'.

Perhaps more than anything, the vernacular bible provided the main meeting-point between old and new. Since the translation of the Wycliffite bible, the English language had developed and the fourteenth-century rendering must have seemed in some ways obscure to sixteenth-century readers. For those newly-interested an up-to-date

---

[1] This mid-fifteenth-century German invention had recently been improved to give speedier production.
[2] Six years later he was burnt in the Lollards' Pit at Norwich.

printed version was needed. In 1526 William Tyndale, an English fugitive in Germany, brought out his translation of the New Testament from the original Greek (and later the Old Testament using the original Hebrew).

The bible in English was still a forbidden book, as Thomas Davy of Cranbrook, Kent, wrote in 1528: '... no man in England may speak of the New Testament on pain of bearing a faggot.' Copies of the recent translation were purchased and brought into the country secretly and this was organised by a Lollard association known as the Christian Brethren. With the experience of more than a century behind them the Lollards had become adept at the surreptitious conveying of illicit literature about the country and it was along their lines of communication that Tyndale's New Testament was carried. Some 64,000 copies were soon in circulation. John Stacey, Lawrence Maxwell and Robert Newton (members of John Hacker's London group), Richard Harman (who hailed from the Lollard town of Cranbrook), and Richard Bayfield (the former monk) were all involved in this, as also was John Tewkesbury, a London leather-merchant, who became the last Lollard martyr (burnt at Smithfield, 1531).

Report of the new bible caused John Tyball and Thomas Hilles, two Lollards from Steeple Bumpstead in Essex, to come up to London to buy a New Testament from Robert Barnes, an Augustinian friar who had become a Lutheran at Cambridge. With them they brought 'certain old books that they had' – gospels and epistles – as evidence of good faith, and were probably disconcerted when Barnes was rather disparaging about these ancient treasures. At this meeting the old dissenters reached out to the men of the 'new learning' and each immediately trusted the other. The two Lollards went away happily with their modern New Testament (having paid the equivalent of the weekly wage of a skilled craftsman for it), after being asked to 'keep it close', for Barnes 'would be loth that it should be known'.

It is likely that at other similar meetings manuscripts written by Lollards themselves were produced. At least ten Lollard texts – such as tracts on Thorpe's and Oldcastle's trials,[1] and the General Prologue to the Wycliffite bible – impressed the new reformers. They were pleased to discover and publish the writings of long-dead predecessors, for they

---

[1] Oldcastle's subsequent reputation as a hero and martyr forced Shakespeare, in 1598, to change the name of Prince Hal's companion in *Henry IV* from Oldcastle to Falstaff. *The Complete Oxford Shakespeare*, ed. S. Wells and G. Taylor (1986) has reversed this in *Henry IV Part I*.

provided early precedents and honourable authorities for their own beliefs and labours. One editor left archaic words unchanged deliberately as proof of antiquity, and said he hoped to come across 'more such holy relics' for his readers.

Through their contacts with Lollards the new reformers realised that they themselves had a long tradition stretching back to Wyclif, who they saw as the 'morning star in the midst of a cloud,' who had 'remained for many days as the faithful witness in the church.'[1] They revered also the noble and dedicated men and women who had suffered before them with no bolt-holes to fly to in Holland, Germany or Switzerland. The vital part that they had played in the long struggle for freedom of worship was told when better days came. John Foxe, who had himself been a refugee from persecution, gave them a deserved place in the history of their troubled times and enshrined their names in his celebrated book, the *Acts and Monuments*. This comprehensive work, more popularly known as Foxe's *Book of Martyrs*, was published in English in 1563, following an earlier Latin version.[2] Carefully collected from bishops' registers, chronicles and eye-witnesses' accounts are the numerous stories of 'the secret multitude of true professors' – those men and women who, down-trodden by a mighty, heartless corporation, yet held firmly to their biblical beliefs; who refused, even as they lived in permanent danger, even as they perished in the flames, to acknowledge that the Church, which had the power to punish and kill them, possessed also the only approach to God. The Lollards had read the gospels in English and believed that Jesus was 'the way, the truth and the life' and that no-one could go to the Father but by Him.

Simon Fish's *Supplication of Beggars* was written in the form of a petition to the king. It was a long tirade against the clergy and the wealth that they amassed by tithes, probates, mortuaries, dispensations, fines, prayers to deliver souls from purgatory and other unjust fees. People who protested, said the author, were called heretics, made to do penance or burned at the stake. The king is advised to whip the 'holy thieves' and set them to work – then should the gospel be preached in England. It was

---

[1] Description given by John Bale in 1548. It was added to by Daniel Neal in a history of the Puritans (1732–8) and became the famous phrase, 'the morning star of the Reformation'.

[2] The Canterbury Convocation of 1571 ordered a copy to be installed in every cathedral church. Many parish churches chose to do the same. Some, perhaps of later editions, are still there, as at Kinver, Staffordshire, and St. Andrew Undershaft, London, for instance. With the Bible and the Prayer Book it was also bought for private homes.

said that the king carried this pamphlet about in his pocket. When it was written the Church still held sway with the same implacable despotism as in previous centuries. But that very year a parliament met that began to demolish the unwieldy structure with the consent of the king. Wyclif had foreseen that the royal leadership was essential for a successful attack on the Church, and now, with the concerted action of king and people, nothing could stop the coming of the longed-for Reformation any longer.

The most important positive contribution of the Lollards to the Reformation was their emphasis on the bible as the fount of religious knowledge and the desirability of its being available to all. Their ancient prayer, 'Would God that every parish church in this land had a good Bible', was answered in 1538. Henry VIII was then so impressed with Coverdale's translation that he said, '... in God's name let it go abroad among our people.' Following the royal permission, hoarded copies of the scriptures must have been brought out from their hiding-places to be openly displayed by proud owners. No longer was an English bible a dangerous possession.

In the Church of England, when it was eventually established in 1559, almost all the reforms that the Lollards had worked for so assiduously were accomplished. There was much for them to thank God for although they must have been disappointed that the new Church was still ruled by a priestly hierarchy – there was no priesthood of all believers. Women, especially, who had played an equal part with men in the teaching of the scriptures and Lollard beliefs and were 'as learned as was the parish priest,' must have felt that they were relegated to the background once more.

As members of a resilient minority the constant and pious Lollards had kept alive, in spite of great tribulation, a marvellous spirit of independence, daring to be different while all about them were meekly accepting orthodoxy. Their ideas influenced the reformers from the continent, who were proud to be linked with them, and the Protestant Church of England recognised its debt to them. Above all, they had made it clear that the medieval Church had been governed by fallible men and that no human-being had the God-given right to dictate how another should worship God.

BIBLIOGRAPHY

ASTON, M. *Lollards and Reformers* (1984).

CATTO, J. I. 'John Wyclif and the Cult of the Eucharist', in *Studies in Church History, Subsidia 4* (1985).
CROSS, C. *Church and People*, 1450–1660 (1976).
CROSS, C. ' 'Great Reasoners in Scripture': The Activities of Women Lollards, 1380–1530', in *Studies in Church History, Subsidia 1* (1978).
CROSS, C. 'Popular Piety and the Records of the Unestablished Churches, 1460–1660', in *Studies in Church History* Vol. II (1975).
DAVIS, J. F. *Heresy and Reformation in the South-east of England, 1520–1559* (1983).
DAVIS, J. F. 'Lollard Survival and the Textile Industry in the South-east of England', in *Studies in Church History*, Vol. 3 (1966).
DAVIS, J. F. 'Lollardy and the Reformation in England', in *Archiv für Reformationgeschichte*, Vol. 73 (1982).
DEANESLY, M. *The Lollard Bible* (1920).
DICKENS, A. G. *The English Reformation* (1964).
DICKENS, A. G. 'Heresy and the Origins of English Protestantism', in *Britain and the Netherlands*, Vol. II (1964).
FINES, J. 'Heresy Trials in the Diocese of Coventry and Lichfield, 1511–12', in *Journal of Ecclesiastical History*, Vol. XIV (1963).
FINES, J. 'William Thorpe: an early Lollard', in *History Today*, Vol. XVIII (1968).
GREEN, V. H. H. *Bishop Reginald Pecock* (1945).
HAINES, R. M. 'Reginald Pecock: a tolerant man in an age of intolerance', in *Studies in Church History*, Vol. 21 (1984).
HAMILTON, B. *The Medieval Inquisition* (1981).
HUDSON, A. (ed.) *Selections from English Wycliffite Writings* (1978).
HUDSON, A. 'A Lollard Compilation and the Dissemination of Wycliffite Thought', in *The Journal of Theological Studies*, New Series, 23 (1972).
HUDSON, A. 'A Lollard Sect Vocabulary?', in *So Meny Longages and Tonges: Philological Essays*, ed. M. Benskin and M. L. Samuels (1981).
HUDSON, A. 'A Lollard Sermon-cycle and its Implications', in *Medium Ævum*, Vol. XI (1971).
HUDSON, A. 'Lollardy: The English Heresy', in *Studies in Church History*, Vol. 18 (1982).
HUDSON, A. 'Some Aspects of Lollard Book Production', in *Studies in Church History*, Vol. 9 (1972).
KENNY, A. *Wyclif* (1985).
LAMBERT, M. D. *Medieval Heresy* (1977).
LEFF, G. *Heresy in the Later Middle Ages* (2 Vols., 1967).
LUXTON, I. 'The Lichfield Court Book: a Postscript', in *Bulletin of the Institute of Historical Research*, Vol. 44 (1971).
McFARLANE, K. B. *Lancastrian Kings and Lollard Knights* (1972).
McFARLANE, K. B. *Wycliffe and English Nonconformity* (1972). First published as *Wycliffe and the Beginnings of English Nonconformity* (1952).
McHARDY, A. K. 'Bishop Buckingham and the Lollards of Lincoln Diocese', in *Studies in Church History*, Vol. 9 (1972).
MOZLEY, J. F. *John Foxe and his Book* (1940).
OGLE, A. *The Tragedy of the Lollards' Tower* (1949).

PARKER, T. M. *The English Reformation to 1558* (1950).
RICHARDSON, H. G. 'Heresy and the Lay Power under Richard II', in *English Historical Review*, Vol. LI (1936).
ROBERTSON, E. *Wycliffe* (1984).
SNAPE, M. G. 'Some evidence of Lollard Activity in the Diocese of Durham in the Early Fifteenth Century', in *Archaeologia Aeliana*, 4th series, XXXIX (1961).
STACEY, J. *John Wyclif and Reform* (1964).
TANNER, N. P. 'Heresy Trials in the Diocese of Norwich, 1428–31'. *Camden Fourth Series*, Vol. 20 (1977).
THOMSON, J. A. F. *The Later Lollards, 1414–1520* (1965).
THOMSON, J. A. F. *The Transformation of Medieval England* (1983).
TREVELYAN, G. M. *England in the Age of Wycliffe* (1899).
WILKS, M. 'Reformatio Regni: Wyclif and Hus as Leaders of Religious Protest Movements', in *Studies in Church History*, Vol. 9 (1972).
WORKMAN, H. B. *John Wyclif* (2 Vols., 1926).

LIST OF ILLUSTRATIONS

Between pages 86 and 87.

1. Marriage at the church door. Painting by an English illuminator in an early fourteenth-century Italian law book. Durham, Dean and Chapter Library MS C.1.6, f. 133. By courtesy of the Dean and Chapter of Durham.

2. Brass of Thomas Wardysworth, vicar (d.1533), at Betchworth church, Surrey.

3. Church, rectory and tithe-barne at Ashleworth, Gloucestershire.

4. Brass of Elyn Bray, a chrisom child (d.1516), in Stoke d'Abernon church, Surrey.

5. The Last Judgement (or Doom). Painting (c.1500) in the church of St. Thomas, Salisbury.

6. A fifteenth-century ivory pax-board, 12 cm. by 8 cm. (Flemish). Ashmolean Museum, Oxford.

7. The penance of Henry II at Becket's tomb, Canterbury. Early fifteenth-century roof boss, north walk of cloisters, Norwich cathedral. By kind permission of the Dean and Chapter of Norwich. Photograph: Philip Howard, Norwich.

8. Ceremonies for the dying and the burial of the dead. British Library MS (Bedford Hours, c.1423), 08, Add. 18850, f. 120. Reproduced by permission of the British Library.

9. Chantry chapel of Bishop Edmund Audley (d.1524) in Salisbury cathedral.

10. Cobham college, Kent, the building of which was begun in 1370.

11. Early fourteenth-century statue of 'the Synagogue', doorway to Chapter Room, Rochester cathedral. Photograph from *Medieval Figure Sculpture in England* (1912), by E. S. Prior and A. Gardner.

12. Elizabeth Herwy, abbess of Elstow (d.1527), drawn from the brass in the church at Elstow, Bedfordshire, the former Benedictine nunnery.

13. Blackfriars, Newcastle-upon-Tyne, c.1789. By kind permission of Newcastle-upon-Tyne City Libraries.

14. The round church of the Knights Hospitaller, Maplestead, Essex, built c.1340.

Acknowledgements are due to the Royal Commission on the Historical Monuments of England for photographs numbered 2, 3, 4, 5, 9, 10, 12 and 14.

INDEX

Abbeys (other than those mentioned under towns): Combermere, Cheshire, 134; Evesham, Worcs., 70, 133; Hailes, Glos., 53; Sheen, Surrey, 79; Syon, Middx., 79, 123; Tewkesbury, Glos., 35; Thorney, Cambs., 186; Winchcombe, Glos., 35
Abingdon, abbot of, 134
Ailred of Rievaulx, abbot, 127
Alban, St., 95
Albert, St., 54
Anne of Bohemia, Queen, 159, 172, 173
Anne Boleyn, Queen, 192
Anselm, abp. Canterbury, 109, 113
Arthur, Prince of Wales, 19, 36, 39, 90
Arundel, Thomas, abp. Canterbury, 62, 106, 163, 168, 170, 173, 178, 185, 187, 188n.
Ashleworth, Glos., 13
Aston, John, 170, 175
Avignon, 54, 157, 158, 159
Aylesford, Kent, friary at, 140

Bacon, Roger, 6
Badby, John, 186–7
Barnes, Robert, 194
Barton, William, 167
Beauforest, Richard, prior, 128
Becket, Thomas, abp, Canterbury, 6, 7, 8, 20, 30, 52, 108, 109, 112, 180
Bede, the Venerable, 12, 52, 96
Benedict, St., 121, 122, 123
Bernard, St., 54, 143
Bernadino of Siena, St., 33
Berwick, 63; Franciscans of, 139
Beverley minster, 62–3, 64–5, 66, 80

Bible, The (The Vulgate, the Wycliffite, Old and New Testaments, the Apocrypha and separate books), 171–3, 174, 177, 178, 179, 180, 193, 194, 196
Bilney, Thoma, 193 and n.
Blanke, Imbert, 147
Blois, Peter of, 51
Blyth, Geoffrey, bp. Coventry and Lichfield, 185
Bonaventure, St., 6, 54, 141
Braybrooke, Northants., 178, 179
Bristol, Glos., 66, 86, 175, 176; abbey, 128; church of St. Philip and St. James, 65
Burgh, Elizabeth de, 137
Bury St. Edmunds, Suffolk, 42, 76, 84, 86; abbey, 53, 134, 192; people of, 134

Calle, Richard, 34, 130n.
Cambridge, churches: St. Benet's, 68; St. Mary's, 72; Franciscans of, 139; university, 80, 125, 193, 194
Campeggio, Cardinal, 62, 157
Canterbury, 30, 58, 61, 109; cathedral priory, 52, 53, 55, 133, 169; monks of, 62; St. Dunstan's church, 43
Cantilupe, Thomas, bp. Hereford, 24, 53
Capgrave, John, 60
Carlisle, cathedral priory, 107n.; diocese, 63, 106
Cathars, 146
Catherine of Aragon, Queen, 36, 39, 90
Chaucer, Geoffrey, 56, 61, 141; *The Canterbury Tales*, 4 and n., 5, 9, 10, 12, 13, 15, 16, 35, 37, 51, 56, 57,

200

61, 63, 73, 79, 81–2, 86, 118, 127, 131, 141–2, 183
Chester, 44, 102
Christian Brethren, 194
Churches (other than those mentioned under towns): Abbots Salford, Warwks., 70; Amesbury, Wilts., 66; Ashburton, Devon, St. Andrew, 45; Ashby-de-la-Zouche, Leics., St. Helen, 56; Bassingbourn, Cambs., 44; Bath, Somerset, St. Michael, 47; Conington, Hunts., 139; Cotterstock, Northants., 80; Crediton, Devon, 80; Denham, Bucks., 142; Exeter, Devon, St. Petrock, 39; Hedon, Yorks., St. Augustine, 43; Henley-on-Thames, Oxon., 35; Hythe, Kent, St. Leonard, 42; Ingatestone, Essex, 27; Ingestre, Staffs., St. Patrick, 39; Knaresborough, Yorks., 36; Pilton, Somerset, St. John Baptist, 37; Rushton, Northants., 144n.; Saint Buryan, Cornwall, 23; Sandwich, Kent, St. Mary, 43, 69; Stoke d'Abernon, Surrey, 22; Thame, Oxon., 69; Tideswell, Derbys., 70; Whitchurch Canonicorum, Dorset, 57; Wiggenhall St. German, Norfolk, 27; Woodham Walter, Essex, 96; Wootton, Northants., 66
Colchester, 50
Colet, John, 6, 192–3
Compostella, 53, 56, 58, 61
Compton, Sir William, 35
Constantine, Emperor, 94
Councils, Church: Constance (1414–18), 159, 173, 174; Ephesus (431), 54; Exeter (1287), 36; Lambeth (1261), 116, (1281), 24; Lateran (1215), 5, 24, 89, 166; Pisa (1409), 159; Trent (Session XIII, 1551), 174; Vienne (1311–12), 62, 148
Courtenay, William, abp. Canterbury, 164, 165, 167, 169, 170, 171, 174
Coventry, Warwks., 44, 176, 179 and n., 181, 182, 183, 188, 189; Martyrs' Memorial, 189n.
Coverdale, Miles, 196
Cowfold, Sussex, 43
Cranbrook, Kent, 194
Cranmer, Thomas, abp. Canterbury, 20, 110
Cratfield, Suffolk, 42
Croscombe, Somerset, 76
Crusades, 59, 86, 143

Dalderby, John, bp. Lincoln, 130
Dante, 148
Dean, Henry, abp. Canterbury, 128
Dioceses, list of, 106n., 107n.
Dionysius Exiguus, 96
Doune, William, archdn., 117
Dunstable, Beds., prior, 134; priory, 72
Dunstan, abp. Canterbury, 112
Durham, bishops of, 112; bishop's court, 38; bishop's prison, 176; cathedral priory, 52, 64, 107 and n., 109, 124, 126; diocese, 63, 106; St. Giles' church, 4

Eastern Orthodox Church, 22, 151n.
Eleanor of Aquitaine, Queen, 39
Elizabeth Woodville, Queen, 67
Elmham, Norfolk, 107
Ely, bishop of, 157; cathedral priory, 53; diocese, 106
England, sovereigns of: Edgar, 112; Edward the Confessor, 53, 57; Edward I, 42, 78, 89, 101, 132, 139; Edward II, 146, 147, 152; Edward III, 111, 139, 152, 157, 164, 165; Edward IV, 34, 104, 142; Edward V, 34, 67; Edward VI (as prince), 21; Elizabeth I (as princess), 18–19, 20, 21, 22; Harold II, 62, 112; Henry I, 35–6, 39, 108, 110, 113, 153; Henry II, 7, 30, 39, 117, 151, 152; Henry III, 84, 88, 89, 112, 139, 145, 153; Henry IV (and Duke of Lancaster), 25, 62, 75, 185; Henry V, 29, 78, 185n., 187, and in *Henry V*, 78; Henry VI,

80; Henry VII, 45, 78, 90; Henry VIII, 36, 39, 67, 110, 157, 192, 196, and in *Henry VIII*, 18–19, 20; John, 39, 100, 111, 151, 152, 153, 154, 155; Mary I, 153; Richard I, 86, 87, 112, 113, 143; Richard II, 62, 67, 75, 78, 159, 164, 165, 173, 185, and in *Richard II*, 112; William I, 7, 62, 83, 103, 110, 112
Erasmus, Desiderius, 108, 192, 193
Eton college, 80
Euphemia, abbess, 131–2
Eusebius, bp. Caesarea, 95
Excommunication, 15–16, 25, 26, 151, 155, 159, 164, 173

Falstolf, Sir John, 9
Fish, Simon, *Supplication of Beggars*, 192, 195
FitzJames, William, bp. London, 190, 191, 193
Flambard, Rannulf, bp. Durham, 108
Fox, John, 176
Fox, Richard, bp. Winchester, 108
Foxe, John, martyrologist, and his *Acts and Monuments*, 195 and n.

Gacoigne, Thomas, 157
George, Duke of Clarence, 82
Gerald of Wales, 6, 60, 70, 88n.
Gifford, John, 80
Gloucester, 86, 141
Godric, St., 4
Gower, John, 10
Grandisson, John, bp. Exeter, 23, 64
Great Yarmouth, 79, 103; church of St. Nicholas, 81
Gregory of Nyssa, St., 52
Grosseteste, Robert, bp. Lincoln, 54, 111–2, 136, 156, 178

Hatfield, Thomas, bp. Durham, 107
Hawley, Sir Robert, 67
Helena, Empress, 95
Hereford, bishop of, 176; cathedral church, 175; Dominican priory, 140; diocese, 116, 128, 187; visitation (1397), 10, 41
Hereford, Nicholas, 169, 172, 175, 185
Heresy, 25, 27, 161–2, 177, 179
Herwy, Elizabeth, abbess, 132
Hoccleve, Thomas, 4
Holgate, Robert, abp. York, 110
Horn, John, 169
Horsey, Dr. William, 191
Hugh of Avalon, St., bp. Lincoln, 70, 100, 128
Hugh of Wells, bp. Lincoln, 77
Hugh, Little St., 86
Hunne, Richard, 189–92
Hus, John, 173

Inquisition, 90, 147, 161
Ipswich, 141, 184, 193
Isabel, Countess of Warwick, 35

Jarrow, monastery, 52
Jerome, St., 52
Jerusalem, 30, 56, 94, 143, 144
Joan, Princess of Wales, 165
John of Gaunt, Duke of Lancaster, 164, 165, 167, 169–70, 171
John of Salisbury, 117, 155
Joseph, Charles, 191

Kemerton, Glos., 178, 186
Kilwardby, Robert, abp. Canterbury, 141
Kirkleatham, Yorks., 156

Lanfranc, abp. Canterbury, 128
Langland, William, and *Piers Plowman*, 4, 8, 9, 30, 38, 63, 79, 100, 117, 134, 138, 139, 141, 142
Langley, Northumberland, 65
Langley, Thomas, bp. Durham, 119
Langton, Stephen, abp. Canterbury, 70
Last Judgement (or Doom), paintings of, 31, 72, 81
Latimer, Sir Thomas, 178, 183
Lincoln, 84, 86, 113, 147; bishop's court, 176; canonry at, 156; cathed-

ral chapter, 157; cathedral church, 86, 100; diocese, 63, 79, 116, 193
Little Maplestead, Essex, 144
Lollards, 169, 174–96
London, 76, 84, 86, 141, 144, 145, 147, 156, 179, 187, 189, 191–2; bishop's court, 138; Blackfriars hall, 169; cathedral church of St. Paul's 36, 79, 147, 165, 175, 186, 191; churches: St. Andrew Hubbard, 46; St. Margaret's, Southwark, 45, 46; St. Mary's Chapel, 147; St. Mary-at-Hill, 46, 47; St. Mary's Spittle, Whitechapel, 189; St. Mildred's, Bread Street, 77; College of St. Martin-le-Grand, 66, 67; diocese, 187, 193; Fulham palace, 190, 191; Highgate almshouse, 81; Lambeth palace, 165, 190; Lollards' Tower, 190, 192; the Minories (nunnery), 137, 138 and n.; priories: of the Hospitallers, 144 and n.; of the Templars, 144–5; Smithfield, 186, 187, 188, 189, 191, 194; the Tower, 67, 108, 187; see also Westminster
Lumby, Elyas de, 63
Luther, Martin, 192, 193
Lyndwood, William, *Provinciale*, 186
Lynn, Norfolk, 86, 140
Lyons, 61
Lytell Geste of Robyn Hode, A, 127

Malebisse, Richard, 87
Malleus Maleficarum, 48
Mare, Thomas de la, abbot, 128
Margaret, Queen, 43
Melton, William, abp, York, 60
Mirk, John, and *Instructions for Parish Priests*, 26, 27, 71, 178
Mitford, Christopher, 37
More, Sir Thomas, 30, 68, 83, 173, 189
More, William de la, 147

Nettleham, Lincs., 101
Newbury, Walter, abbot, 128

Newcastle-upon-Tyne, 44, 176; Blackfriars, 140
Northampton, 66, 88, 176
Norwich, 84, 85, 86, 134; Carrow nunnery, 131; cathedral priory, 85, 125; Dominican friary, 140; Lollards' Pit, 188 and n., 193n.; St. Peter Hungate Church and Museum, 32n., 131, 172
Nunneries (other than those mentioned under towns): Barking, Essex, 131; Blackborough, Norfolk, 130n.; Bruisyard, Suffolk, 137; Dartford, Kent, 137; Denney, Cambs., 137, 138; Elstow, Beds., 132; Kirklees, Yorks., 130; Markyate, Herts., 130; Nunburnholme, Yorks., 122; Polesworth, Warwks., 131; Seton, Cumberland, 129; Shaftesbury, Dorset, 129, 131; Wherwell, Hants., 132
Nuremberg Chronicle, 69

Oldcastle, Sir John (Lord Cobham), 187, 194n.
Osmund, St., bp. Salisbury, 54
Oxford, 170; colleges: Balliol, 162; Corpus Christi, 108; Lincoln, 74; Merton, 162; New, 108, 109, 111; Queen's 162; St. Edmund's Hall, 173; Franciscans of, 139; Osney abbey, 89 and n.; university, 80, 125, 135, 162, 165, 166, 167–8, 169, 170, 173, 174

Paris, Matthew, 95, 136, 155
Parliament, 25, 68, 78, 113, 154, 157, 174, 185 and n., 191 and n., 192
Paston family, 67; John, 20, 57, 73, 131; Margaret, 57; Margery, 34, 130n.
Payne, Peter, 173
Peasants' Revolt, 134, 140, 167
Pecham, John, abp. Canterbury, 141, 155
Pecock, Reginald, bp. Chichester, 186
Peterborough, abbot of, 139

Peter's Pence, 41–2, 115, 154
Philip IV, king of France, 146, 148
Place-names, 122, 144
Plumpton, Sir William, 36
Plymouth, 66
Pole, Reginald, Cardinal, 110, 153
Poore, Richard, bp. Salisbury, 38
Popes: Alexander III, 53; Alexander VI, 152; Boniface VIII, 61; Boniface IX, 186; Clement V, 62, 146, 148, 158; Clement VI, 148, 157; Clement VII, 159; Gregory the Great, 108, 109; Gregory VII, 110; Gregory XI, 158, 165; Hadrian IV, 3, 155; Innocent III, 25, 151, 155; Innocent IV, 136; Innocent VI, 106; Martin V, 159; Urban II, 59; Urban V, 64, 166; Urban VI, 158–9
Portsmouth, 66
Prague, 173, 178
Priories (other than those mentioned under towns): Brinkburn, Northumberland, 119; Bromholm, Norfolk, 53, 73; Dorchester, Oxon., 128; Hexham, Northumberland, 64, 65
Purgatory, 27, 28, 29, 32, 59, 63, 64, 71, 72, 73, 75, 77, 81, 82, 163, 176
Purvey, John, 168–9, 172, 175, 185, 186

Reading, abbey, 133; St. Lawrence's church, 40, 44
Repingdon, Philip, bp. Lincoln, 169, 174
Richard, Earl of Arundel, 37
Richard of Stretton, bp. Coventry and Lichfield, 129
Rigg, Robert, 169
Ripon, 64
Robert the Devil, Duke of Normandy, 30
Robin Hood, 130
Rochester, 56, 192; cathedral priory, 83; diocese, 116, 187
Rome, 54, 56, 60, 61, 94, 110, 151, 155, 156, 158, 165

St. Albans, abbey, 49, 53, 128, 133, 134; people of, 134
Salisbury, 141, 184; cathedral church, 78; diocese, 193; St. Edmund's church, 42, 44, 47
Samson of Bury, abbot, 127
Sawtry, William, 186
Shakespeare, William, works by: *Hamlet*, 27–8, 29, 42, 74–5; *Henry IV, Part One*, 194n.; *Henry V*, 22, 78, 185n.; *Henry VI, Part Two*, 73; *Henry VIII*, 18–19, 20; *King John*, 35; *Merry Wives of Windsor, The*, 12; *Midsummer Night's Dream, A*, 38; *Richard II*, 112; *Romeo and Juliet*, 71–2; *Taming of the Shrew, The*, 35, 37; *Twelfth Night*, 12; *Winter's Tale, The*, 19
Sleaford, Lincs., gild at, 101
Spalding, John, 191
Stamford, Lincs., 86; nunnery, 129
Statutes: *De Heretico Comburendo*, 186; Mortmain, 78; *Praemunire*, 158, 190, 192; Provisors, 157, 158
Stigand, abp. Canterbury, 110
Stratford-on-Avon (and gild at), 81–2
Straw, Jack, 140
Street-names, from friaries, 140–1; from the Jewry, 84
Strood, Kent, 144
Sudbury, Simon, abp. Canterbury, 165, 167
Swinderby, William, 175–6, 187
Swinfield, Richard, bp. Hereford, 53, 101

Terrington, St. John's, Norfolk, 80
Thetford, Norfolk, 107
Thomas Aquinas, St., 6, 18, 54, 161
Thomas, Duke of Gloucester, 172
Thorpe, William, 168, 176, 185, 188n.
Towneley Plays, The, 15
Throckmorton, Elizabeth, abbess, 138
Transubstantiation, 5, 22, 32, 166–7, 193
Trent, Dorset, 80

True Cross, 53, 94–5
Tunstall, Cuthbert, bp. London, 193
Tweng, Sir Robert, 156
Tydd St. Giles, Cambs., 81
Tyndale, William, 194

Uxbridge, Middx., 184, 193

Vergil, Polydore, 192
Villeneuf, Elyan de, 148

Waldensians, 146, 161–2, 172
Walsingham, Norfolk, 55, 57, 58, 183
Walsingham, Thomas, 140
Ware, 63
Warwick, 84; St. Mary's church, 78
Westminster, abbey, 35–6, 57, 75, 78, 86, 133, 145, 185; hall, 113, 185; palace, 67, 113; St. Margaret's church, 44; sanctuary, 66, 67
William, bp. St. Andrews, 5
William, prior, 119
William of Malmesbury, 59
William of Newburgh, 87–8
William of Norwich, St., 85, 86, 90
William of Perth, 56
William of Wykeham, bp. Winchester, 108, 109, 111
Wimborne minster, Dorset, 53
Winchester, 84; archdeacon's court, 117; cathedral priory, 53; school, 111
Winkfield, Berks., 134
Wolsey, Thomas, Cardinal, 129, 153, ' 191
Wyche, Richard, 176, 189
Wyclif, John, and works, 141, 162–74, 177, 178, 183, 193, 195 and n., 196
Wkyes, Thomas, 90

York, 86, 87–8, 89, 113, 147; archbishop's court, 38; diocese, 63, 106; Franciscan friary, 139; minister, 87, 147; *Mystery Plays*, 12, 44, 61; St. Mary's abbey, 122, 127